KS3 Success

Maths

Practice Test Papers

Age 11-14

Trevor Dixon

Contents

Introduction

How to Use the Practice Test Papers

About these Practice Test Papers

At the end of Key Stage 3, or Year 9, tests will be used by your teachers to determine your level of achievement in maths.

In this book, there are three sets of test papers that will allow you to track your progress in Key Stage 3 Maths. They will also help you to identify your strengths and weaknesses in the subject.

Sets A, B and C each provide one complete assessment and comprise:
* Test Paper 1: **1 hour** (no calculator allowed)
* Test Paper 2: **1 hour** (calculator allowed)

The test papers will:
* test your knowledge and understanding of the subject, and how you use this knowledge to answer questions
* provide practice questions in all maths topics
* help to familiarise you with the different question styles that appear in test papers
* highlight opportunities for further study and skills practice that will lead to improvement
* record results to track progress.

How to Use the Test Papers

The questions in these test papers have been written in the style that you will see in actual tests.

While you should try to complete the different sections in each set in the same week, you should complete sets A, B and C **at intervals** through Key Stage 3, or Year 9.

Make sure you leave a reasonable amount of time between each assessment – it is unrealistic to expect to see much improvement in just a few weeks. Spreading out the sets will mean you have an opportunity to develop and practise any areas you need to focus on. You will feel much more motivated if you wait for a while, because your progress will be much more obvious.

If you want to re-use the papers, write in pencil and then rub out the answers. However, don't repeat the set too soon or you will remember the answers and the results won't be a true reflection of your abilities.

How to Prepare for the Tests

Revision:
After covering the necessary maths topics, read through your notes from school, or course notes. Perhaps use a revision guide to recap the key points. You could also add notes and diagrams to a mind map.

Equipment you will need:
- pen(s), pencil and rubber
- ruler
- protractor
- pair of compasses
- calculator
- a watch or clock to keep track of the pace at which you are answering questions.

When you feel that you're properly prepared, take the first set of test papers.

Taking the Tests

1. Each set of tests is made up of **two** test papers. Each paper is worth **60 marks**. You should spend **60 minutes** on **each** paper, meaning that one set will take you **two hours**.
2. Check the information about formulae at the end of this introduction.
3. Choose a time to take the first paper when you can work through it in one go. Make sure you have an appropriate place to sit and take the test, where you will be uninterrupted.
4. Answer **all** the questions in the test. If you are stuck on one question, move on and come back to it later. Tests often start with easier questions. The questions become more complex and cover more than one topic as you work through the test papers.
5. Read the questions **carefully**, so that you understand exactly what you need to do. Don't spend too long on any one question.
6. Write the answers in the spaces provided. The space provided for you to write your answer will also give you an indication of how detailed your answer needs to be.
7. The number of marks allocated to each question is shown. This will tell you how many key points the examiner is looking for.
8. Remember that marks may be awarded for key points or working out even if your final answer isn't correct, so **always show your working**, and keep it neat. It may be that if you get the answer wrong, you could still be awarded one mark for showing your working. Sometimes, the second mark for a calculation could be for the **units of measurement**, so make sure you include these.
9. Stay calm! Don't be fazed by questions. Read the question carefully and think it through.

How to Use the Mark Scheme

When you've taken the test, you, or a parent or guardian, should use the mark scheme to mark it. You could mark the test together. It's often helpful for you to discuss the answers with someone as you go through the mark scheme.

The answers and mark scheme will:
- give you an answer to the question **in full**. Any words shown in brackets aren't necessary to obtain the full marks, but should help your understanding of the question
- tell you where alternative answers are acceptable. If it's possible to use different words or terms in an answer, these will be separated by a forward slash, e.g. / . Sometimes when an answer isn't fully correct, certain alternatives may be acceptable
- provide Helpful Hints on answering particular questions.

When you've gone through the test paper, add up the marks to give you your total.

Tips for the Top

After sitting a test paper:
1. Try to analyse your performance. For questions that were incorrect, identify where you went wrong. Are there gaps in your knowledge and understanding? Were there topics where you were under-prepared? Have you misunderstood some of the maths?
2. Pay attention to the Helpful Hints in the answers and mark scheme. These will give you revision tips, and important information about answering a question on a topic. They will also help you to avoid errors made by many students sitting tests.

Check through the following ideas, as they'll help you to do better next time:
1. Make sure your number skills are good – knowing number facts, remembering and using formulae, and being confident with calculation methods will help you to avoid making mistakes.
2. Make sure your knowledge of mathematical facts is accurate – such as knowing metric measures and the meaning of mathematical terms.
3. Check through the paper you have completed.
   - Look for any careless mistakes and try to identify where you went wrong.
   - Look for questions you got wrong – you may not have answered them or you may not have understood.
   - Make a note of the topics and try to focus on these areas to develop your understanding.

Formulae:
You'll be expected to know some formulae, such as those for finding the area and perimeter of rectangles, the area of triangles and parallelograms, and the area and circumference of circles.

Make sure you learn these and can use them. Remember that many questions at Key Stage 3 will ask you to use two of these; for example, finding the area of a compound shape made from a rectangle and a triangle.

We have provided you with two formulae that you'll need to use. Make sure you understand how to use these.

When you've assessed your performance in the first test paper, do any additional work you need to. When you sit the second, and finally the third test, check to see how your performance is improving by comparing marks.

Set **A**

KEY STAGE 3

TEST 1

Maths

Test Paper 1

Test Paper 1

Calculator **not** allowed

First name _Dripti_

Last name _Hemant_

Date _∅ any time or day_

Instructions:

- The test is 1 hour long.
- Find a quiet place where you can sit down and complete the test paper undisturbed.
- You **may not** use a calculator for any question in this test.
- You will need: a pen, pencil, rubber and a ruler. You may find tracing paper useful.
- This test starts with easier questions.
- Write your answers where you see this symbol: ✏
- Try to answer all the questions.
- The number of marks available for each question is given in the margin.
- Write all your answers **and working** on the test paper. Marks may be awarded for working.
- Check your work carefully.
- Check how you have done using pages 103–112 of the Answers and Mark Scheme.

You might need to use these formulae:

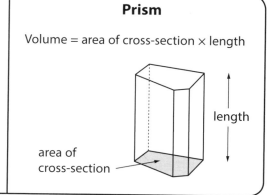

Trapezium	Prism
Area $= \frac{1}{2}(a + b)h$	Volume = area of cross-section × length

MAXIMUM MARK	60	ACTUAL MARK	

1. Write one of the signs <, >, = in each circle to complete these statements.

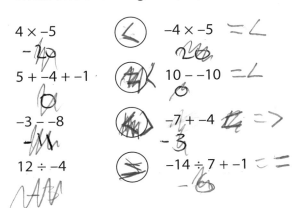

4×-5 ⊘(<) -4×-5 =∠

$5 + -4 + -1$ ⊘ $10 - -10$ =∠

$-3 - -8$ ⊘ $-7 + -4$ =>

$12 \div -4$ ⊘ $-14 \div 7 + -1$ = =

2. Join equivalent numbers with straight lines.

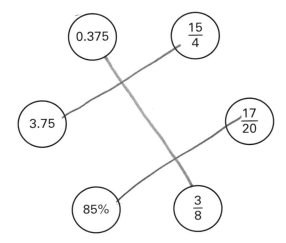

3. Calculate the perimeter and area of this shape.

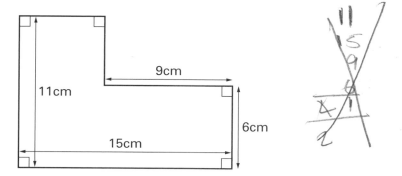

(a) Perimeter:

52 _____ cm

(b) Area:

120 _____ cm²

4. Dave and Ali are going to share the cost of a present.

They agree to share the cost in the ratio of 5 : 4.

Dave pays £12.

(a) How much does Ali pay?

£15

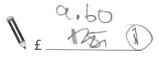

£ _____

(b) How much did the present cost?

£ _____

5. A maths group completed a test.

Their scores are:

15	14	14	19	19
20	16	16	13	14

(a) What is the mean score?

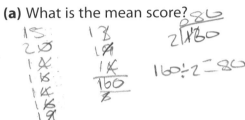

_80_

1 mark

(b) What is the median score?

_320_

1 mark

(c) What is the modal score?

_480_

1 mark

(d) What is the range of the scores?

the range of scores are all end in zero so The range of scores are all even numbers. This is because all even numbers end or have 2, 4, 6, 8, 10 etc.

even

1 mark

9

SUBTOTAL

6. **(a)** Solve:

$7g + 12 = 21 + g$

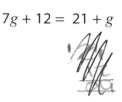

$7g + 12 = 21 + g$
$\quad -g \qquad\qquad -g$
$6g + 12 = 21$
$\qquad -12 \quad -12$
$\dfrac{6g}{6} = \dfrac{9}{6}$
$g = 1.5$

$6\overline{)9\,.^39\,^30\,0} \quad 1.5$

✏ $g = \cancel{9}\ 1.5$

(b) Simplify this expression.

$6n + 3p^2 + 5p - p^2 - 4p + 4n$

I used shapes to help 8 rom working out!

$6n + 4n = 10n$
$10n$

$3p^2 - p^2 = 2p^2$
$2p^2$

$5p - 4p = 1p$
$1p$

$10n + 2p^2 + 4p =$ answers

✏ $10n + 2p^2 + p$

(c) Find the value of $2a^2 + a^3b$, when $a = 4$ and $b = 5$.

Need Help ✗

16
4
64

$2a^2 = 8^2 = 64$

$a^3b = 4^3b = 4^3 \cdot 5$

64

✏ _____

7. Find the volume of this cylinder.

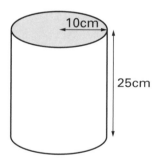

10cm

25cm

Use $\pi = 3$

Give your answer as a whole number.

working out

$10 \times 25 = 250$

250
$\times 10$
$\overline{000}$
$\overline{2500}$

2500
$\times 25$
12500
50000
62500
7500

✏ 7500 cm³

10

8. **(a)** Express 24 as a product of its prime factors.

12 × 2
4 × 2
2 × 2

2 × 2 × 3 × 2

(b) Find the highest common factor of 36 and 96.

12
24
36
48
60
72
84
96

12)36 0 3
12)96 0 8

12

(c) Find the lowest common multiple of 15 and 24.

15, 30, 45, 60, 75, 90, 105, 120
24, 48, 72, 96, 120

120

90
15
105

105
15
120

9. A regular polygon has 12 sides.

(a) Lines are drawn from one vertex to other vertices to make triangles. **Some** lines have been drawn for you.

How many triangles will there be altogether?

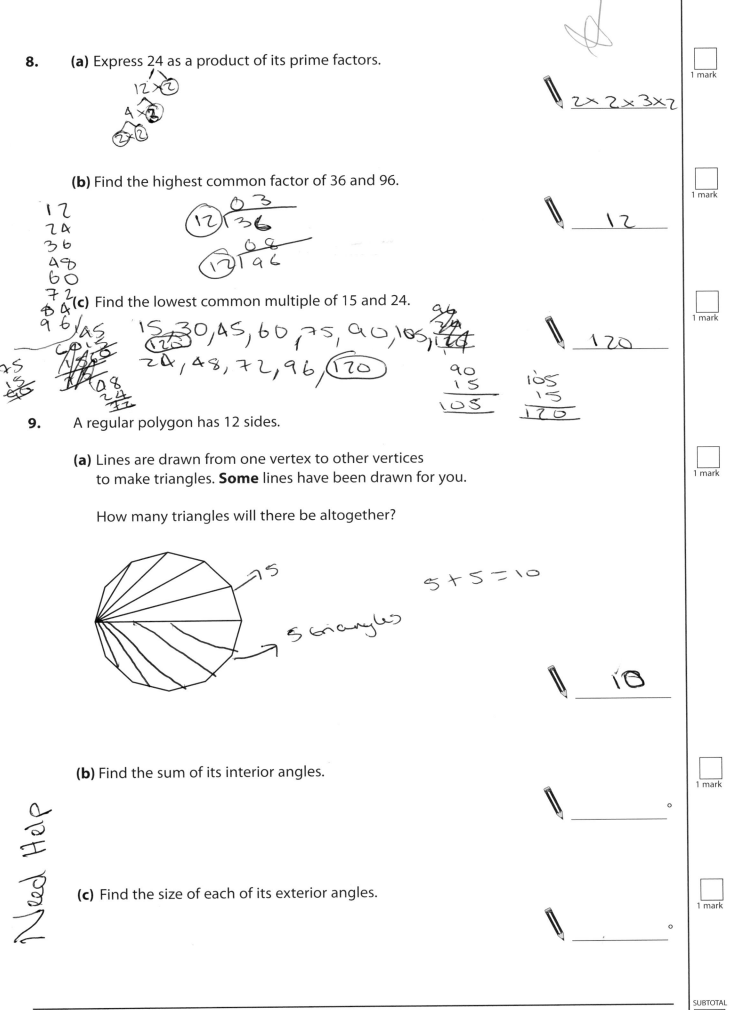

75

5 + 5 = 10

5 triangles

10

(b) Find the sum of its interior angles.

_____ °

(c) Find the size of each of its exterior angles.

_____ °

Need Help

10. There are some red, blue, black and white counters in a bag.

There are 12 blue counters.

One counter is selected at random. The probability of it being a certain colour is as follows:

handwritten: There are 30 counters in the bag

- A red counter   0.2
- A blue counter   0.4   *handwritten: 12 ÷ 2 = 6*
- A black counter   0.1   *handwritten: 6 ÷ 2 = 3, 12 + 6 + 3 = 21*

handwritten near red counter: 12

(a) Explain why it is impossible for there to be 25 counters in the bag.

handwritten: The probability of being a black counter is 0.1 and that 25 × 0.1 does not equal a whole number

(b) What is the probability of taking a white counter from the bag?

_____

(c) How many white counters are in the bag?

_____

Margin: 1 mark (×3), Need Help

12

11. *ABC* and *DEF* are similar triangles.

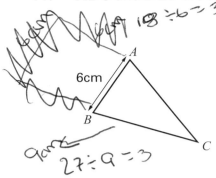

18 ÷ 6 = 3

Not to scale

6cm

27 ÷ 9 = 3

18cm

24cm

27cm

(a) What is length of the side *BC*?

9 _____ cm

(b) A third similar triangle is drawn by increasing *DEF* by a scale factor of 4.

Write the lengths of the sides of the third similar triangle.

72 _____ cm, 96 _____ cm, 108 _____ cm

1 mark

2 marks

SUBTOTAL

12. Sally trials rolling a die.

The probability of the die landing on a number is shown in the table.

Number on die	1	2	3	4	5	6
Probability	0.2	0.05	0.1	0.05	0.1	0.5

(a) Complete this table to show the expected number of successes for rolling a number.

Number rolled on die	Number of trials	Expected number of successes
1	25	5
2	40	2
3	90	9

(b) Sally says, 'The dice is fair because any number can be rolled.'

Is Sally correct?

Circle YES or NO.

YES / NO

Explain your answer.

It is not fair because there 4 expected number of successes but 2 and 1 are less. It would be fair if all of the number in the dice had a correct number of successes.

14

13. This frequency table shows the scores in a maths test.

Score	Frequency	Score × frequency
20	1	20
19	2	38
18	3	54
17	7	119
16	4	64
15	3	45
Totals	20	340

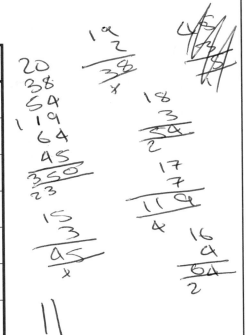

(a) Complete the table.

3 marks

(b) Find the median number on this stem and leaf diagram.

3	2	6	7		
4	6	8			
5	1	5	8	9	
6	2	2	5	7	9
7	8				

Need Help

1 mark

SUBTOTAL

14. **(a)** Draw lines to join the inverse functions.

① $x \to 2x + 3$ $y \to \dfrac{y-2}{3}$ ③

② $x \to 2x - 3$ $y \to \dfrac{y+2}{3}$ ④

③ $x \to 3x + 2$ $y \to \dfrac{y-3}{2}$ ①

④ $x \to 3x - 2$ $y \to \dfrac{y+3}{2}$ ②

(b) Give the inverse function of this equation in the form $y =$

$$\frac{(x+5)}{4} \qquad \to \qquad y = 4y + 5$$

15. Sally and Yasmin like to make a drink from a mixture of pear and apple juice.

Sally likes to mix the pear and apple juice in the ratio of 2 : 3.   P A

Yasmin prefers the mixture to have the ratio of 3 : 2.   P A

(a) What fraction of Sally's drink is made from apple juice?

2 : 3

2 + 3 = 5   3/5

3/5

(b) Yasmin uses 450 ml of apple juice.

What is the difference between the amount of apple and pear juice in Yasmin's drink?

Give your answer in millilitres (ml).

225
× 3
675
x

$2\overline{)4^{1}5^{5}0}$

3 : 2

225 + 225

225ml

(c) Sally makes 1 litre of her mixture.

She drinks half of her juice mixture.

How many millilitres of pear juice will Yasmin have to add to the rest so it makes her mixture?

225

300 ÷ 2 = 150   +100

= 250

250ml

16. The lengths of four sides on this hexagon are identified.

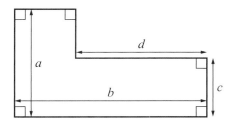

(a) Tick (✓) the expression that does **not** represent a way of finding the area of the hexagon.

(i) ☐ $ab - d(a - c)$

(ii) ☐ $a(b - d) + cd$

(iii) ☑ $a(b - d) + bc$

(iv) ☐ $(a - c) \times (b - d) + bc$

1 mark

(b) Write a formula to find the length b when the perimeter P and width a are known.

1 mark

$$b = \frac{P - 2a}{2}$$

SUBTOTAL

17. AB is the diameter of the circle and is 20cm.

Use $\pi = 3$

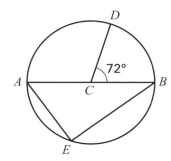

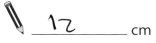

(a) Calculate the length of the arc BD.

 12 _____ cm

(b) Calculate the area of the sector BCD.

Give your answer as a whole number.

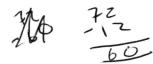

 60 _____ cm²

(c) $\angle ABE = 38°$

Calculate $\angle BAE$.

_____ °

Need Help

18

18. Cuboids A, B and C are similar.

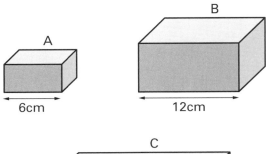

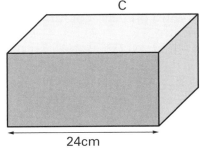

The ratio of length : width : height is 3 : 2 : 1 in these cuboids.

(a) Calculate the ratio volume of A : volume of B.

1 : 8

2 marks

(b) Calculate the ratio volume of A : volume of C.

1 : 64

2 marks

SUBTOTAL

19. These spinners are identical.

Spinner 1   Spinner 2

The chart shows the probability of the spinners landing on each colour.

Yellow	Red	Blue
0.1	0.5	0.4

Calculate these probabilities.

(a) The probability of spinning yellow on both spinners.

$0.1 \times 0.1 = 0.01$

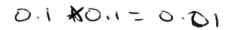 0.81

(b) The probability of not spinning yellow on both spinners.

$1 - 0.01$

0.99

(c) The probability of spinning red on Spinner 1 and blue on Spinner 2.

0.5×0.4
$= 0.2$

 0.2

20. Convert these numbers to standard form.

(a) $(3 \times 10^5) \times (5 \times 10^3)$

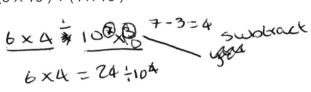

$3 \times 5 \times 10^5 \times 10^3$

$3 \times 5 = 15 \times 10^8$

1.5×10^9

(b) $(6 \times 10^7) \div (4 \times 10^3)$

$6 \times 4 \div 10 \quad 7 - 3 = 4 \quad \text{subtract}$

$6 \times 4 = 24 \div 10^4$

1.5×10^4

21.

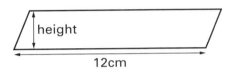

height

12cm

The area of this parallelogram is 30 cm².

The length is 12 cm.

What is the height of the parallelogram?

$30 \div 12 = 2.5$

$\begin{array}{r} 12 \\ 24 \\ \hline 36 \end{array}$

2.5

Test Paper 2

Calculator allowed

First name _____

Last name _____

Date _____

Instructions:

- The test is 1 hour long.
- Find a quiet place where you can sit down and complete the test paper undisturbed.
- You **may** use a calculator for any question in this test.
- You will need a pen, pencil, rubber, ruler, a pair of compasses and a scientific or graphic calculator.
- This test starts with easier questions.
- Write your answers where you see this symbol:
- Try to answer all the questions.
- The number of marks available for each question is given in the margin.
- Write all your answers **and working** on the test paper. Marks may be awarded for working.
- Check your work carefully.
- Check how you have done using pages 103–112 of the Answers and Mark Scheme.

You might need to use these formulae:

Trapezium	Prism
Area $= \frac{1}{2}(a + b)h$	Volume = area of cross-section × length

Trapezium diagram: height (h), b (top), a (bottom)

Prism diagram: length, area of cross-section

MAXIMUM MARK	60	ACTUAL MARK	

1. **(a)** Write the next three terms in this sequence.

19 ～ 12 ～ 5 ～ $\underline{\ \ -2\ \ }$ $\underline{\ \ -9\ \ }$ $\underline{\ \ -16\ \ }$
-7   -7   -7   -7   -7

(b) To find the next number in this sequence, double the number and subtract 4.

Write the next three terms.

5 ___ 6 ___ 8 ___ $\underline{\ \ 11\ \ }$ $\underline{\ \ 15\ \ }$ $\underline{\ \ 20\ \ }$
 +1   +2

(c) To find the next term in this sequence, follow this rule: $3n - 7$

Write the next three terms.

−4   −1   2 $\underline{\hspace{3cm}}$ $\underline{\hspace{3cm}}$ $\underline{\hspace{3cm}}$

2. A fruit dessert is made using 200 g of oranges, 120 g of apples and 160 g of pears.

(a) What is the ratio of oranges to apples to pears?

Write the ratio in its simplest terms.

$\underline{\hspace{2.5cm}} : \underline{\hspace{2.5cm}} : \underline{\hspace{2.5cm}}$

(b) What fraction of the dessert is apple?

Write the fraction in its simplest terms.

$\underline{\hspace{2cm}}$

1 mark

1 mark

1 mark

1 mark

1 mark

SUBTOTAL

3. This bag contains coloured counters.

(a) What is the probability that a counter taken from the bag will **not** be yellow?

(b) A yellow counter and a green counter are taken from the bag.

What is the probability that the third counter taken from the bag will be blue?

(c) Five black counters are added to the original bag of counters.

What is the probability that a blue counter will be taken from the bag?

4. Here is a train timetable.

London King's Cross	14:00	14:35	15:05	15:40	16:05	16:25	16:55
Peterborough		15:36	15:58			17:18	17:49
Doncaster	15:35	16:22				17:39	
York	16:27	16:57	17:23	17:35		18:35	
Newcastle	17:31	18:04	18:19		19:02	19:32	19:48
Edinburgh		19:42	19:58	20:12		20:55	21:20

(a) Ewan arrives at London King's Cross station at 4pm to catch a train to Newcastle.

When should he arrive in Newcastle?

_____

1 mark

(b) Milly has to be in York for six o'clock in the evening.

Which would be the best train to catch from Peterborough?

_____

1 mark

(c) Dev catches the 14:00 from London King's Cross. He gets off in York and spends one hour meeting someone at York Station. He then gets the next train to Newcastle.

When will he arrive in Newcastle?

_____

1 mark

SUBTOTAL

5. A cuboid measures 12cm × 8cm × 4cm.

(a) How many edges will be 12cm long?

(b) What will the surface area of the cuboid be?

_____ cm²

6. The curved lines in this shape are the circumferences of two semi-circles joined by two straight lines.

Give your answers correct to 2 decimal places.

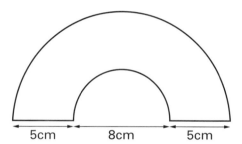

5cm   8cm   5cm

(a) Find the area of the shape.

_____ cm²

(b) Find the perimeter of the shape.

_____ cm

7. Multiply out the brackets in these expressions.

(a) $4(s^2 - 5s)$

_______________ 1 mark

(b) $(r + 6)\ (r + 7)$

_______________ 1 mark

Factorise.

(c) $10t + 25$

_______________ 1 mark

8. **(a)** 60% of a number is 360.

What is the number?

_______________ 1 mark

(b) Jack spent $\frac{3}{8}$ of his savings on buying DVDs.

He spent £19.50

How much of his savings did he have left?

_______________ 1 mark

SUBTOTAL

9. This table shows the numbers of jumpers on sale in a shop.

The sizes and colours of the jumpers are shown.

		Colour			
		Brown	Blue	Green	Red
Size	Extra large	2	4	4	1
	Large	3	3	6	5
	Medium	4	6	5	5
	Small	3	4	3	2

(a) A jumper is chosen at random.

What is the probability that the jumper chosen will be brown?

(b) The brown jumper is replaced. A jumper is chosen at random.

What is the probability that the jumper chosen will be medium?

(c) Martha thinks about picking a jumper at random.

She says, 'Picking a large, red jumper is a mutually exclusive event.'

Is Martha correct? Circle YES or NO   YES / NO

Explain your answer.

10. This table shows the cost of sending letters and parcels by post.

	Letters			
	First class		Second class	
	Letter	Large letter	Letter	Large letter
0–100 g	60p	90p	50p	69p
101 g–250 g		£1.20		£1.10
251 g–500 g		£1.60		£1.40
501 g–750 g		£2.30		£1.90
	Parcels			
	First class		Second class	
	Small parcel	Medium parcel	Small parcel	Medium parcel
Up to 1 kg	£3.00	£5.65	£2.60	
1 kg–2 kg	£6.85	£11.90	£5.60	£8.90
2 kg–5 kg		£15.10		£12.92
5 kg–10 kg		£21.25		£15.92
10 kg–15 kg		£32.40		£22.46
15 kg–20 kg		£32.40		£27.68
20 kg–25 kg				£38.48
25 kg–30 kg				£42.50

SUBTOTAL

(a) Mr Jones sends the following:

- 2 first-class letters.

- 3 second-class large letters weighing 300g each.

- 1 first-class medium parcel weighing 8kg.

What does Mr Jones have to pay?

£ _____

(b) Mrs Singh pays £26.40 for the following:

- 4 second-class large letters weighing 400g.

- 2 medium parcels.

Circle the prices she paid for the 2 medium parcels.

	First class	**Second class**
	Medium parcel	Medium parcel
Up to 1kg	£5.65	
1kg–2kg	£11.90	£8.90
2kg–5kg	£15.10	£12.92
5kg–10kg	£21.25	£15.92
10kg–15kg	£32.40	£22.46
15kg–20kg	£32.40	£27.68
20kg–25kg		£38.48
25kg–30kg		£42.50

11. Solve:

(a) $\dfrac{5x + 13}{6} = 8$

 $x =$ _____

(b) $\dfrac{4x - 2}{3} = \dfrac{3x + 9}{4}$

 $x =$ _____

12. Use a calculator to solve the following.

Round your answer to two decimal places.

$$\dfrac{35.78 \, (56.7 - 7.08)}{3.4 + 2.3 \times 8.32}$$

 _____

13. Look at this sequence.

5   8   13   20   29

Tick (✓) the expression that describes the nth term in the sequence.

☐ $n^2 + 3$

☐ $n^2 + 4$

☐ $2n + 3$

☐ $3n + n^2$

☐ $2n^2 + 3$

2 marks

2 marks

1 mark

1 mark

SUBTOTAL

14. Find two pairs of quadrilaterals that will join to make two similar rectangles.

Not to scale

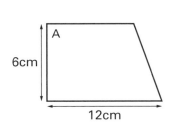

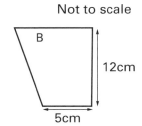

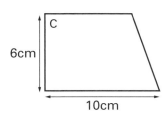

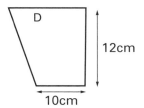

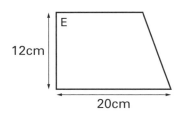

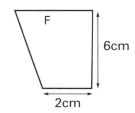

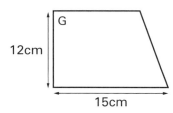

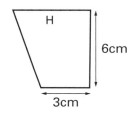

_____ and _____ make a rectangle similar to _____

and _____

15. Tom wants to buy a game console.

The full price is £225

The price is reduced to £180

(a) What is the percentage decrease?

_____

1 mark

Tom buys the game console at the reduced price. He pays a deposit of £30

The shop adds a percentage to the balance left to pay.

He decides to pay the rest in 12 instalments.

Tom has to pay 12 instalments of £13.25

(b) What is the percentage increase the shop has added to pay by instalments?

_____

2 marks

The shop also has computer games for sale.

Each game costs £40

The price for a pack of three games is £72

(c) What is the percentage saving when buying a pack of three games instead of buying three separate games?

_____

2 marks

SUBTOTAL

16.

(a) Here are 7 number cards. They are all integers.

| 12 | 15 | 8 | 20 | 34 | ? | ? |

The mean of the seven numbers is 16.

What could the other two numbers be?

_____ and _____

(b) Here are 7 number cards. They are all integers.

| 13 | 15 | 6 | 12 | 7 | 20 | ? |

The range of the numbers is 18.

What could the other number be?

_____ and _____

(c) Here are 7 number cards. They are all integers.

| 12 | 10 | 9 | 9 | 10 | ? | ? |

The mode of the numbers is 9, the median is **not** 9 and the range is 3.

What are the other two numbers?

_____ and _____

17. **(a)** Here are two expressions.

$$4a + 3 \qquad 5a - 1$$

What value of a would make the expressions equal?

$a =$ _____

(b) Solve these simultaneous equations.

$$5b - 2c = 17$$

$$8b + 2c = 48$$

$b =$ _____ and $c =$ _____

(c) The lengths of the triangle are shown.

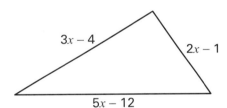

(i) Write an expression for the perimeter (P) of the triangle.

$P =$ _____

(ii) The perimeter of the triangle is 53cm.

Find the lengths of the three sides.

The sides are _____ cm, _____ cm and _____ cm

18. The options for a sports lesson are shown in this two-way table.

Sports	Male	Female	Total
Football	17	15	32
Basketball	15	13	28
Swimming	14	16	30
Total	46	44	90

(a) A boy is chosen at random. What is the probability that he is playing basketball?

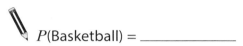 P(Basketball) = _____

(b) A pupil is chosen at random. What is the probability that they are swimming?

P(Swimming) = _____

(c) When it rains, football is played in the Sports Hall.

P(raining) = 0.2

Complete the tree diagram to calculate the probability it will **not** rain on two consecutive days.

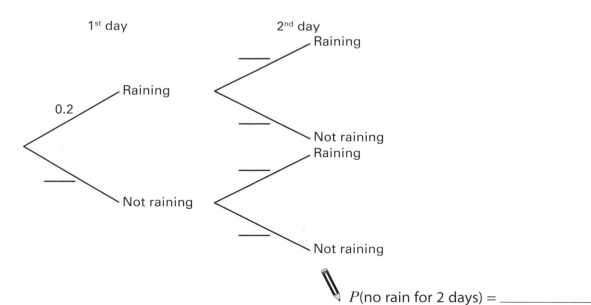

P(no rain for 2 days) = _____

19. A school carried out a survey to find how far children lived from school.

There are 600 students in the school.

The data is presented in a cumulative frequency graph.

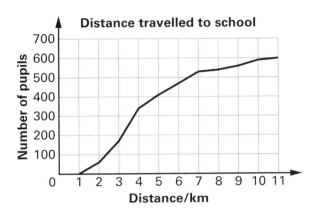

Use the graph to work out:

(a) the median distance travelled to school.

_____

(b) the interquartile range for the school's data.

_____

20. Simplify the following:

(a) $6d^{-3} \times 3d^{-2}$

_____

(b) $24c^7 \div 8c^{-2}$

_____

(c) $\dfrac{10a^3b^4}{2ab^2}$

_____

Test Paper 1

Calculator **not** allowed

First name _____

Last name _____

Date _____

Instructions:

- The test is 1 hour long.
- Find a quiet place where you can sit down and complete the test paper undisturbed.
- You **may not** use a calculator for any question in this test.
- You will need: a pen, pencil, rubber and a ruler. You may find tracing paper useful.
- This test starts with easier questions.
- Write your answers where you see this symbol:
- Try to answer all the questions.
- The number of marks available for each question is given in the margin.
- Write all your answers **and working** on the test paper. Marks may be awarded for working.
- Check your work carefully.
- Check how you have done using pages 103–112 of the Answers and Mark Scheme.

You might need to use these formulae:

Trapezium	Prism
Area $= \frac{1}{2}(a + b)h$	Volume = area of cross-section × length

MAXIMUM MARK	60		ACTUAL MARK	

1. Tim needs to cut a 4m plank of wood into five equal lengths to make some shelves.

(a) How long will each shelf be?

_____

(b) Tim is going to use the shelves for his DVDs.

Each DVD is 1.5cm wide.

How many DVDs will fit on each shelf?

_____

2. Calculate $683 \div 17$.

Give your answer correct to two decimal places.

_____

SUBTOTAL

3. These two triangles are congruent.

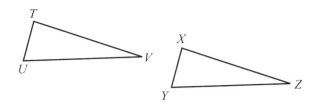

$\angle TUV = 75°$

$\angle YXZ = 87°$

(a) Calculate $\angle XZY$

_____ °

(b) Explain why TUV and XYZ are **not** isosceles triangles.

_____

_____

_____

(c) There are two possible isosceles triangles that could have at least one angle of 76°.

Write the three angles of each of these triangles.

_____ °, _____ ° and _____ °

and

_____ °, _____ ° and _____ °

4. **(a)** The lengths of the sides of this rectangle are shown by expressions.

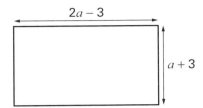

Write an expression for the area (A) of the rectangle.

 $A =$ _____

(b) This design is made from nine rhombuses.

The length of each side of a single rhombus is $2b + 1$.

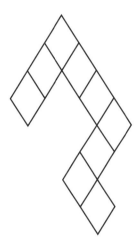

Find the perimeter (P) of the design if $b = 8$ cm.

 $P =$ _____

5. This pie chart shows how 720 children travel to school.

Travelling to school

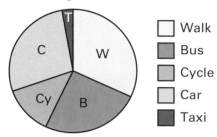

☐ Walk
◼ Bus
◻ Cycle
☐ Car
◼ Taxi

(a) Estimate the number of children who get the bus to school.

(b) Which means of transport represents about 12.5% of the children?

6. This bar chart shows the weekly wages of the staff at an office.

(a) How many office workers earn between £101 and £300 a week?

The office manager wants to make a pie chart of this information.

(b) What fraction of the pie chart would be shown by the workers who earn between £401 and £500 a week?

_____

(c) What would be the angle at the centre of the sector for the workers who earn between £301 and £400 a week?

_____ °

7.   A map has a scale of 1 : 50 000.

(a) A walk is 4 kilometres long. How long is the walk on the map?

Give your answer in centimetres (cm).

_____ cm

(b) On the map, two towns are 25 cm apart. How far are the towns apart in real life?

Give your answer in kilometres (km).

_____ km

8.   A number is divided by 26 and the answer is 43.6

What is the number?

_____

SUBTOTAL

9. Nisha has two fair 1 to 6 dice.

She asks herself these questions about the trials she is trying.

Tick (✓) the correct statement for each question.

(a) 'How can I describe the events of "rolling a 6" with each dice?'

These are independent events.	These are mutually exclusive events.	These are dependent events.

(b) 'What is the probability of totalling both scores to reach 12?'

The probability is $\frac{1}{6}$	The probability is $\frac{1}{12}$	The probability is $\frac{1}{36}$

(c) 'What is the probability of rolling one die and the number being < 2 and even?'

This is an independent event.	This is a mutually exclusive event.	This is a dependent event.

(d) 'What is the probability of rolling a number < 3 on one dice and an even number on the second dice?'

The probability is $\frac{1}{2}$	The probability is $\frac{1}{5}$	The probability is $\frac{1}{6}$

10. Mark, Barry and Carla have some marbles.

Barry has three times as many marbles as Mark.

Carla has four times as many marbles as Mark.

(a) Write a formula to show the total number of marbles, M, and let the number of Mark's marbles be x.

$M =$ _____

(b) Carla has 140 marbles.

How many marbles do Mark and Barry have?

Mark has _____ marbles and Barry has _____ marbles.

11. Manisha completed a test. She got 17 questions out of 20 right. Her teacher wrote her score as a percentage.

(a) What was her percentage score?

_____

(b) Manisha's friend Sally scored 70%.

How many out of 20 did Sally score?

_____

(c) Dev completed a different test. He got 18 out of 25 questions right.

Dev says, 'I scored more than Manisha, so I did best.'

Manisha says, 'No, I did best.'

Explain why Manisha is correct.

_____

_____

_____

1 mark

1 mark

1 mark

1 mark

1 mark

SUBTOTAL

12. Garden fertiliser uses a ratio to show the amount of nitrogen (N), phosphorus (P) and potassium (K) it contains. It is called the NPK ratio.

A 6 : 4 : 4 ratio means the fertiliser contains 6% nitrogen, 4% phosphorus and 4% potassium. The remaining percentage is a filler.

(a) A pack of fertiliser has an NPK ratio of 25 : 2 : 8.

The pack has 160g of potassium.

What is the mass of the full pack, including the filler?

Give your answer in kilograms (kg).

_____ kg

(b) There is 200g **each** of nitrogen, phosphorus and potassium.

How much fertiliser can be made if the fertiliser has an NPK ratio of 25 : 2 : 8?

Give your answer in kilograms (kg).

_____ kg

13. By rounding to 1 significant figure, estimate the answers to these calculations.

(a) 831 × 0.709

_____

(b) (4811 + 4427) ÷ 27

_____

14. There are three pairs of triangles.

Tick (✓) the pairs that are congruent and give the condition of congruency you are using.

	Tick (✓) if congruent	Condition of congruency

(i)

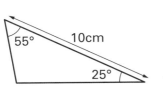

(ii)

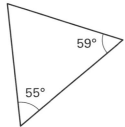

(iii)

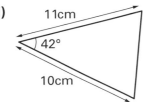

SUBTOTAL

15. A nursery teacher has a set of shapes.

All the shapes are pentagons. There are three different sizes:

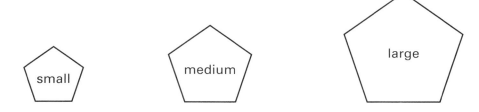

Each of the sizes comes in four different colours:

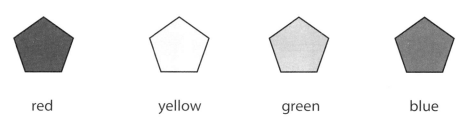

The teacher takes **some** of the shapes.

The probability of picking the shapes the teacher selected at random is listed in the table.

Pentagon	Probability	Pentagon	Probability
Small red	0.1	Small green	0.05
Medium red	0.125	Medium green	0.15
Small yellow	0.25	Large green	0.125
Large yellow	0.15	Small blue	0.05

(a) The probability of selecting a medium red pentagon is 0.125

There are 10 medium red pentagons.

How many pentagons did the teacher select altogether?

(b) The teacher did not select every type of pentagon.

Use the table to identify the types of pentagon the teacher did **not** select.

16. **(a)** Solve:

$$3(5x + 3) + 4(3x - 3) = 105$$

$x =$ _____

1 mark

(b) Solve this pair of simultaneous equations.

$$5x + 2y = 26$$

$$2x + 2y = 14$$

$x =$ _____ , $y =$ _____

(c) Make f the subject of this equation.

$$e + 4 = \frac{d^2}{f} + 7$$

$f =$ _____

17. The mean of five numbers was 21.

Here are some facts about the five numbers:

- The largest number was 40.

- The median number and the mode were both 16.

- The range was 28.

(a) When the five numbers were arranged in order, from lowest to highest, what was the fourth number?

_____

A sixth number was added to the group.

The new mean was 24.

(b) What was the sixth number added to the group?

_____

18. *ABG*, *ACF* and *ADE* are all similar triangles.

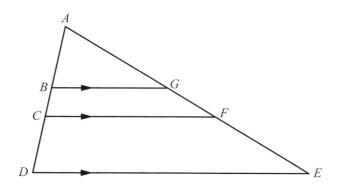

- Line *AG* is 10cm

- Line *AD* is 15cm

- Line *BG* is 8cm

- Line *DE* is 20cm

- Line *EF* is 10cm

Calculate the lengths of:

(a) *GF*

_____ cm

(b) *CF*

_____ cm

(c) *BC*

_____ cm

19. This is an octagonal prism.

It is 15cm long.

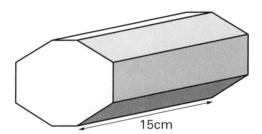

15cm

The end face is not a regular octagon, but does have two lines of symmetry.

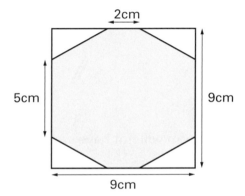

2cm

5cm

9cm

9cm

(a) Calculate the area of the end face of the octagonal prism.

 _____ cm²

(b) Calculate the volume of the prism.

 _____ cm³

20. 125 students were asked about how they spent the previous evening.

Their answers were recorded in a sorting diagram.

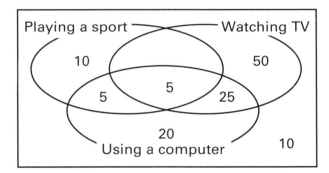

(a) What is the probability that a student chosen at random will have been using a computer?

(b) What is the probability that a student chosen at random will not have watched TV?

The same group of students was surveyed again one week later.

This time the probability that a student did not take part in any activity was 0.04

(c) How many students did not take part in any activity?

(d) Explain why the probability of a student in the second survey using a computer could not be 0.1

21. The scatter graph shows the relationship between the height and shoe size of some students.

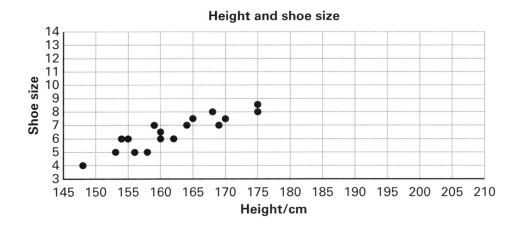

(a) Describe the correlation of the graph.

 _____

1 mark

(b) On the graph, draw a line of best fit.

1 mark

(c) Estimate the shoe size for someone who is 195cm tall.

 _____

1 mark

(d) Holly says, 'This graph shows that all students who are 160cm tall would never wear shoes that are size 10.'

Is Holly correct?

Circle YES or NO   YES / NO

Explain your answer:

 _____

_____

_____

1 mark

SUBTOTAL

Test Paper 2

Calculator allowed

First name _____

Last name _____

Date _____

Instructions:

- The test is 1 hour long.
- Find a quiet place where you can sit down and complete the test paper undisturbed.
- You **may** use a calculator for any question in this test.
- You will need a pen, pencil, rubber, ruler, a pair of compasses and a scientific or graphic calculator.
- This test starts with easier questions.
- Write your answers where you see this symbol: ✏
- Try to answer all the questions.
- The number of marks available for each question is given in the margin.
- Write all your answers **and working** on the test paper. Marks may be awarded for working.
- Check your work carefully.
- Check how you have done using pages 103–112 of the Answers and Mark Scheme.

You might need to use these formulae:

Trapezium	Prism
Area $= \frac{1}{2}(a + b)h$	Volume = area of cross-section × length

MAXIMUM MARK	60		ACTUAL MARK	

1. Calculate the missing angles.

(a) Find $\angle r$

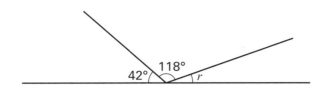

$r =$ _____°

(b) Find $\angle s$

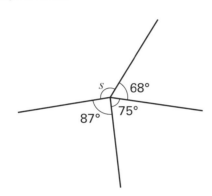

$s =$ _____°

(c) Find $\angle t$

$t =$ _____°

1 mark

1 mark

2 marks

SUBTOTAL

2. Glen's music collection is made up from CDs and downloads.

He has 5 downloads for every 7 CDs.

Glen has 35 CDs.

(a) How many downloads does he have?

_____

Glen's friend Ben has twice as many CDs, but the same number of downloads.

(b) What is the ratio of Ben's CDs to downloads in its simplest terms?

_____ : _____

3. A bag has 5 counters; 3 of the counters are black and 2 are white.

(a) A counter is drawn at random; what is the probability that the counter is black?

Give your answer in its simplest terms.

_____

(b) A black counter is drawn and is not replaced in the bag.

What is the probability that the next counter drawn at random will be black?

_____

4. Here are six number cards.

The sixth card is turned over.

| 4 | 4 | 4 | 4 | 4 | |

The mean of the six numbers is 5.

(a) What is the number on the sixth card?

_____

Here are another six number cards, again the sixth card is turned over.

| 6 | 3 | 7 | 4 | 7 | |

The range of the six numbers is 6.

(b) What are the two numbers that the sixth card could be?

_____ or _____

5. **(a)** Find the value of $\dfrac{6a + 12}{a}$ when $a = 1.5$

_____

(b) Solve:

$2b + 6 = 5c + 8$ when $c = 0.5$

$b =$ _____

6.   **(a)** Find $\frac{4}{5}$ of £28.

(b) £28 is $\frac{4}{5}$ of an amount.

What is the amount?

7.   Using a ruler and compasses:

(a) construct the perpendicular bisector of this line.

A —————————————— B
9cm

(b) construct the bisector of this angle.

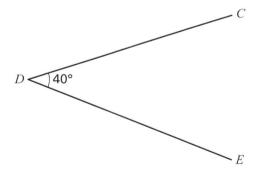

8. Barry has £75 in his bank account.

He takes £30 from the account.

(a) Calculate the ratio, in its simplest terms, of the money he has taken out to the money he has left in his account.

_____ : _____

Barry decides to spend $\frac{1}{3}$ of the money.

(b) Re-calculate the ratio, in its simplest terms, of the money he now has left to the money left in his account.

_____ : _____

9. Calculate:

(a) $5\frac{2}{3} + 6\frac{7}{8} =$

_____

(b) $6\frac{2}{5} - 3\frac{2}{3} =$

_____

10.

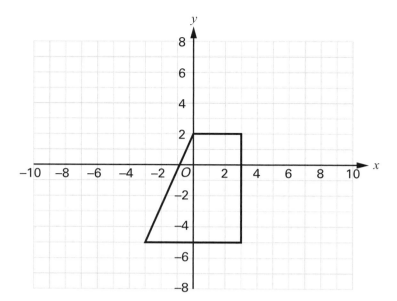

(a) What are the coordinates of the quadrilateral?

(_____ , _____), (_____ , _____),

(_____ , _____), (_____ , _____)

(b) The quadrilateral is reflected in the *y*-axis.

What are the new coordinates?

(_____ , _____), (_____ , _____),

(_____ , _____), (_____ , _____)

1 mark

1 mark

11. This is a triangular spinner.

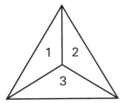

It is a biased spinner.

Spinning a 2 is twice as likely as spinning a 1.

Spinning a 3 is twice as likely as spinning a 2.

What is the probability of spinning a 1?

_____

2 marks

12. The ages of members of a gym club are shown.

2 marks

Ages															
Male	21	32	26	21	34	45	46	19	53	24	33	40	61	49	53
Female	24	27	39	40	18	27	45	61	26	35	37	49	34	21	62

Complete this two-way table to show the frequencies.

	Male	**Female**
$10 < A \leq 20$		
$20 < A \leq 30$		
$30 < A \leq 40$		
$40 < A \leq 50$		
$50 < A \leq 60$		
$60 < A \leq 70$		

SUBTOTAL

13. Four circles fit exactly into this square.

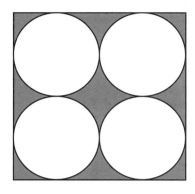

The area of the square is 625cm².

(a) Find the area of one circle.

Give your answer correct to 2 decimal places.

 _____ cm²

(b) Calculate the shaded area.

 _____ cm²

14. Factorise:

(a) $5x - 25$

 _____

(b) $4ab^2 + 2bc$

 _____

$$\text{Area} = 12d^2 \qquad 4d$$

(c) Write a simplified expression for the length of this rectangle.

_____

15. A cake has this nutritional information.

(a) Complete the missing values in the table.

Write the values to 1 decimal place.

	Per 120g	Per 50g
Protein	9g	3.75g
Carbohydrates	79.4g	_____ g
of which sugars	_____ g	8.7g
Fat	2.1g	_____ g
of which saturates	0.6g	0.25g
Fibre	_____ g	1.8g

(b) The cake weighs 900g.

(i) How much protein does it contain?

_____ g

(ii) How much saturated fat does it contain?

_____ g

16. Milly has a money box with 60 coins.

There are no 2p or 1p coins.

This table shows the probabilities of picking a coin at random.

Coin	Probability
£1	0.3
50p	0.25
20p	0.2
10p	0.1
5p	0.15

(a) Explain why it is impossible that Milly has any £2 coins in her money box.

_____

_____

_____

(b) Calculate how much money Milly has altogether.

 £ _____

17. This table shows the results of a school maths test.

Score	Frequency
⩽ 20%	2
> 20% ⩽ 40%	4
> 40% ⩽ 60%	8
> 60% ⩽ 80%	12
> 80% ⩽ 100%	6

(a) What fraction of the scores were in the > 20% ⩽ 40% category?

Give your answer as a simplified fraction.

(b) Use this circle to display the information from the table in a pie chart.

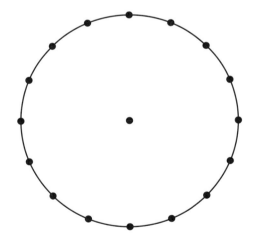

(c) Calculate the angle at the centre of the sector for the > 60% ⩽ 80% category.

SUBTOTAL

18. **(a)** Here are possible lengths for a triangle.

5cm   6cm   7cm

8cm   9cm   10cm

Which three lengths could be used for a right-angled triangle?

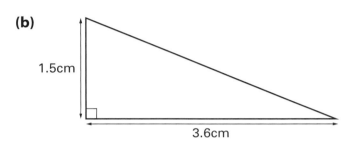 _____ cm, _____ cm and _____ cm

(b)

1.5cm

3.6cm

Calculate the area of this triangle.

 _____ cm²

(c) The square of the hypotenuse of a right-angled **isosceles** triangle is 800cm².

Calculate the length of one of the other sides.

 _____ cm

19. **(a)** Write the first 3 numbers in the sequence $5n^2 - 4$.

1 mark

_____ , _____ , _____

(b) Write the expression that is shown by the curve on the graph.

1 mark

_____

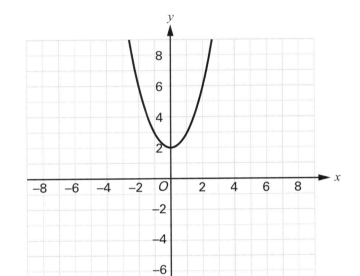

(c) On the graph, draw a curve representing the equation $y = x^2 - 3$.

1 mark

SUBTOTAL

20. The amount of money raised during a charity fun run is recorded in a table.

Amount raised per person (n)	Frequency	Cumulative frequency
$0 < n \leqslant 50$	5	
$50 < n \leqslant 100$	12	
$100 < n \leqslant 150$	28	
$150 < n \leqslant 200$	20	
$200 < n \leqslant 250$	18	
$250 < n \leqslant 300$	12	
$300 < n \leqslant 350$	4	
$350 < n \leqslant 400$	1	

(a) Draw a cumulative frequency graph of this data.

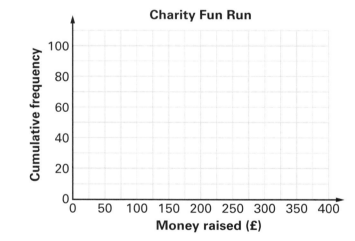

(b) Estimate the median amount of money raised.

✎ £ _____

(c) Give the interquartile range.

✎ _____ – _____

(d) An extra runner has raised £350.

If this is included with the others, describe the effect that this will have on the mean.

✎ _____

_____

21. In 2011 the populations of countries in the United Kingdom were:

- England   53 012 456

- Scotland   5 295 000

- Wales   3 063 456

- N. Ireland   1 810 863

(a) What percentage of the population of the United Kingdom lived in England?

✎ _____

(b) In 2001, the population of England was 49 138 831.

By how many percent had the population of England increased?

✎ _____

SUBTOTAL

Test Paper 1

Calculator **not** allowed

First name _____

Last name _____

Date _____

Instructions:

- The test is 1 hour long.
- Find a quiet place where you can sit down and complete the test paper undisturbed.
- You **may not** use a calculator for any question in this test.
- You will need: a pen, pencil, rubber and a ruler. You may find tracing paper useful.
- This test starts with easier questions.
- Write your answers where you see this symbol:
- Try to answer all the questions.
- The number of marks available for each question is given in the margin.
- Write all your answers **and working** on the test paper. Marks may be awarded for working.
- Check your work carefully.
- Check how you have done using pages 103–112 of the Answers and Mark Scheme.

You might need to use these formulae:

Trapezium	Prism
Area $= \frac{1}{2}(a + b)h$	Volume = area of cross-section × length

Trapezium diagram: with top side b, height (h), bottom side a

Prism diagram: with length and area of cross-section labelled

MAXIMUM MARK	60		ACTUAL MARK	

1. **(a)** Ewan has £60 and spends £15

What percentage of his original amount has he spent?

(b) Milly has £60 left after spending £15

What percentage of her original amount does she have left?

(c) Scott has spent 15% of his £60

How much money does he have left?

2. Here are two cuboids.

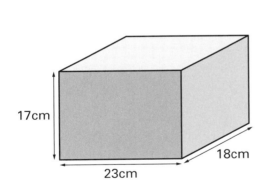

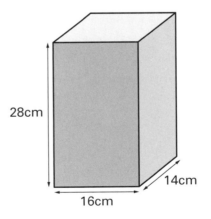

What is the difference between the volumes of the two cuboids?

Give your answer in cubic centimetres (cm³).

 _____ cm^3

3. Here are two spinners.

Spinner A

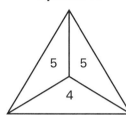

Spinner B

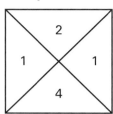

(a) Explain why it is more likely to spin a 4 on Spinner A than on Spinner B.

_____

_____

Kirsty uses both spinners and totals the number from each spinner.

(b) What is the probability that Kirsty will score 10?

(c) What is the probability that Kirsty will score 6?

4. Tower A and Tower B are made with identical blocks.

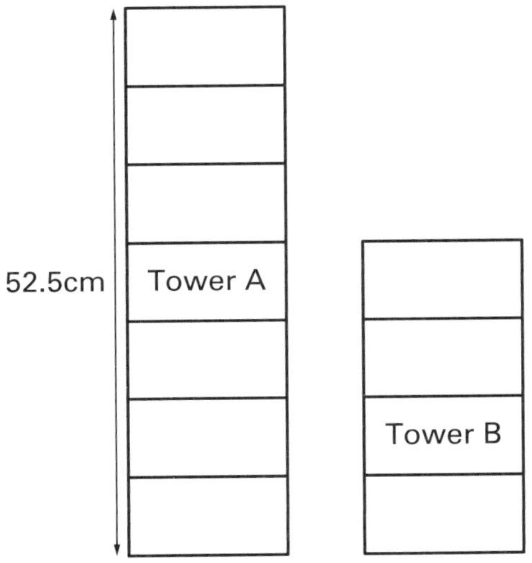

52.5cm Tower A

Tower B

Tower A is 52.5cm tall.

(a) How tall is Tower B?

_____

2 marks

The ratio of the length to width of each block is 2 : 1.

(b) How long is each block?

_____

1 mark

SUBTOTAL

5. Solve:

1 mark

(a) $5x - 7 = 2x + 8$

1 mark

(b) $6(y + 3) = 10(y - 3)$

1 mark

6. **(a)** Ravi divides a number by 1.25 and multiplies it by 2.5.

Which number could Ravi use to multiply by that would have the same effect?

Max has a recipe that makes enough for 12 people.

1 mark

(b) He multiplies the quantities of the ingredients by 0.25.

How many people will there be enough food for?

1 mark

(c) He divides the quantities of the ingredients by $1\frac{1}{3}$.

How many people will there be enough food for?

7. An experiment records the height of some seedlings and the number of hours of light that the seedlings receive each day.

This scatter graph shows the results after one week.

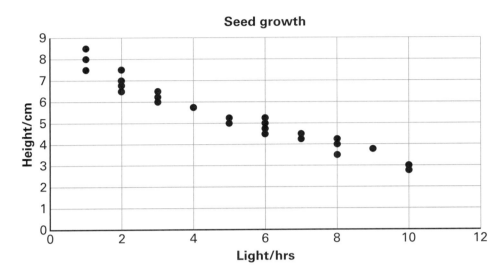

(a) Describe the correlation between the height of the seedlings and the amount of light they have received.

_____

_____

1 mark

(b) Describe the relationship between the height of the seedlings and the amount of light they receive.

_____

_____

2 marks

(c) On the graph, draw a line of best fit.

1 mark

SUBTOTAL

8. Triangle ABC is an isosceles triangle.

Lines DE and FG are parallel.

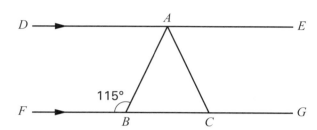

Calculate these angles.

(a) $\angle ACB =$ _____ °

(b) $\angle CAE =$ _____ °

(c) $\angle BAC =$ _____ °

9. Change these metric measures to the units shown.

(a) 6m² = _____ cm²

(b) 1cm³ = _____ mm³

(c) A fish tank is 80cm long, 50cm wide and 60cm high.

How many litres of water can it hold?

_____ *l*

1 mark

1 mark

1 mark

1 mark

1 mark

1 mark

10. A gym club opened six years ago.

The club wants to know for how many months its members have been in the club.

Membership is recorded in a cumulative frequency table for the first six years.

Length of membership in years, Y	Members	Cumulative frequency
$0 < Y \leqslant 1$	40	
$1 < Y \leqslant 2$	60	
$2 < Y \leqslant 3$	110	
$3 < Y \leqslant 4$	100	
$4 < Y \leqslant 5$	80	
$5 < Y \leqslant 6$	90	

(a) Complete the cumulative frequency column.

1 mark

(b) Draw the cumulative frequency graph.

(There is a blank graph on the next page.)

2 mark

(c) Use your graph to estimate the median length of membership.

1 mark

(d) Use your graph to estimate the interquartile range.

1 mark

SUBTOTAL

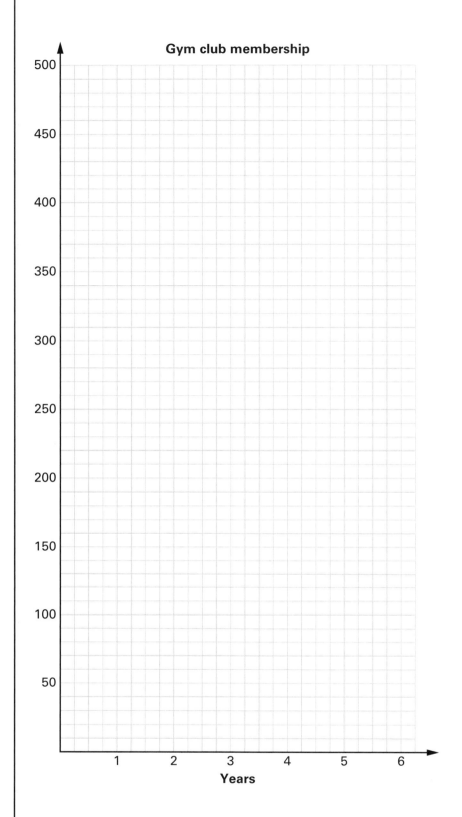

Gym club membership

Years

11. Here is a sequence of patterns.

| Pattern number 1 | Pattern number 2 | Pattern number 3 | Pattern number 4 |

(a) How many squares will be needed to make the next pattern in the sequence?

_____

(b) Write a formula to show the number of squares in any pattern.

Begin your formula with s, where $s =$ the number of squares and use $p =$ the pattern number.

_____

(c) Use your formula to find out how many squares would be needed in pattern number 48.

_____

12. Yousef uses this spinner.

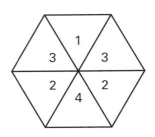

(a) Complete the table showing the theoretical probability of spinning each number.

Number	1	2	3	4
Theoretical probability	_____	_____	_____	_____

(b) Complete this table showing the number of times you would theoretically spin each number.

	After 100 spins			
Number	**1**	**2**	**3**	**4**
Theoretical probability	_____	_____	_____	_____

(c) Yousef spun his spinner 150 times. Give the number of times the spinner should theoretically land on an even number.

_____

13. Describe fully the rotation of the shape from Shape A to Shape B.

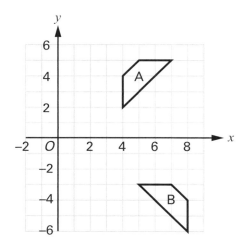

_____

_____

14. Linda sets out on a journey by car.

She leaves at 13:45 and arrives at 16:25. The journey is 120 miles.

(a) At what speed did Linda travel?

A formula for making an approximate change of miles to kilometres is:

$$Kilometres = \frac{8 \times miles}{5}$$

(b) What was Linda's speed in kilometres per hour?

(c) Linda's return journey was quicker and she travelled at 60mph.
If she left at 12:45 the next day, at what time did she arrive home?

15. The triangle ABC is enlarged by a scale factor of $\frac{1}{5}$.

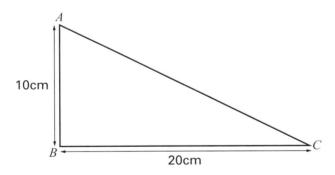

(a) What would the lengths of the sides AB and BC be?

$AB =$ _____ cm and $BC =$ _____ cm

(b) By what scale factor would the lengths of the new triangle have to be multiplied to
return it to being the first triangle?

16. Two identical bags both contain three white balls and two black balls.

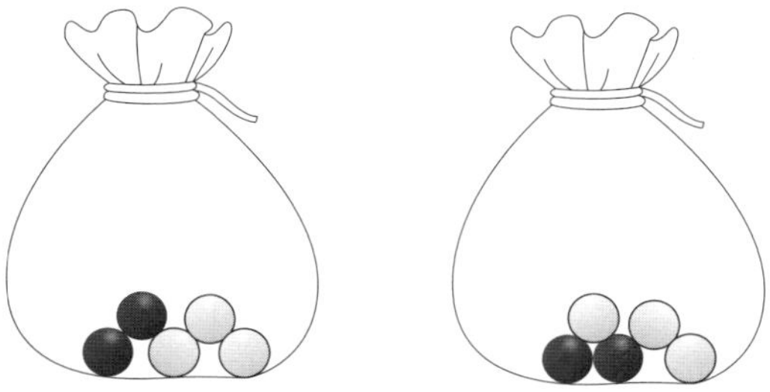

Maria pulls a ball from each bag.

1 mark

(a) Calculate the probability that both balls will be white.

____

1 mark

(b) Calculate the probability that both balls will be black.

____

Maria just uses one of the bags.

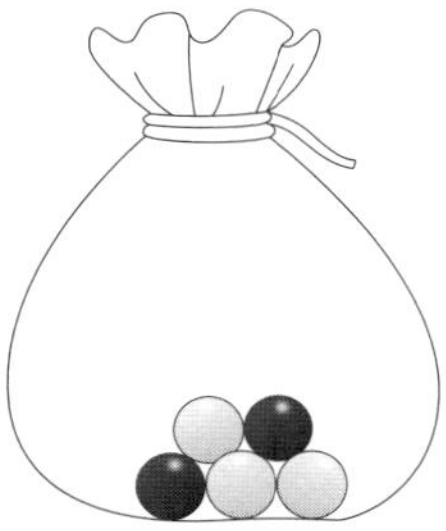

She pulls one ball from the bag, keeps the ball and then pulls another ball.

1 mark

(c) Calculate the probability that both balls will be white.

____

1 mark

(d) Calculate the probability that both balls will be black.

____

17. A school collects tokens from a local supermarket.

48 000 tokens are collected and need to be put into bundles of 100.

It takes 6 students $2\frac{1}{2}$ hours to count the tokens.

(a) How long would it take 10 students to count the tokens?

(b) How many students would be needed to complete the task in 60 minutes?

18. The line shows the equation $y = x - 2$.

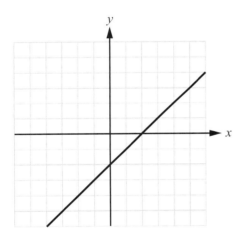

(a) Use the graph to give the value of y if $x = -3$.

  $y =$ _____

SUBTOTAL

(b) Use the same graph to give the value of x if $y = -4$.

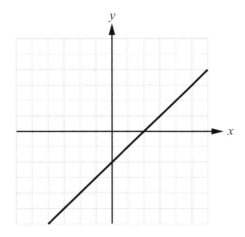

$x =$ _____

(c) Write the equation shown by this graph.

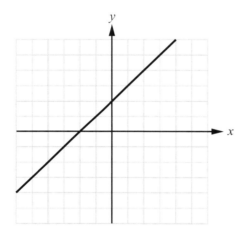

$y =$ _____

19. This cumulative frequency graph shows the ages of 160 passengers on an aeroplane.

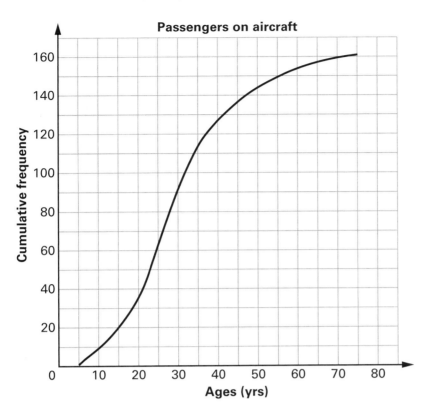

(a) Draw a box plot of the information in the cumulative graph.

2 marks

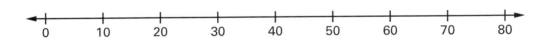

(b) Give the median age of the passengers.

1 mark

(c) Give the interquartile range of the ages of the passengers.

1 mark

SUBTOTAL

Test Paper 2

Calculator allowed

First name _____

Last name _____

Date _____

Instructions:

- The test is 1 hour long.
- Find a quiet place where you can sit down and complete the test paper undisturbed.
- You **may** use a calculator for any question in this test.
- You will need a pen, pencil, rubber, ruler, a pair of compasses and a scientific or graphic calculator.
- This test starts with easier questions.
- Write your answers where you see this symbol:
- Try to answer all the questions.
- The number of marks available for each question is given in the margin.
- Write all your answers **and working** on the test paper. Marks may be awarded for working.
- Check your work carefully.
- Check how you have done using pages 103–112 of the Answers and Mark Scheme.

You might need to use these formulae:

Trapezium	Prism
Area $= \dfrac{1}{2}(a + b)h$	Volume = area of cross-section × length

Trapezium diagram with sides labelled b (top), height (h), a (bottom).

Prism diagram with labels "length", "area of cross-section".

MAXIMUM MARK	60	ACTUAL MARK	

1. **(a)** Ula earns £7.60 an hour.

She works 35 hours a week.

She is given a rise of 5%.

What will her new weekly wage be?

✎ £ _____

(b) Ben earns £8 an hour.

He works 30 hours a week.

He gets a pay rise of £12 a week.

What is this pay rise as a percentage?

✎ £ _____

2. The time in Italy is 1 hour ahead of time in the United Kingdom.

A plane leaves Manchester at 16:48.

The flight takes 2 hours and 17 minutes.

At what time does the plane land in Italy?

✎ _____

SUBTOTAL

3. This is the end of a building.

The roof is 6.5m high.

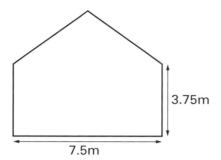

3.75m

7.5m

Calculate the area of the end wall.

Give your answer correct to 2 decimal places.

_____ m²

4. Here are three parcels. They are the same size but weigh different amounts.

| A | B | C | D |

- Parcel A weighs one quarter of parcel C.

- Parcel A weighs three times parcel B.

- Parcel B weighs half of parcel D.

- Parcel D weighs 4.5kg.

What is the weight of all four parcels?

_____ kg

5. This bar chart shows the number of times players played for their rugby club during a season.

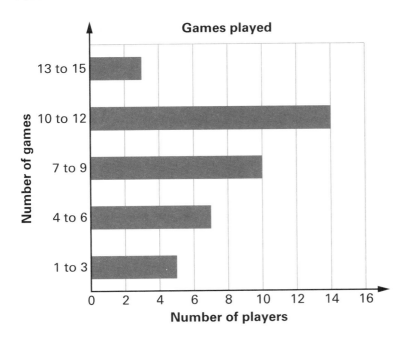

(a) How many players played in 7 or more games?

1 mark

(b) How many played at least one game?

1 mark

(c) 'At least 1 person played in all 15 games.'

1 mark

Is this statement correct?

Explain your answer.

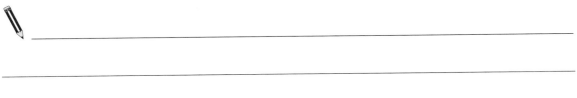

6. Solve:

$$12(2t - 3) = 4t - 31$$

$t =$ _____

2 marks

7. A sandwich shop makes sandwiches in batches of 20.

The owner works out the cost of each sandwich by using the formula:

$$S = \frac{F + B}{20} + 2.8$$

where S is the cost of one sandwich in pounds, F is the cost of the fillings in £ and B is the cost of the bread in £.

(a) Find the cost of 1 cheese and tomato sandwich where the cost of the fillings is £9.25 and the cost of the bread is £4.75

£ _____

1 mark

(b) Find the cost of 12 egg and salad sandwiches, where the cost of the fillings is £5.25 and the cost of the bread is £4.75

£ _____

1 mark

(c) A sandwich sells for £3.90 If the bread cost £4.80, what was the cost of the fillings?

£ _____

1 mark

8. **(a)** Calculate the area of this trapezium.

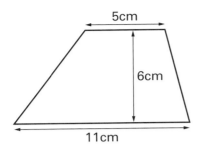

_____

(b) This right-angled triangle has an area of 56cm².

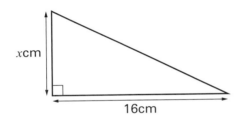

What is the height of the triangle?

_____ cm

SUBTOTAL

9. **(a)** Write the ratio 72 : 48 : 36 in its simplest form.

_____ : _____ : _____

(b) These cans of beans come in three sizes.

One can
•   Weight: 200g
•   Cost: 35p

One pack of three cans
•   Total weight: 750g
•   Cost: £1

One can
•   Weight: 450g
•   Cost: 55p

Compare the unit amounts to decide which is the best value for money.

Give the unit cost per gram and tick the best-value option.

	Unit cost per gram	Best value Tick (✓)
An individual can weighing 200g		
A pack of 3 cans each weighing 250g		
An individual can weighing 450g		

10. A castle is open to visitors 5 days a week.

This pie chart shows the number of visitors.

Castle visitors

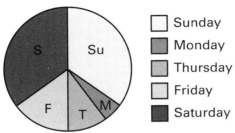

- ☐ Sunday
- ▨ Monday
- ▨ Thursday
- ☐ Friday
- ■ Saturday

There were 1000 visitors during the week.

(a) The sector showing Thursday has an angle of 36° at the centre.

How many visitors were there on Thursday?

1 mark

(b) A bar chart is drawn of the same information, but two blocks are missing.

Draw the missing blocks.

1 mark

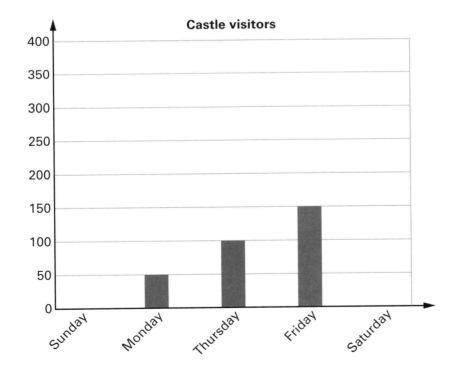

11. In a box of 200 coloured straws, there are blue, red, orange, green and yellow straws.

Straws are chosen at random.

The probabilities of taking a colour are:

- blue: $\frac{1}{8}$

- red: $\frac{1}{10}$

- orange: $\frac{1}{5}$

(a) Explain why it is impossible for there to be an equal number of green and yellow straws.

_____

_____

There are 35 green straws in the box.

Give the probability that a straw taken at random is:

(b) green

_____

(c) yellow

_____

12. This model of a steam engine is built to a scale of 1 : 80.

15.5cm

(a) How long is the real-life steam engine?

Give your answer in metres.

 _____ m

(b) The real-life carriages are 18m long.

The model carriages are made to the same scale.

How long is a model carriage?

Give your answer in centimetres.

 _____ cm

SUBTOTAL

13. This is a line graph showing the journey of two cars.

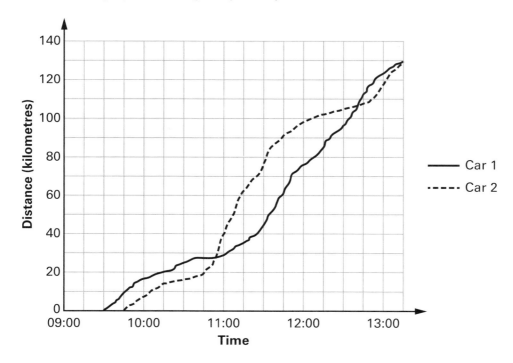

(a) After nearly 30 kilometres, Car 2 passes Car 1. At what time does this happen?

(b) What was the mean speed for Car 1's journey?

(c) Calculate the mean speed of Car 2 between 10:45 and 11:15.

(d) At about 12:40 Car 1 passes Car 2. How far had the cars travelled when this happened?

14. This design is made up from four semi-circles and a 5cm square.

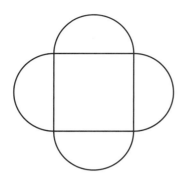

Calculate:

(a) the perimeter of the design.

Give your answer correct to 2 d.p.

(b) the area of the design.

Give your answer correct to 2 d.p.

15. Solve the following inequalities and show their solutions on the number line.

Use the correct symbols.

(a) $r + 6 < 5$

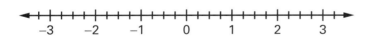

(b) $2s + 6 \geqslant 5$

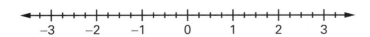

(c) $4(t - 2) \leqslant 2$

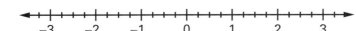

16. A spinner is made from a regular pentagon and is numbered 1 to 5.

(a) What is the theoretical probability that a 5 is rolled?

 _____

Another spinner is used but is numbered differently.

The number of times that the spinner lands on 5 are recorded in this table.

(b) Complete the table to show the relative frequencies of landing on a 5.

Number of spins	10	20	30	40	50
Number of times landing on a 5	5	7	12	12	21
Relative frequency	_____	_____	_____	_____	_____

(c) How many of the sections on the second spinner would you expect to be numbered 5?

 _____

17. A quadrilateral is drawn on this grid.

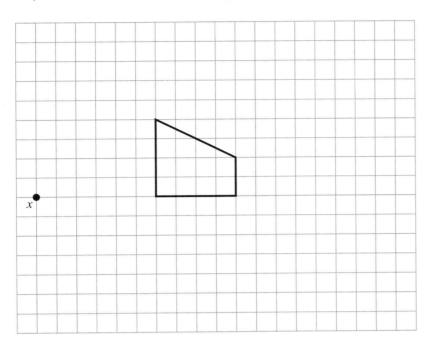

(a) Enlarge the quadrilateral by a scale factor of 1.5 about the centre of enlargement x.

Draw the quadrilateral on the grid.

2 marks

(b) Enlarge the quadrilateral by a scale factor of 0.5 about the centre of enlargement x.

Draw the quadrilateral on the grid.

2 marks

SUBTOTAL

18. In each circle, the centre of the circle is c.

Calculate the missing angles.

(a)

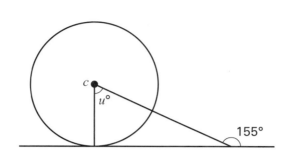

✎ $u =$ _____ °

(b)

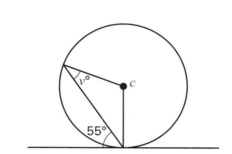

✎ $v =$ _____ °

(c)

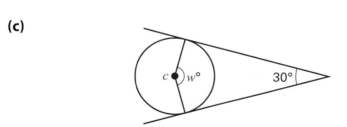

✎ $w =$ _____ °

1 mark

1 mark

1 mark

19. There are three bags with black and white balls.

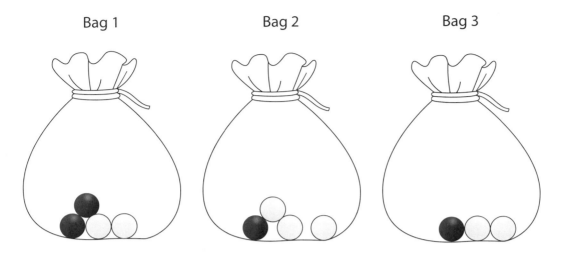

Bag 1   Bag 2   Bag 3

(a) Complete this tree diagram.

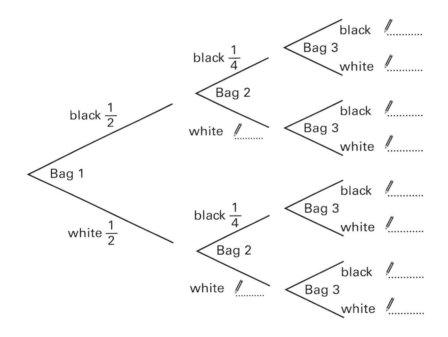

(b) What is the probability of pulling a black ball from each bag at random?

(c) What is the probability of pulling a white ball from each bag at random?

101

20. **(a)** Bill bought a car for £8000.

He ran the car for three years and each year the car lost 12% of its value.

What was the value of the car after the third year?

Answer to the nearest £10.

(b) Calculate:

$$5.2(-7.2 - 8.45) \times \frac{(5.35 - 6.8)}{2^2}$$

Answer to 1 d.p.

(c) Calculate:

$$81^{\frac{1}{2}}$$

(d) Calculate:

$$\left(\frac{3}{4} + \frac{2}{5}\right) \div \left(\frac{3}{8} - \frac{1}{6}\right)$$

1 mark

1 mark

1 mark

1 mark

Answers and Mark Scheme

Set A, Test Paper 1

1. Signs in order should be:
$<\ <\ >\ =$ (*2 marks. 1 mark: three symbols correct*)

2. Circles joined: (*2 marks. 1 mark: 1 or 2 lines correctly drawn*)

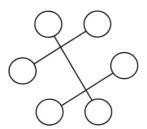

3. (a) 52cm   (*2 marks. 1 mark: Correct method e.g. 2 (15 + 11 = error or 15 + 11 + 9 + 6 + 6 + 5 = error)*)
   (b) 120cm^2 (*2 marks. 1 mark: Correct method e.g. 2 (15 + 11 = error or 15 + 11 + 9 + 6 + 6 + 5 = error)*)

4. (a) £9.60 (Do not accept £9.6)   (*1 mark*)
   (b) £21.60   (*1 mark*)

5. (a) 16   (*1 mark*)
   (b) 15.5   (*1 mark*)
   (c) 14   (*1 mark*)
   (d) 7   (*1 mark*)

6. (a) $g = 1.5$ (*1 mark*)
   (b) $10n + 2p^2 + p$ (*1 mark*)
   (c) 352   (*1 mark*)

7. 7500cm^3 (*2 marks. 1 mark: Correct method e.g. $\pi \times 10^2 \times 25$ = error*)

8. (a) $2 \times 2 \times 2 \times 3$ or $2^3 \times 3$ (*1 mark*)
   (b) 12   (*1 mark*)
   (c) 120   (*1 mark*)

9. (a) 10   (*1 mark*)
***Helpful hint** Remember the number of triangles in any polygon is always two less than the number of sides.*
   (b) 1800°   (*1 mark*)
   (c) 30°   (*1 mark*)
***Helpful hint** The exterior angle of any regular polygon is 360° ÷ by the number of sides of the polygon.*

10. (a) Explanation could use the fact that: (*1 mark*)
- the probability of there being a black counter is 0.1 and 25 × 0.1 does not equal a whole number.

- the probability of a blue counter is 0.4 and there are 12 blue counters, therefore there are 30 counters.

   (b) $1 - (0.2 + 0.4 + 0.1) = 0.3$ (*1 mark*)
   (c) 9 white counters   (*1 mark*)

11. (a) 9cm   (*1 mark*)
   (b) 72cm, 96cm, 108cm   (*2 marks. 1 mark: Two correct lengths*)
   Answers can be given in any order.

12. (a) 1: 5 expected successes
2: 2 expected successes
3: 9 expected successes   (*2 marks. 1 mark: two correct answers*)
   (b) No. Explanation needs to refer to the table: the expected probabilities are not the same, which they would be on a fair dice.   (*1 mark*)

13. (a) Total of frequencies = 20   (*1 mark*)
   Score × frequency column completed from top to bottom as follows: 20, 38, 54, 119, 64, 45, 340   (*2 marks. 1 mark: 4 or more correct multiplications*)
   (b) 58   (*1 mark*)

14. (a) The pattern of the lines should be: (*2 marks. 1 mark: Two or three lines correctly drawn*)

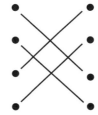

   (b) $y = 4x - 5$ (*1 mark*)

15. (a) $\frac{3}{5}$ (*1 mark*)
   (b) 225ml   (*1 mark*)
   (c) 250ml   (*2 marks. 1 mark: Correct method e.g. Sally has 200ml of pear juice and 300ml of apple juice. To find Yasmin's juice, 300 ÷ 2 = 150, 150 × 3 = error, error – 200*)

16. (a) (iii) $a(b - d) + bc$ (*1 mark*)
   (b) $b = \dfrac{P - 2a}{2}$ (*1 mark*)

17. (a) 12cm   (*1 mark*)
   (b) 60cm^2 (*1 mark*)

(c) 52° *(1 mark)*

Helpful hint *The two chords AE and BE will always form a right angle when they meet on the circumference and join the ends of the diameter.*

18. (a) 1 : 8 *(2 marks. 1 mark: Correct method e.g. $6 \times 4 \times 2 = $ error 1, $12 \times 8 \times 4 = $ error 2, error 2 ÷ error 1)*

(b) 1 : 64 *(2 marks. 1 mark: Correct method e.g. $6 \times 4 \times 2 = $ error 1, $24 \times 16 \times 8 = $ error 2, error 2 ÷ error 1)*

19. (a) $0.1 \times 0.1 = 0.01$ *(1 mark)*
(b) $1 - 0.01 = 0.99$ *(1 mark)*
(c) $0.5 \times 0.4 = 0.2$ *(1 mark)*

Helpful hint *Remember to multiply probabilities to find the outcome of two independent events.*

20. (a) 1.5×10^9 *(1 mark)*
(b) 1.5×10^4 *(1 mark)*

Helpful hint *Re-arrange expressions, e.g. $(3 \times 10^5) \times (5 \times 10^3) = 3 \times 5 \times 10^5 \times 10^3$ Indices are added when multiplying*
$$= 15 \times 10^8$$
Indices are subtracted when dividing.

21. 2.5cm *(1 mark)*

Set A, Test Paper 2

1. (a) −2, −9, −16 *(1 mark)*
(b) 12, 20, 36 *(1 mark)*
(c) 5, 8, 11 *(1 mark)*

2. (a) 5 : 3 : 4 *(1 mark)*
(b) $\frac{1}{4}$ *(1 mark)*

3. (a) $\frac{3}{5}$ or 0.6 *(1 mark)*
(b) $\frac{3}{8}$ or 0.375 *(1 mark)*
(c) $\frac{1}{5}$ or 0.2 *(1 mark)*

4. (a) 19:02 *(1 mark)*
(b) 15:58 *(1 mark)*
(c) 19:32 *(1 mark)*

Helpful hint *On a timetable, empty spaces mean the train doesn't stop.*

5. (a) 4 edges *(1 mark)*
(b) 352cm² *(2 marks. 1 mark: Correct method e.g. $2 (12 \times 8) = 2 (12 \times 4) + 2 (8 \times 4)$)*

6. (a) 102.10cm² *(2 marks. 1 mark: Correct method e.g. $\frac{(\pi \times 9^2)}{2} - \frac{(\pi \times 4^2)}{2}$)*
(b) 50.84cm *(2 marks. 1 mark: Correct method e.g. $\frac{(\pi \times 18)}{2} + \frac{(\pi \times 8)}{2} + (2 \times 5)$)*

7. (a) $4s^2 - 20s$ *(1 mark)*
(b) $r^2 + 13r + 42$ *(1 mark)*
(c) $5(2t + 5)$ *(1 mark)*

8. (a) 600 *(1 mark)*
(b) £32.50 *(1 mark)*

Helpful hint *When you read from a calculator and the answer refers to money, two numbers are always needed after the decimal point. So, £32.5 would be a wrong answer.*

9. (a) 0.2 or $\frac{1}{5}$ or $\frac{12}{60}$ *(1 mark)*

(b) $0.\dot{3}$ or $\frac{1}{3}$ or $\frac{20}{60}$ *(1 mark)*

(c) No. Explanation needs to show that it is possible to pick a jumper that is red and large at the same time. *(1 mark)*

Helpful hint *Mutually exclusive events are ones that can't happen at the same time: e.g. tossing a coin and the result being both a head and a tail.*

10. (a) £26.65 *(1 mark)*
(b) The following should be circled:
• £11.90 (1st class, 1kg–2kg)
• £8.90 (2nd class, 2kg–5kg) *(2 marks. 1 mark: Correct method e.g. 26.40 − 5.60)*

11. (a) 7 *(2 marks. 1 mark: Works to correct equation e.g. $5x + 13 = 45$)*
(b) 5 *(2 marks. 1 mark: Works to correct equation e.g. $16x − 8 = 9x + 27$)*

12. 78.78 *(1 mark)*

13. Second box indicated only. *(1 mark)*

14. A + H and E + D *(1 mark)*

15. (a) 20% *(1 mark)*
(b) 6% *(2 marks. 1 mark: Correct method e.g. $(13.25 \times 12) − 150 = $ error; error ÷ 150 × 100)*
(c) 40% *(2 marks. 1 mark: Correct method e.g. $40 \times 3 = $ error 1, error 1 − 72 = error 2, error 2 ÷ error 1 × 100)*

Helpful hint *When finding percentages, remember you need to make a fraction. In this case, the whole price is £120. The price has been reduced by £48 (120 − 72)*

So the fraction is $\frac{48}{120}$ and the calculation becomes $48 ÷ 120 \times 100 = 40$

16. The order of these answers is not important.
(a) Any two numbers that total 23, e.g. 1 and 22, 2 and 21, 3 and 20 … *(1 mark)*

Helpful hint If the mean is 16 and there are 7 numbers, the total of the numbers must be 112 (16 × 7).
The given numbers total 89, so the other two numbers must total 23 (112 – 89).

    (b) 2 or 24   *(1 mark)*

Helpful hint The range is 16, which could mean either
- 6 (the lowest number) + 18 = 24
- 20 (the highest number) – 18 = 2

    (c) 9 and 11 or 9 and 12 (ignoring the order)   *(1 mark)*

Helpful hint Arrange the numbers in order –
          9   9   10   10   12
Another 9 must be added to make the mode 9.
The range is 3, but the other number cannot be 9 since this would make the median 9, and it cannot be 10 as this would make the mode 9.5.
So the other number could be 11 or 12.

17. (a) 4   *(2 marks. 1 mark: Forms correct equation e.g. 4a + 3 = 5a – 1)*

    (b) $b = 5$ and $c = 4$ *(2 marks. 1 mark: Works to correct equation e.g. 13b = 65)*

(c) (i) $P = 10x - 17$ *(1 mark)*
    (ii) 23 cm, 17 cm, 13 cm   *(1 mark)*

18. (a) $0.1\dot{6}$ or $\frac{1}{6}$ or $\frac{15}{90}$ *(1 mark)*

    (b) $0.\dot{3}$ or $\frac{1}{3}$ or $\frac{30}{90}$ *(1 mark)*

    (c) The probability of it not raining on the first day is 0.8   *(2 marks. 1 mark: Correct method e.g. 0.8 × 0.8)*
The probabilities of 0.2 and 0.8 also apply on the second day and should be written in spaces provided.
P(no rain for 2 days) = 0.8 × 0.8 = 0.64

19. (a) Accept an answer ≥3.6 km and ≤3.9 km   *(1 mark)*

    (b) Accept answers ≥ 2.6, ≤ 2.9 and ≥5.6, ≤ 5.9   *(2 marks. 1 mark for each outlier)*
Accept also answers in the range of 2.7–3.3 inclusive.

20. (a) $18d^{-5}$ *(1 mark)*
    (b) $3c^{9}$ *(1 mark)*
    (c) $5a^{2}b^{2}$ *(1 mark)*

Set B, Test Paper 1

1. (a) 0.8m or 80cm   *(1 mark)*
    (b) 53 DVDs   *(2 marks. Accept follow through from 1(a) 1 mark: Correct method e.g. 80 ÷ 1.5 = error)*
Helpful hint Remainders here do not apply. You can't put one-third of a DVD on a shelf.

2. 40.18 (to 2 d.p.)   *(2 marks. 1 mark: Correct method with no more than one arithmetical error)*

3. (a) 18°   *(1 mark)*
    (b) Explanation should indicate that isosceles triangles have two equal angles.
    Do **not** accept: They don't look like it.   *(1 mark)*
    (c) • 28°, 76°, 76°
        • 52°, 52°, 76°   *(2 marks. 1 mark for each set of correct angles)*

4. (a) $(2a - 3)(a + 3) = 2a^{2} + 3a - 9$ *(1 mark)*
    $(2a - 3)(a + 3)$ is not sufficient for the mark.
    (b) 340cm or 3.4m   *(1 mark)*

5. (a) 180 ± 2   *(1 mark)*
Helpful hint The angle of this sector is a right angle.
    (b) Cycle   *(1 mark)*
Helpful hint 12.5% is $\frac{1}{8}$

6. (a) 36   *(1 mark)*
    (b) $\frac{1}{12}$ or $\frac{5}{60}$ *(1 mark)*
    (c) 72°   *(1 mark)*
Helpful hint 12 out of 60 = $\frac{1}{5}$
$\frac{1}{5}$ of 360° = 72°

7. (a) 8cm   *(2 marks. 1 mark: Correct method e.g. 4 ÷ 50 000 × 1000 × 100 = error)*
    (b) 12.5km   *(2 marks. 1 mark: Correct method e.g. 25 × 50 000 ÷ 100 ÷ 1000 = error)*

8. 1133.6   *(1 mark)*

9. (a) ☑ ☐ ☐
    (b) ☐ ☐ ☑
    (c) ☐ ☑ ☐
    (d) ☐ ☐ ☑   *(2 marks. 1 mark for three correct answers)*

10. (a) $M = x + 3x + 4x = 8x$ *(1 mark)*
    (b) Mark has 35 marbles and Barry has 105 marbles.   *(1 mark)*

11. (a) 85%   *(1 mark)*
    (b) 14   *(1 mark)*
    (c) Explanation should show that $\frac{18}{25} = 72\%$ and that 72% < 85%   *(1 mark)*

12. (a) 2kg   *(1 mark)*
    (b) 0.8kg   *(2 marks. 1 mark: Correct method e.g. Nitrogen is 25% (1/4) of the total amount of fertiliser. Therefore 200g × 4 = 800g)*

13. (a) 560   *(1 mark)*
    (b) 300   *(1 mark)*

14. (i) Is not congruent.

   (ii) Is not congruent.

Helpful hint *The three angles are the same, but this has no effect on the length of the sides.*

   (iii) Are congruent.

       Condition of congruency:

       side, angle, side (SAS) *(3 marks. 1 mark for correct ticks; 1 mark for correct condition for congruency)*

15. (a) 80   *(2 marks. 1 mark: Correct method e.g. 1 ÷ 0.125 = error, error × 10 = error)*

   (b) The teacher did not select: *(2 marks. 1 mark: 3 correct answers)*

     • Large red pentagons
     • Medium yellow pentagons
     • Medium blue pentagons
     • Large blue pentagons

16. (a) $x = 4$ *(1 mark)*

   (b) $x = 4$, $y = 3$ *(1 mark)*

   (c) $f = \dfrac{d^2}{e-3}$ Accept $f = \dfrac{d^2}{e+4-7}$ *(1 mark)*

17. (a) 21   *(1 mark)*

   (b) 39   *(1 mark)*

18. (a) GF = 5cm   *(1 mark)*

   (b) CF = 12cm   *(1 mark)*

   (c) BC = 3cm   *(1 mark)*

Helpful hint *Add the lengths you know to the diagram. Use ratio to find the other lengths.*

19. (a) 67cm^2 *(2 marks; 1 mark: Finding correct triangle 3.5cm × 2cm; 1 mark: Correct method e.g. $92 - 4 \times \frac{(3.5 \times 2)}{2})$*

   (b) 1005cm^3 *(2 marks. 1 mark: Answer from 19 (a) × 15 = error)*

20. (a) 0.44 or $\dfrac{11}{25}$ or $\dfrac{55}{125}$ *(1 mark)*

   (b) 0.36 or $\dfrac{9}{25}$ or $\dfrac{45}{125}$ *(1 mark)*

   (c) 5 students   *(1 mark)*

   (d) Explanation should show that 0.1 of 125 would be 12.5 or $12\frac{1}{2}$ and it would be impossible to have 0.5 or $\frac{1}{2}$ of a student.   *(1 mark)*

21. (a) The graph shows a positive correlation.   *(1 mark)*

   (b)

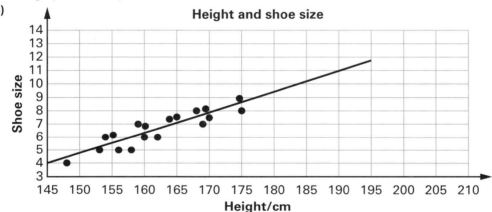

                                              (1 mark)

   (c) 11 or 12 (in the context of the question, these are the nearest possible sizes)   *(1 mark)*

   (d) No. Explanation to include that these are only statistical trends.   *(1 mark)*

Set B, Test Paper 2

1. (a) 20°   *(1 mark)*

   (b) 130°   *(1 mark)*

   (c) 155°   *(2 marks. 1 mark: Correct method e.g. (180 – 115) + 90 = error 1; 180 – error 1 = error 2; 180 – error 2)*

2. (a) 25 downloads   *(1 mark)*

   (b) 14 : 5   *(1 mark)*

Helpful hint *Ben has 25 downloads and 70 CDs (35 × 2). The ratio is 25 : 70; simplified, this is 5 : 14.*

3. (a) 0.6 or $\dfrac{3}{5}$ *(1 mark)*

   (b) 0.5 or $\dfrac{1}{2}$ or $\dfrac{2}{4}$ *(1 mark)*

4. (a) 10   *(1 mark)*

   (b) 1 or 9   *(2 marks. 1 mark for each answer)*

5. (a) 14   *(1 mark)*

   (b) $b = 2.25$ (Accept $2\frac{1}{4}$ or $\frac{9}{4}$)   *(1 mark)*

6. (a) £22.40   *(1 mark)*

      £22.4 is **not** an acceptable answer.

   (b) £35   *(1 mark)*

7. You should use a pair of compasses and show how you draw your answers. Add a pair of construction marks on the horizontal line, both the same distance from the centre point.

(a)

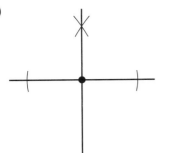

(1 mark)

(b)

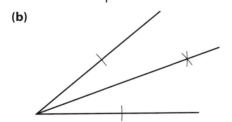

(1 mark)

8. (a) 2 : 3   *(2 marks. 1 mark: 30 : (75 – 30 = error))*
  (b) 4 : 9   *(2 marks. 1 mark: 75 – 30 = error 1,*
30 × 23 = error 2, error 2 : error 1)

9. (a) $12\frac{13}{24}$ *(1 mark)*

  (b) $2\frac{11}{15}$ *(1 mark)*

10. (a) (0, 2) (3, 2) (–3, –5) (3, –5)   *(1 mark)*
  (b) (0, 2) (–3, 2) (–3, –5) (3, –5)   *(1 mark)*

11. $\frac{1}{7}$ *(2 marks. 1 mark: Correct method e.g. use*
of algebra, let 1 = x, so x + 2x + 4x = 7x)
Helpful hint *Think of spinning a 1 as x, then spinning a 2 will*
be 2x and spinning a 3 will be 4x (twice as likely as spinning a 2).
So, the total is x + 2x + 4x = 7x; x is $\frac{1}{7}$ of 7x

12.   *(2 marks. 1 mark for 9–11 correctly completed cells)*

	Male	Female
$10 < A \leqslant 20$	1	1
$20 < A \leqslant 30$	4	5
$30 < A \leqslant 40$	4	5
$40 < A \leqslant 50$	3	2
$50 < A \leqslant 60$	2	0
$60 < A \leqslant 70$	1	2

Helpful hint *Don't forget the 0.*

13. (a) 122.72cm^2 *(2 marks. 1 mark: Use of correct*
formula, πr^2)
  (b) 134.13cm^2 *(2 marks. 1 mark: Allow follow through*
from 13(a) or Correct method e.g. 625 – 4 × area of circle)

14. (a) $5(x – 5)$ *(1 mark)*
  (b) Accept $2b(2ab + c)$ or
     $2(2ab^2 + bc)$ or $b(4ab + 2c)$ *(1 mark)*
  (c) $3d$ *(1 mark)*

15. (a)   *(2 marks. 1 mark: 2 or 3 correct answers)*

	Per 120g	Per 50g
Protein	9g	3.75g
Carbohydrates of which sugars	79.4g 20.9g	**33.1g** 8.7g
Fat of which saturates	2.1g 0.6g	**0.9g** 0.25g
Fibre	**4.3g**	1.8g

  (b) (i) 67.5g
     (ii) 4.5g *(2 marks. 1 mark for each correct answer)*

16. (a) Explanation should show that the probabilities
     given total 1.   *(1 mark)*
  (b) £28.95   *(2 marks. 1 mark: Correct identification of*
number of 3 or 4 coins, £1 (18), 50p (15), 20p (12), 10p (6), 5p (9))
Helpful hint *Having used the probability to work out*
the number of coins, don't forget to turn it into money.
E.g. 15 50p coins = £7.50.

17. (a) $\frac{1}{8}$ or $\frac{4}{32}$ *(1 mark)*
  (b)   *(2 marks. 1 mark: 3 or 4 correctly named*
sectors or correct sectors but not named)

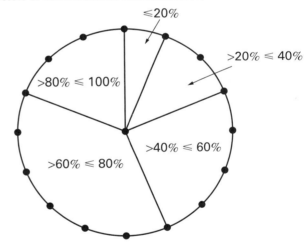

  (c) 135°   *(1 mark)*

18. (a) 6cm, 8cm, 10cm   *(1 mark)*
  (b) 2.7cm^2 *(2 marks. 1 mark: Correct method e.g.*
(1.5 × 3.6) ÷ 2 = error)
  (c) 20cm   *(1 mark)*

19. (a) 1, 16, 41   *(1 mark)*
  (b) $y = x^2 + 2$ *(1 mark)*
Helpful hint *You should recognise this type of curve as*
representing a quadratic equation. This means it involves
square numbers.
Find the coordinates you can find easily:
(0, 2) (1, 3) (2,6) (3, 11)
(0, 2) is useful; if x = 0, then x^2 also equals 0, 2 is added in
the y-axis.

(c) *(1 mark)*

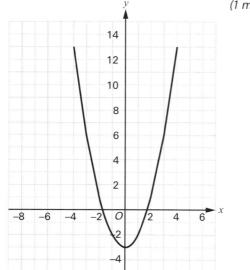

(a) *(1 mark)*

Charity Fun Run

(Graph: Cumulative frequency (y-axis, 0 to 100) vs Money raised (£) (x-axis, 0 to 400))

(b) In the range of £155–£170 inclusive *(1 mark)*
(c) In the range £110 (±5) – £230 (±5) inclusive *(1 mark)*
(d) Explanation should show that as £350 is above the mean, so the mean will increase. *(1 mark)*

21. (a) 83.9% (to one d.p.) *(1 mark)*
(b) 7.9% (to one d.p.) *(1 mark)*

20.

Amount raised per person (n)	Frequency	Cumulative frequency
$0 < n \leqslant 50$	5	**5**
$50 < n \leqslant 100$	12	**17**
$100 < n \leqslant 150$	28	**45**
$150 < n \leqslant 200$	20	**65**
$200 < n \leqslant 250$	18	**83**
$250 < n \leqslant 300$	12	**95**
$300 < n \leqslant 350$	4	**99**
$350 < n \leqslant 400$	1	**100**

Set C, Test Paper 1

1. (a) 25% *(1 mark)*
(b) 80% *(1 mark)*
(c) £51 *(1 mark)*

2. 766cm³ *(2 marks. 1 mark: Correct method e.g. (23 × 18 × 17) – (28 × 16 × 14) = error)*

3. (a) Explanation should show that the probability of spinning a 4 on Spinner 1 is $\frac{1}{3}$ and spinning a 4 on Spinner 2 is $\frac{1}{4}$ **and** $\frac{1}{3} > \frac{1}{4}$ Accept: The angle at centre of Spinner 1 is 120°; at the centre of Spinner 2 the angle is 90° and 120° > 90°. *(1 mark)*
(b) 0 (It is impossible to total 10 from the numbers on the spinners.) *(1 mark)*

(c) 0.42 (2 d.p.) or $\frac{5}{12}$ *(1 mark)*

4. (a) 30cm *(2 marks. 1 mark: Correct method e.g. 52.5 ÷ 7 × 4 = error)*
(b) 15cm *(1 mark)*

5. (a) $x = 5$ *(1 mark)*
(b) $y = 12$ *(1 mark)*

6. (a) 2 *(1 mark)*
(b) 3 *(1 mark)*
(c) 9 *(1 mark)*

7. (a) There is a negative correlation. *(1 mark)*

(b) The less light the seedlings receive, the higher they grow.

or

The more light the seedlings receive, the less they grow. *(2 marks. 1 mark: Incomplete statement e.g. The less light the seedlings receive affects their growth.)*

(c) *(1 mark)*

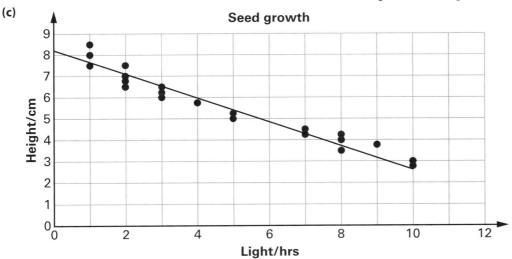

8. (a) 65° *(1 mark)*
(b) 65° *(1 mark)*
(c) 50° *(1 mark)*

9. (a) 60 000cm^2 *(1 mark)*
(b) 1000mm^3 *(1 mark)*
(c) 240l *(1 mark)*

10. (a) *(1 mark)*

Length of membership in years, Y	Members	Cumulative frequency
$0 < Y \leqslant 1$	40	**40**
$1 < Y \leqslant 2$	60	**100**
$2 < Y \leqslant 3$	110	**210**
$3 < Y \leqslant 4$	100	**310**
$4 < Y \leqslant 5$	80	**390**
$5 < Y \leqslant 6$	90	**480**

(b) *(2 marks. 1 mark for a correct graph using (incorrect) data from 10 (a))*

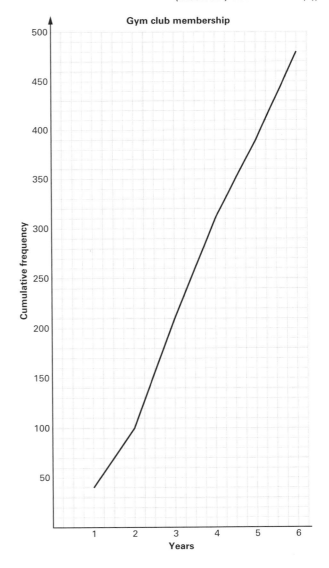

109

(c) In the range $\geqslant 3.1$, $\leqslant 3.4$ *(1 mark)*
(d) In the range from $\geqslant 2.1$ years, $\leqslant 2.4$ years to
> 4 years, < 4.25 years *(1 mark)*

11. (a) 16 squares *(1 mark)*
(b) $s = 3p + 1$ *(1 mark)*
Helpful hint *The pattern is growing by 3 at each step, so 3 must be the multiplier in the formula.*
Looking back to pattern number 1, the first multiple of 3 is 3. There is 1 extra square, which gives + 1.
(c) 145 squares *(1 mark)*

12. (a) Probability of spinning *(1 mark)*
- 1: $\frac{1}{6}$ or $0.1\dot{6}$
- 2: $\frac{1}{3}$ or $\frac{2}{6}$ or $0.\dot{3}$
- 3: $\frac{1}{3}$ or $\frac{2}{6}$ or $0.\dot{3}$
- 4: $\frac{1}{6}$ or $0.1\dot{6}$

(b) Theoretical probability of spinning
each number: *(1 mark)*
- 1: 16.7 or $16\frac{2}{3}$ or 17
- 2: 33.3 or $33\frac{1}{3}$ or 33
- 3: 33.3 or $33\frac{1}{3}$ or 33
- 4: 16.7 or $16\frac{2}{3}$ or 17

(c) 75 *(1 mark)*

13. A clockwise rotation of 90° about the point (2, −1) or an anti-clockwise rotation of 270° about the point (2, −1) *(2 marks. 1 mark: identification of point (2, −1); 1 mark: correct description of rotation)*

14. (a) 45mph *(1 mark)*
(b) 72km/h *(1 mark)*
(c) 14:45 *(1 mark)*

15. (a) $AB = 2$cm, $BC = 4$cm
(2 marks. 1 mark for each correct length)
(b) 5 *(1 mark)*

16. (a) 0.36 or $\frac{9}{25}$ *(1 mark)*
Helpful hint *Remember to multiply the probabilities to find the probability of two events. In this case:*
- 0.6×0.6
- $\frac{3}{5} \times \frac{3}{5}$

(b) 0.16 or $\frac{4}{25}$ *(1 mark)*
(c) 0.3 or $\frac{3}{10}$ *(1 mark)*
Helpful hint *Remember: having kept one ball, the probability of the second ball being white is now $\frac{1}{2}$ or $\frac{2}{4}$.*
(d) 0.1 or $\frac{1}{10}$ *(1 mark)*

17. (a) $1\frac{1}{2}$ hours or 90 minutes *(2 marks. 1 mark: Correct method e.g. $150 \times \frac{3}{5}$ = error)*
Helpful hint *The number of tokens is a distractor and not relevant.*

The key facts are 6 students take 150 minutes ($2\frac{1}{2}$ hours).

The question asks how long 10 students will take.

The number of students has increased by $1\frac{2}{3}$ or $\frac{5}{3}$

To find the time taken we need to increase the time taken by the reciprocal of $\frac{5}{3}$.

You can find this by inverting $\frac{5}{3}$, this is $\frac{3}{5}$.

$150 \times \frac{3}{5} = 90$ minutes or $1\frac{1}{2}$ hours.

(b) 15 students *(2 marks. 1 mark: Correct method e.g. $6 \times \frac{5}{2}$ = error)*
Helpful hint *The time has been multiplied by $\frac{2}{5}$, so we need to multiply the number of students by the reciprocal of $\frac{2}{5}$; which is $\frac{5}{2}$ or 2.5; $6 \times 2.5 = 15$*

18. (a) $y = -5$ *(1 mark)*
(b) $x = -2$ *(1 mark)*
(c) $y = x + 2$ *(1 mark)*

19. (a) *(2 marks)*

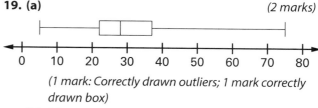

(1 mark: Correctly drawn outliers; 1 mark correctly drawn box)
(b) 28 years *(1 mark)*
(c) 15 years *(1 mark)*

Set C, Test Paper 2

1. (a) £279.30 *(2 marks. 1 mark: Correct method e.g. 7.6×35 = error; error + $\frac{5}{100}$ of error)*
£279.3 is **not** acceptable.
(b) 5% *(2 marks. 1 mark: Correct method e.g. $12 \div (8 \times 30) \times 100$)*

2. 20:05 *(2 marks. 1 mark: 18:05 or 19:05)*

3. 38.44m^2 *(2 marks)*
(1 mark: Correct method e.g.
$6.5 - 3.75$ = error 1
$(7.5 \times 3.75) + \left(\frac{7.5 \times error\ 1}{2}\right)$ = error 2

4. 40.5kg *(2 marks)*

(1 mark: Two correctly identified weights:)
- A = 6.75kg
- B = 2.25kg
- C = 27kg

Helpful hint *Start with the given fact:*
D = 4.5kg.
B is half of D.
B = 4.5 ÷ 2 = 2.25kg.
A is three times B.
A = 2.25 × 3 = 6.75kg.
A is a quarter of C.
C = 6.75 × 4 = 27kg.

5. (a) 27 players *(1 mark)*
(b) 39 players *(1 mark)*
(c) This statement is incorrect, so NO. Explanation needs to show that the 13–15 group only indicates players within that group, not the specific number of games. E.g. all three players in this section may have played 13 games. *(1 mark)*

6. $t = 0.25$ or $\frac{1}{4}$ *(2 marks. 1 mark: Correct expression e.g. 24t − 36 = 4t − 31)*

7. (a) £3.50 *(1 mark)*
£3.5 is **not** an acceptable answer.
(b) £39.60 *(1 mark)*
£39.6 is **not** an acceptable answer.
(c) £17.20 *(1 mark)*
£17.2 is **not** an acceptable answer.

8. (a) 48cm^2 *(1 mark)*
(b) 7cm *(1 mark)*

9. (a) 6 : 4 : 3 *(1 mark)*
(b)

	Best value Tick (✓)	Unit cost per gram
An individual can weighing 200g		0.175p
A pack of 3 cans each weighing 250g		0.13̇p
An individual can weighing 450g	✓	0.12̇p

(2 marks. 1 mark for correct best value indicated. 1 mark for three correct unit costs per gram)

10. (a) 100 visitors *(1 mark)*
(b) The blocks for Sunday and Saturday should both be drawn to 350. *(1 mark)*

11. (a) Blue straws $= \frac{1}{8}$ of 200 = 25; red straws $= \frac{1}{10}$ of 200 = 20; orange straws $= \frac{1}{5}$ of 200 = 40
25 + 20 + 40 = 85
200 − 85 = 115, and 115 cannot be divided equally between green and yellow straws.
(2 marks. 1 mark: Correct method e.g. $1 - (\frac{1}{8} + \frac{1}{10} + \frac{1}{5}) = $ error. Error × 200)
(b) $\frac{7}{40}$ or 0.175 *(1 mark)*
(c) $\frac{2}{5}$ or 0.4 *(1 mark)*

12. (a) 12.4m *(1 mark)*
(b) 22.5cm *(1 mark)*

13. (a) 10:50–10:55 *(1 mark)*
(b) 34.7km/h *(1 mark)*
(c) 114km/h ±4km/h *(1 mark)*
(d) 107 ±2km *(1 mark)*

14. (a) 31.42cm *(2 marks. 1 mark: Correct method e.g. 2 × πd)*
(b) 64.27cm^2 *(2 marks. 1 mark: Correct method e.g. 2 × πr^2 + 5^2)*

15. (a) 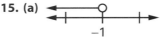 *(1 mark)*

(b) 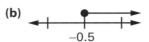 *(1 mark)*

(c)  *(1 mark)*

Helpful hint *Remember that the symbols for inequalities consist of two parts:*
- *An arrow – this tells you the direction of the values; they may be increasing (to the right) or decreasing (to the left)*
- *A circle – this tells you whether the number indicated is included in the inequality; a shaded circle indicates it is; an empty circle indicates that it is not.*

16. (a) 0.2 or $\frac{1}{5}$ *(1 mark)*
(b) *(1 mark)*

Number of spins	10	20	30	40	50
Number of times landing on a 5	5	7	12	12	21
Relative frequency	0.5	0.35	0.4	0.3	0.42

(c) 2 *(1 mark)*

17. (a)

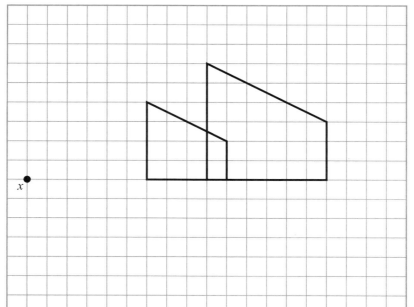

(2 marks. 1 mark: Correct enlargement incorrectly placed)

(b)

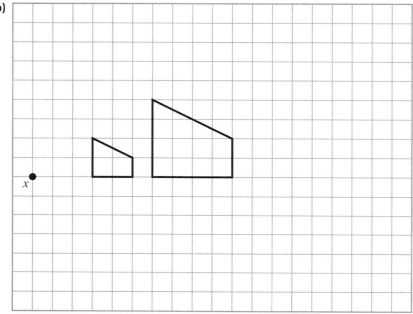

(2 marks. 1 mark: Correct enlargement incorrectly placed)

18. (a) $u = 65°$ *(1 mark)*
  (b) $v = 35°$ *(1 mark)*
  (c) $w = 150°$ *(1 mark)*

19. (a) For Bag 2   *(2 marks. 1 mark: Correct probabilities for Bag 2; 1 mark: Correct probabilities for Bag 3)*
     • white $= \frac{3}{4}$

    For Bag 3

     • black $= \frac{1}{3}$

     • white $= \frac{2}{3}$

  (b) $\frac{1}{24}$ *(1 mark)*

  (c) $\frac{1}{4}$ or $\frac{6}{24}$ *(1 mark)*

20. (a) £5450   *(1 mark)*
  (b) 29.5   *(1 mark)*
  (c) 9   *(1 mark)*
  (d) $5\frac{13}{25}$ or 5.52   *(1 mark)*

KS3 Success

English

Practice Test Papers

Age 11-14

Paul Burns

Contents

Introduction

How to Use the Practice Test Papers

About these Practice Test Papers

At the end of Key Stage 3, tests will be used by your teachers to determine your level of achievement in English.

In this book, you have three sets of test papers that will allow you to track your progress in Key Stage 3 English. They will help you to identify your strengths and weaknesses in the subject.

The test papers will:
- test your knowledge and understanding of reading, writing and comprehension
- provide practice on how to answer questions on these topics by helping to familiarise you with the different question styles that appear in test papers
- highlight opportunities for further study and skills practice that will lead to further improvement
- record results to track progress.

How to Use the Test Papers

- The questions in these test papers have been written in the style that you will see in actual tests.
- While you should try to complete the different sections in each set in the same week, you should complete sets 1, 2 and 3 **at intervals** through Key Stage 3, or Year 9.
- Make sure you leave a reasonable amount of time between each assessment – it is unrealistic to expect to see much improvement in just a few weeks. Spreading out the sets will mean you have an opportunity to develop and practise any areas you need to focus on. You will feel much more motivated if you wait for a while, because your progress will be much more obvious.
- If you want to re-use the papers, write in pencil and then rub out the answers. However, don't repeat the set too soon or you will remember the answers and the results won't be a true reflection of your abilities.

Each set of papers (A, B and C) provides one complete assessment. Each set includes:
1. a reading test paper, including reading material on which the questions are based (1 hour 15 minutes)
2. a writing test paper, which consists of a longer writing task and a shorter writing task (1 hour 15 minutes)
3. three Shakespeare test papers: one on *Romeo and Juliet;* one on *As You Like It*; and one on *Macbeth*, including extracts from the scenes on which the questions are based (45 minutes).

English

Introduction

How to Prepare for the Tests

Revision:
After covering the necessary topics, read through your notes from school or course notes. Perhaps use a revision guide to recap the key points. You could also add notes and diagrams to a mind map.

Equipment you will need:
- pen(s), pencil and rubber
- ruler
- a watch or clock to time yourself.

When you feel that you're properly prepared, take the first set of test papers.

Taking the Tests

1. Remember, each set of tests is made up of **three** test papers. The following table will give you the time you should spend on each, and the marks they are worth:

Paper	Reading test paper	Shakespeare test paper	Writing test paper
Time	75 mins	45 mins	75 mins
Marks	32	18	50 (20/30)

2. Choose a time to take the first paper when you can work through it in one go. Make sure you have an appropriate place to sit and take the test, where you will be uninterrupted.
3. Answer **all** the questions in the test. If you are stuck on one question, move on and come back to it later. Tests often start with easier questions. These become more complex, and cover more than one topic, as you work through the test papers.
4. Read the questions **carefully**, so that you understand exactly what you need to do. Don't spend too long on any one question.
5. The number of marks allocated to each question is shown. This will tell you how many key points are needed in the answer.
6. Stay calm! Don't be fazed by questions. Read the question carefully and think it through.

Approaching the Reading Test

The reading tests can be quite intimidating when you first see them. Each of them comes with five pages of reading material, on three topics. Don't worry. The reading material can easily be read in the 15 minutes allowed, and there is plenty of time to answer all the questions. Here are some tips to help you to do your best:
1. Use the whole of the 15 minutes allocated to read through the reading material. In a real exam, you will not be allowed to open your question and answer booklet until the 15 minutes are up. While you are reading, you might find it helpful to underline or highlight parts that you find interesting.
2. Remember that you can and **should** refer back to the reading material once the 15 minutes are up.
3. Timing is key. There are three sections, each containing questions on one of the texts. Therefore, you should try to spend no more than 20 minutes on each section. It is not uncommon for students to do well on the first few questions but fail to complete the paper, and end up with low marks as a result.

4. Within each section, note how many marks are awarded for each answer. Some questions might give you only one mark, while others can gain you five. The number of marks is usually reflected in the amount of space you are given for the answer.

During the Test

To do well in any test or exam you need to understand what each question requires you to do. In these papers, the questions test a variety of skills that you use when reading. You need to know what the 'instruction' words in the questions mean so you can show that you possess these skills. Here are some words and phrases that the questions might use, with a brief explanation of what they mean:

1. **Pick out a phrase/phrases or word/words:** Take the words directly from the text. A phrase is a group of words.
2. **Support with a quotation:** Again, use exact words from the text, and use quotation marks.
3. **Identify:** Give an example or quotation.
4. **Evidence from the text:** This can be a quotation or it can be put in your own words – a quotation is usually safer.
5. **Explain:** Don't just repeat what's already there – make it clearer, showing that you understand what it means.
6. **Give reasons:** Support your point by referring back to the text, either using quotations or your own words.
7. **What is the effect of/explain the effect:** What is the effect on you, the reader? How does it make you feel, for example? What does it make you think about?
8. **How does the writer...?** This will be about how the writer uses language. Think about the choice of words, how different words or phrases might affect you, and how the text is set out.
9. **Fill in the box or complete a chart:** Make sure you know exactly what you are required to do and you put your answers in the correct spaces.
   Five-mark questions usually have bullet points underneath. These are there to help you and you cannot get good marks if you do not cover all the points. It is a good idea to write a paragraph on each bullet point and support each with at least one quotation from the text and a comment on each quotation.

Approaching the Shakespeare Test

Which Papers Should You Do?

- Each set of practice test papers in this book includes three Shakespeare papers: one on *Romeo and Juliet*; one on *As You Like It*; and one on *Macbeth*.
- While there are three plays in the set, only do the **one you have studied at school**. There will be two scenes from it to read, and one question on them.
- It is possible that you go to a school where the teachers are teaching a different Shakespeare play. If you are in this position, it will still be helpful to look at the questions in this book to give you an idea of the type of question you can expect. You might even be able to make up your own question, in a similar style, for the play you have studied. When you take the test for real, you will be asked about the play you have studied!
   Similarly, you may have studied one of the three plays used here but have focused on particular scenes which are different from those used in these practice papers. It will still be useful to have a go at the tests in this book, but you may also want to try out the questions using the scenes you have concentrated on in class, rather than the extracts printed here.

- Make sure you know the play you have studied. If you have not yet covered it when you want to start doing practice tests, you should leave the Shakespeare test and come back to it when feel you have enough knowledge to have a go.

During the Test

1. Read the question carefully, making sure you understand what you need to do. It may focus on language, character, themes or performance. Underline or highlight key points.
2. Skim-read the extracts you have been given and make notes on the page, underlining or highlighting useful quotations.
3. Plan your answer. Do not take too long doing this and do it in whatever way suits you best. Your plan is not marked.
4. Make sure you **use a quotation to support every point you make**. Remember PEE: Point, Evidence, Explanation.
5. Write about both of the extracts, paying special attention to any differences between them.
6. Write in paragraphs, in good, clear English.
7. When you have finished, read through your work to make sure that you have included everything you wanted to.

Approaching the Writing Test

This test assesses your ability to adapt your writing to different forms, purposes and audiences, as well as testing the accuracy of your spelling, grammar and punctuation.

People often find it difficult to revise for writing tests. There are two main things you can do:

1. Revise what is required for different audiences, purposes and forms. You might be asked to write in order to:
   - explain or describe something
   - argue a point of view or persuade someone to your point of view
   - give advice
   - entertain your readers, by using your imagination.

   Or you could be asked to write in different forms, for example:
   - a letter
   - a story
   - a diary
   - a leaflet.

   Sometimes the question will specify an audience, for example:
   - teenagers
   - children
   - adults – such as parents, teachers or a head teacher.

   All these things affect the organisation and the style of your writing. Make sure you know what the expected layout of each form looks like, and use it.

2. Look carefully over the written work you have done in the past and make a list of errors you tend to make in spelling, punctuation and grammar. Then work hard at putting them right.

There are two tasks on each paper and you should make sure you allocate your time properly, spending more time on the longer task than on the shorter task.

The two tasks will be very different from each other. For example, one might be in the form of a letter and the other in the form of a short story. One might be about trying to argue a point, while the other might ask you to explain something.

Remember that your marks are not based on how much you write. **Aim for quality, not quantity.**

During the Test

1. Read the question carefully, making sure you understand what you are being asked to do:
   - What is its purpose?
   - Who is the intended audience?
   - What form should it be in?
2. Quickly plan your answer. For the longer task, you might be provided with a planning frame but you can plan in whatever way suits you best.
3. Make sure you write in paragraphs and try to connect them with appropriate words and phrases.
4. Pay close attention to correct spelling, punctuation and grammar.
5. When you have finished, check your work carefully and correct any errors that you spot.

How to Use the Answers and Mark Scheme

When you've sat the test, you, or a parent or guardian, should use the mark scheme to mark it. You could mark the test together. It's often helpful for you to discuss the answers with someone as you go through the mark scheme.

You should:
- read the suggested answers and marks given in the section at the back of this book
- look at your own answers and decide what mark you deserve for each one
- add up the marks to give you your overall score out of 100
- keep your mark for next time, so that you can compare how you do after each set.

Tips for the Top

After sitting a test paper:
1. Try to analyse your performance. For questions that only gained a low mark, identify where you went wrong. Are there gaps in your knowledge and understanding? Were there areas where you were under-prepared?
2. Go back through your test papers and make a note of all the questions where you lost marks and the reasons for losing them.
3. Use study guides and workbooks at home to reinforce your learning and develop your skills.
4. Undertake another set after a reasonable amount of time has passed. Go back to your last practice set and compare your results to see how far you have progressed and what you may still need to concentrate on.

Set

A

KEY STAGE 3

Reading Test
Paper

English

Into the Woods!

Reading Test Paper

Into the Woods!

First name _____

Last name _____

Date _____

Instructions

- Before you start to write, you have 15 minutes to read the reading material (pages 9–14). There are three texts. Make sure you read all three.

- During this time you should not look at the questions on the following pages.

- You then have **1 hour** to answer all the questions on pages 15–21.

- Answer all the questions.

- Write your answers in the spaces provided.

- When you have finished, check your work carefully.

After you have completed the test, you can mark your answers using pages 107–110 of the Answers and Mark Scheme section of this book.

Enter the marks for each answer in the small box next to your answer.

At the bottom of each page put the total marks for that page.

Enter your marks in the boxes below and add them up to get your total out of 32.

Page	15	16	17	18	19	20	21	Total mark	Maximum mark
Score									32

Reading Material

Contents

People have always been fascinated by woods and forests. In old stories and tales they are places of mystery, creating fear and excitement. Some people still find them scary places.

Others see them as places of adventure, where you can go on long walks and enjoy nature, or take part in activities like canoeing and abseiling.

In these texts we see what going into the woods means to different people (or animals), and how it makes them feel.

"The Way Through the Woods"

In this poem, Rudyard Kipling describes a place where a road used to run through some woods. The road was closed many years ago and has now disappeared altogether under trees and undergrowth . . .

They shut the way through the woods
Seventy years ago.
Weather and rain have undone it again,
And now you would never know
5 There was once a road through the woods
Before they planted the trees.
It is underneath the coppice[1] and heath
And the thin anemones.
Only the keeper[2] sees
10 That, where the ring-dove broods,
And the badgers roll at ease,
Stanz 2 There was once a road through the woods.

Yet, if you enter the woods
Of a summer evening late,
15 When the night-air cools on the trout-ringed pools
Where the otter whistles his mate,
(They fear not men in the woods,
Stanz 2 Because they see so few)
You will hear the beat of a horse's feet,
20 And the swish of a skirt in the dew,
Steadily cantering[3] through
The misty solitudes,
As though they perfectly knew
The old lost road through the woods . . .
25 But there is no road through the woods.

Rudyard Kipling

---

[1]Coppice – an area of undergrowth and small trees
[2]Keeper – the gamekeeper, whose job it is to look after and control birds and animals for a landowner
[3]Cantering – (a horse) going at a medium pace, between a trot and a gallop

Home   **Gallery**   **About Us**   **Contact Us**

WESTERLY WOODS ADVENTURE PARK: a world of adventure waiting for you!

Fun and adventure on your doorstep

Wondering what to do in the school holidays? Fancy a few days away not too far from home? Or would you just like a day out with family or friends? Here at Westerly Woods we've got something for everyone.

The woods themselves are beautiful all the year round: when the first flowers are appearing in spring; in the full glory of summer; when the leaves turn red and gold in the autumn; and even when the ground is covered in a blanket of snow. Whatever the time of year, you're welcome to enjoy Nature's bounty at Westerly.

[handwritten: a good place for a half term holiday]

[handwritten: talks about the 3 seasons]

Walks in the woods

There are miles of well-maintained footpaths through the woods. They're all well sign-posted and you're welcome to set off on your own. However, if you prefer company and the guidance of an expert, you can book one of our guided walks.

Our well-trained and experience Woodland Rangers offer a wide variety of walks, for all levels of experience. You can book them as an individual or as a group of any size. Click here for more details.

Adventure trails

If you're looking for a bit more of an adrenaline buzz, you might want to have a go at one of the Westerly Adventure Trails.

If you're one of life's thrill-seekers, you'll love our trails! These are walks through the woods with a difference. Around every corner there's a new challenge – swinging on ropes, battling through swamps or hurtling down slides. All this and more is waiting for you at Westerly Woods.

Whether you're young or old, with your family or a group of friends, we can organise an adventure to suit you. Scouts and Guides, school and youth groups, work colleagues – even stag and hen parties – can be catered for at Westerly. Find out more by clicking here!

Stay a while

Sometimes a day out just isn't enough – especially when there's as much to see and do as there is at Westerly Woods. So why not stay a while? Spend the night, the weekend or even longer. Make yourself at home.

Try one of our log cabins

Here at Westerly we've built a whole village of rustic log cabins, clustered around the tranquil natural lake that lies at the centre of the woods. They can sleep anything from two to eight people, are built from traditional materials and finished to the highest standards. Inside you'll find every modern convenience to make your stay comfortable and stress-free. Get in touch here for details of prices and availability.

[handwritten note: old looking]

Or what about a camping barn?

For bigger groups we've got two specially designed camping barns. A bit less sophisticated than our cabins, these are designed to take large parties. Basic cooking and bathroom facilities are provided, but everything else you bring yourselves. It's just like camping but without a tent!

These barns make superb venues for corporate adventure weekends as well as being ideal for groups of young people. Click here for details.

Education through fun

For school and youth groups, we can provide tailor-made educational activities. Young people learn just from being here, and we aim to help them develop physical and mental skills through fun. But we also have a team of well-qualified and enthusiastic Woodland Rangers. They not only instruct and supervise young people on the adventure trails, but also have a wealth of knowledge about nature and the environment to share with them. For details of educational activities and resources, click here.

So what are you waiting for? Get in touch today and we'll guarantee you the adventure of a lifetime!

"The Wild Wood"

"The Wild Wood" from *The Wind in the Willows* by Kenneth Grahame

The Wind in the Willows *describes the adventures of a group of animals that live on the banks of a river, near the Wild Wood. One afternoon, Mole, who has never been into the Wild Wood before, leaves his friend Ratty's house to explore the woods, ignoring Ratty's warnings . . .*

It was a cold still afternoon with a hard steely sky overhead, when he slipped out of the warm parlour into the open air [. . .] and with great cheerfulness of spirit he pushed on towards the Wild Wood, which lay before him low and threatening, like a black reef in some still southern sea.

There was nothing to alarm him at first entry. Twigs crackled under his feet, logs tripped him, funguses on stumps resembled caricatures, and startled him for the moment by their likeness to something familiar and far away; but that was all fun, and exciting. It led him on, and he penetrated to where the light was less, and trees crouched nearer and nearer, and holes made ugly mouths at him on either side.

Everything was very still now. The dusk advanced on him steadily, rapidly, gathering in behind and before; and the light seemed to be draining away like flood-water.

Then the faces began.

It was over his shoulder, and indistinctly, that he first thought he saw a face: a little evil wedge-shaped face, looking at him from a hole. When he turned and confronted it, the thing had vanished.

He quickened his pace, telling himself cheerfully not to begin imagining things, or there would be simply no end to it. He passed another hole, and another, and another; and then – yes! – no! – yes! Certainly a little narrow face, with hard eyes, had flashed up for an instant from a hole, and was gone. He hesitated – braced himself up for an effort and strode on. Then suddenly, and as if it had been so all the time, every hole, far and near, and there were hundreds of them, seemed to possess its face, coming and going rapidly, all fixing on him evil glances of malice and hatred: all hard-eyed and evil and sharp.

If he could only get away from the holes in the banks, he thought, there would be no more faces. He swung off the path and plunged into the untrodden places of the wood.

Then the whistling began.

Very faint and shrill it was, and far behind him, when first he heard it; but somehow it made him hurry forward. Then, still very faint and shrill, it sounded far ahead of him, and made him hesitate and want to go back. As he halted in indecision it broke out on either side, and seemed to be caught up and passed on throughout the whole length of the wood to its furthest limit. They were up and alert and ready, evidently, whoever they were! And he – he was alone, and unarmed, and far from help; and the night was closing in.

Then the pattering began.

He thought it was only falling leaves at first, so slight and delicate was the sound of it. Then as it grew it took a regular rhythm, and he knew it for nothing else but the pat-pat-pat of little feet, still a very long way off. Was it in front or behind? It seemed to be first one, then another, then both. It grew and it multiplied, till from every quarter as he listened anxiously, leaning this way and that, it seemed to be closing in on him. As he stood still to hearken,[1] a rabbit came running hard towards him through the trees. He waited, expecting it to slacken pace, or to swerve from him into a different course. Instead the animal almost brushed him as it dashed past, his eyes staring. 'Get out of this, you fool, get out!' the mole heard him mutter as he swung round a stump and disappeared down a friendly burrow.

---

[1]*Hearken – listen*

Questions 1–5 are about "The Way Through the Woods" by Rudyard Kipling (on page 10 of the reading material).

1. The way through the woods has disappeared, partly because of nature and partly because of people.

   Give two ways in which people are responsible.

   You should be sensible and if you would like to stay that then only 7 to 8 peopu can sleep.

2. In the first stanza (lines 1–12), the poet gives examples of animals and plants that live in the woods. From the first stanza pick out examples of:

   (a) a flower ___`Before they planted trees`___

   (b) a bird ___`Only the keepers see`___

   (c) a mammal ___`And the thin anemones`___

3. The phrase 'only the keeper sees' (line 9) suggests the keeper is different from other people. How do you think he is different?

   The keeper is different from the other people because the keeper is called the game keeper. The game keepers job is to look after and control birds and animals for a land owner. The keeper does a compute different job then the other people.

4. The second stanza of the poem ends with an ellipsis (…) before the final line. What effect does this have?

   The second stanza starts talking about the old road in the woods but after the ellipsis it says that there is no road This makes the reader feel that there was a road a long ago but now there is no road. It is a really good ending and keeps the reader amused.

5. How does the poet use language to give an impression of mystery and the supernatural?

You should comment on:

- words and phrases he uses to describe the wood in the first stanza
- what he says you will hear in the woods
- the effect his language has on the reader.

_____

_____

_____

_____

_____

_____

_____

_____

_____

_____

_____

_____

_____

Questions 6–10 are about Westerly Woods Adventure Park (pages 11–12 of the reading material).

6. How does the writer describe the woods in winter?

_____

1 mark

7. According to the section headed "Walks in the woods", why might some people prefer to go on a guided walk rather than setting off on their own? Give two reasons.

_____

_____

_____

1 mark

8. Look at the section headed "Try one of our log cabins". In the chart below are descriptions of people who might be attracted to the log cabins. In column 2 write down a phrase from the paragraph that would appeal to these people. The first one is done for you.

2 marks

People being appealed to	Phrase from the text
People who like their 'home comforts'	_Every modern convenience_
People who feel they need a good rest	
People who like to meet new people on holiday	
People who like to feel they're close to nature	

SUBTOTAL

9. Explain why the camping barns at Westerly Woods might appeal to large groups of young people.

2 marks

_____

_____

_____

_____

_____

10. Look again at the section headed "Adventure trails". How does the writer use language to make the trails sound exciting and fun?

3 marks

Refer to specific words and phrases from the section and comment on them.

_____

_____

_____

_____

_____

_____

_____

_____

Questions 11–16 are about "The Wild Wood" (pages 13–14 of the reading material).

11. Write down a phrase from the first paragraph which shows that Mole is happy and optimistic.

1 mark

_____

12. Pick out two phrases from the second paragraph which 'personify' the woods, giving the impression that the woods are alive.

1 mark

_____

_____

13. What do the following quotations tell us about Mole's attitude to the faces in the woods? Complete the following table. The first one has been done for you.

2 marks

He quickened his pace, telling himself not to begin imagining things . . .	_Mole thinks that the 'faces' are not real and that, if he is confident, they will go away._
And then – yes! – no! – yes!	
Certainly a little narrow face, with hard eyes, had flashed up	
. . . all fixing on him with evil glances of malice and hatred	

SUBTOTAL

14. Read the last paragraph again.

(a) The first sentence states: 'He thought it was only falling leaves at first'. How does the writer imply that the sound is **not** that of falling leaves?

_____

_____

(b) What might the reader expect to be making the noise before Mole sees the rabbit?

_____

_____

15. Which of the following statements about the text are true and which are false? Write 'True' or 'False' in the box. The first one has been done for you.

Mole knows the Wild Wood very well.	False
Mole imagines the faces.	
The faces and noises are all made by the rabbit.	
At the end of the extract we do not know whose faces they are.	
At the end of the extract Mole is safe.	
At the end of the extract the rabbit is safe.	

1 mark

1 mark

2 marks

16. How does the author, Kenneth Grahame, create an atmosphere of fear and tension in "The Wild Wood"?

Think about:
- Mole's feelings when he sets off on his walk
- the things that happen that worry him
- how Mole's feelings change from the beginning to the end of the extract
- the language used to describe the woods and Mole's feelings.

_____

_____

_____

_____

_____

_____

_____

_____

_____

_____

_____

_____

_____

_____

Set
A

KEY STAGE 3

Shakespeare
Test Paper

English

*Romeo and Juliet, As
You Like It and Macbeth*

Shakespeare Test Paper

Romeo and Juliet, As You Like It and *Macbeth*

First name _____

Last name _____

Date _____

Instructions

In the following pages you will find three questions which assess your reading and understanding of Shakespeare. Each is on a different play:

Romeo and Juliet	page 23
As You Like It	page 28
Macbeth	page 33

- **Only** answer the question on the play you have studied.

- Read the question carefully.

- Write your answer on lined paper.

- You have **45 minutes** to complete the task.

- When you have completed the test, you can mark your answer using pages 115–118 of the Answers and Mark Scheme section of this book.

- Enter your mark below:

MAXIMUM MARK	18		ACTUAL MARK	

Romeo and Juliet

What impressions might an audience get of Juliet and her feelings for Romeo from the way she speaks and acts in these extracts?

Support your ideas by referring to both of the extracts which are printed on the following pages.

Please note that line numbers may not be the same as those in the edition you used in class.

Romeo and Juliet

Act 3, Scene 2, lines 1–71

In this extract, after Friar Lawrence has married them, Juliet is waiting for Romeo.

JULIET   Gallop apace, you fiery-footed steeds,
Towards Phoebus' lodging. Such a wagoner
As Phaeton would whip you to the west
And bring in cloudy night immediately.
Spread thy close curtain, love-performing night,   5
That runaways' eyes may wink, and Romeo
Leap to these arms, untalked of and unseen.
Lovers can see to do their amorous rites
By their own beauties; or, if love be blind,   10
It best agrees with night. Come, civil night,
Thou sober-suited matron, all in black,
And learn me how to lose a winning match
Played for a pair of stainless maidenhoods.
Hood my unmanned blood bating in my cheeks,   15
With thy black mantle, till strange love grow bold,
Think true love acted simple modesty.
Come night, come Romeo, come thou day in night,
For thou wilt lie upon the wings of night
Whiter than new snow upon a raven's back.   20
Come gentle night, come loving, black-browed night,
Give me my Romeo; and when he shall die
Take him and cut him out in little stars,
And he will make the face of heaven so fine
That all the world will be in love with night,   25
And pay no worship to the garish sun.
O, I have bought the mansion of a love
But not possessed it, and though I am sold,
Not yet enjoyed. So tedious is this day
As is the night before some festival   30
To an impatient child that has new robes
And may not wear them. O, here comes my Nurse
And she brings news, and every tongue that speaks
But Romeo's name speaks heavenly eloquence.

Enter NURSE *with cords*

How, Nurse, what news? What hast thou there? The cords
That Romeo bid thee fetch?

NURSE   Ay, ay, the cords.   35

JULIET	Ay me! What news? Why dost thou wring thy hands?	
NURSE	Ah, well-a-day! He's dead, he's dead, he's dead!	
	We are undone, lady, we are undone!	
	Alack the day! He's gone, he's kill'd, he's dead!	
JULIET	Can heaven be so envious?	40
NURSE	Romeo can,	
	Though heaven cannot. O Romeo, Romeo,	
	Whoever would have thought it? Romeo!	
JULIET	What devil art thou that dost torment me thus?	
	This torture should be roar'd in dismal hell.	45
	Hath Romeo slain himself? Say thou but 'Ay',	
	And that bare vowel 'I' shall poison more	
	Than the death-darting eye of cockatrice:	
	I am not I, if there be such an 'Ay',	
	Or those eyes shut, that makes thee answer 'Ay'.	50
	If he be slain, say 'Ay'; or if not, 'No':	
	Brief sounds determine of my weal or woe.	
NURSE	I saw the wound, I saw it with mine eyes –	
	God save the mark – here on his manly breast.	
	A piteous corse, a bloody piteous corse;	55
	Pale, pale as ashes, all bedaub'd in blood –	
	All in gore-blood. I swounded at the sight.	
JULIET	O break, my heart! Poor bankrupt, break at once!	
	To prison, eyes, ne'er look on liberty!	
	Vile earth, to earth resign. End motion here;	60
	And thou and Romeo press one heavy bier!	
NURSE	O Tybalt, Tybalt, the best friend I had.	
	O courteous Tybalt! Honest gentleman!	
	That ever I should live to see thee dead!	
JULIET	What storm is this that blows so contrary?	65
	Is Romeo slaughter'd and is Tybalt dead?	
	My dear-loved cousin and my dearer lord?	
	Then, dreadful trumpet sound the general doom!	
	For who is living, if these two are gone?	
NURSE	Tybalt is gone and Romeo banished;	70
	Romeo that kill'd him, he is banished.	

Act 3, Scene 5, lines 1–59

In this extract, Romeo is leaving Juliet after they have spent their first night together.

JULIET   Wilt thou be gone? It is not yet near day.
         It was the nightingale and not the lark
         That pierced the fearful hollow of thine ear.
         Nightly she sings on yon pomegranate tree.
         Believe me, love, it was the nightingale.   5

ROMEO   It was the lark, the herald of the morn,
         No nightingale. Look, love, what envious streaks
         Do lace the severing clouds in yonder east.
         Night's candles are burnt out, and jocund day
         Stands tiptoe on the misty mountain tops.   10
         I must be gone and live, or stay and die.

JULIET   Yon light is not daylight, I know it, I.
         It is some meteor that the sun exhales
         To be to thee this night a torchbearer,
         And light thee on thy way to Mantua.   15
         Therefore stay yet: thou need'st not be gone.

ROMEO   Let me be ta'en. Let me be put to death.
         I am content, so thou wilt have it so.
         I'll say yon grey is not the morning's eye,
         'Tis but the pale reflex of Cynthia's brow.   20
         Nor that is not the lark whose notes do beat
         The vaulty heaven so high above our heads.
         I have more care to stay than will to go.
         Come death, and welcome. Juliet wills it so.
         How is't, my soul? Let's talk. It is not day.   25

JULIET   It is, it is. Hie hence! Be gone, away!
         It is the lark that sings so out of tune,
         Straining harsh discords and unpleasing sharps.
         Some say the lark makes sweet diversion.
         This doth not so, for she divideth us.   30
         Some say the lark and loathed toad change eyes.
         O, now I would they had changed voices too,
         Since arm from arm that voice doth us affray,
         Hunting thee hence with hunt's-up to the day.
         O, now be gone; more light and light it grows.   35

ROMEO   More light and light: more dark and dark our woes

NURSE	Madam.	
JULIET	Nurse?	
NURSE	Your lady mother is coming to your chamber.	
	The day is broke; be wary, look about.	40

Exit

JULIET	Then, window, let day in and let life out.	
ROMEO	Farewell, farewell. One kiss and I'll descend.	

They kiss; ROMEO descends

JULIET	Art thou gone so? Love, lord, ay husband, friend,	
	I must hear from thee every day in the hour,	
	For in a minute there are many days.	45
	O, by this count I shall be much in years	
	Ere I again behold my Romeo.	
ROMEO	Farewell.	
	I will omit no opportunity	
	That may convey my greetings, love, to thee.	50
JULIET	O think'st thou we shall ever meet again?	
ROMEO	I doubt it not, and all these woes shall serve	
	For sweet discorses in our times to come.	
JULIET	O God, I have an ill-divining soul!	
	Methinks I see thee, now thou art so low,	55
	As one dead in the bottom of a tomb.	
	Either my eyesight fails, or thou look'st pale.	
ROMEO	And trust me, love, in my eye so do you.	
	Dry sorrow drinks our blood. Adieu, adieu.	

Exit

As You Like It

As You Like It

Act 1, Scene 1, lines 1–79
Act 2, Scene 3, lines 30–77

In the first extract, Orlando confronts his brother, Oliver, about his behaviour since the death of his father. In the second, Orlando's servant, Adam, warns him about the danger he is in from Oliver.

What do these scenes tell us about the themes of family love and loyalty in the play?

Support your ideas by referring to both of the extracts printed on the following pages.

As You Like It

Act 1, Scene 1, lines 1–79

In this extract (which opens the play), Orlando confronts his older brother, Oliver, about the way he has treated him since their father's death.

Enter ORLANDO and ADAM

ORLANDO   As I remember, Adam, it was upon this fashion
bequeathed me by will but poor a thousand crowns,
and, as thou sayest, charged my brother, on his
blessing, to breed me well: and there begins my
sadness. My brother Jaques he keeps at school, and   5
report speaks goldenly of his profit. For my part,
he keeps me rustically at home, or, to speak more
properly, stays me here at home unkept. For call you
that keeping for a gentleman of my birth, that
differs not from the stalling of an ox? His horses   10
are bred better; for, besides that they are fair
with their feeding, they are taught their manage,
and to that end riders dearly hired. But I, his
brother, gain nothing under him but growth; for the
which his animals on his dunghills are as much   15
bound to him as I. Besides this nothing that he so
plentifully gives me, the something that nature gave
me his countenance seems to take from me. He lets
me feed with his hinds, bars me the place of a
brother, and, as much as in him lies, mines my   20
gentility with my education. This is it, Adam, that
grieves me; and the spirit of my father, which I
think is within me, begins to mutiny against this
servitude. I will no longer endure it, though yet I
know no wise remedy how to avoid it.   25

ADAM   Yonder comes my master, your brother.

ORLANDO   Go apart, Adam, and thou shalt hear how he will
shake me up.

Enter OLIVER

OLIVER   Now, sir! What make you here?

ORLANDO   Nothing. I am not taught to make anything.   30

OLIVER   What mar you then, sir?

ORLANDO	Marry, sir, I am helping you to mar that which God made, a poor unworthy brother of yours, with idleness.	
OLIVER	Marry, sir, be better employed, and be naught awhile.	
ORLANDO	Shall I keep your hogs and eat husks with them? What prodigal portion have I spent, that I should come to such penury?	35
OLIVER	Know you where you are, sir?	
ORLANDO	O, sir, very well; here in your orchard.	
OLIVER	Know you before whom, sir?	40
ORLANDO	Ay, better than him I am before knows me. I know you are my eldest brother; and, in the gentle condition of blood, you should so know me. The courtesy of nations allows you my better, in that you are the first-born; but the same tradition takes not away my blood, were there twenty brothers betwixt us. I have as much of my father in me as you; albeit, I confess, your coming before me is nearer to his reverence.	45
OLIVER	What, boy! (*strikes him*)	50
ORLANDO	Come, come, elder brother, you are too young in this. (*seizes him*)	
OLIVER	Wilt thou lay hands on me, villain?	
ORLANDO	I am no villain. I am the youngest son of Sir Rowland de Boys. He was my father, and he is thrice a villain that says such a father begot villains. Wert thou not my brother, I would not take this hand from thy throat till this other had pulled out thy tongue for saying so. Thou hast railed on thyself.	55
ADAM	Sweet masters, be patient. For your father's remembrance, be at accord.	60
OLIVER	Let me go, I say.	
ORLANDO	I will not, till I please. You shall hear me. My father charged you in his will to give me good education. You have trained me like a peasant, obscuring and hiding from me all gentleman-like	65

qualities. The spirit of my father grows strong in
me, and I will no longer endure it. Therefore allow
me such exercises as may become a gentleman, or
give me the poor allottery my father left me by
testament; with that I will go buy my fortunes. 70

OLIVER   And what wilt thou do? Beg, when that is spent?
Well, sir, get you in. I will not long be troubled
with you. You shall have some part of your will. I
pray you, leave me.

ORLANDO   I will no further offend you than becomes me for my good. 75

OLIVER   Get you with him, you old dog.

ADAM   Is 'old dog' my reward? Most true, I have lost my
teeth in your service. God be with my old master!
He would not have spoke such a word.

Exeunt ORLANDO *and* ADAM

Act 2, Scene 3, lines 30–77

*In this extract, Adam has just warned Orlando not to return home because of the danger he is in from
his brother.*

ORLANDO   Why, whither, Adam, wouldst thou have me go? 30

ADAM   No matter whither, so you come not here.

ORLANDO   What? Wouldst thou have me go and beg my food?
Or with a base and boisterous sword enforce
A thievish living on the common road?
This I must do, or know not what to do. 35
Yet this I will not do, do how I can.
I rather will subject me to the malice
Of a diverted blood and bloody brother.

ADAM   But do not so. I have five hundred crowns,
The thrifty hire I saved under your father, 40
Which I did store to be my foster-nurse
When service should in my old limbs lie lame
And unregarded age in corners thrown.
Take that, and He that doth the ravens feed,
Yea, providently caters for the sparrow, 45
Be comfort to my age! Here is the gold.
And all this I give you. Let me be your servant.
Though I look old, yet I am strong and lusty;
For in my youth I never did apply

31

Hot and rebellious liquors in my blood,　　　　　　50
Nor did not with unbashful forehead woo
The means of weakness and debility.
Therefore my age is as a lusty winter,
Frosty, but kindly. Let me go with you.
I'll do the service of a younger man　　　　　　　55
In all your business and necessities.

ORLANDO　O good old man, how well in thee appears
The constant service of the antique world,
When service sweat for duty, not for meed!
Thou art not for the fashion of these times　　　　60
Where none will sweat but for promotion,
And having that, do choke their service up
Even with the having. It is not so with thee.
But, poor old man, thou prunest a rotten tree
That cannot so much as a blossom yield　　　　　　65
In lieu of all thy pains and husbandry.
But come thy ways. We'll go along together,
And ere we have thy youthful wages spent,
We'll light upon some settled low content.

ADAM　Master, go on, and I will follow thee　　　　　70
To the last gasp, with truth and loyalty.
From seventeen years till now almost fourscore
Here lived I, but now live here no more.
At seventeen years many their fortunes seek,
But at fourscore it is too late a week.　　　　　　75
Yet fortune cannot recompense me better
Than to die well, and not my master's debtor.

Exeunt

32

Macbeth

How does Macbeth's language convey his feelings and attitudes in these two extracts?

Support your ideas by referring to both of the extracts printed on the following pages.

Macbeth

Act 2, Scene 2, lines 14–61

In this extract, Macbeth has just killed Duncan.

MACBETH	I have done the deed. Didst thou not hear a noise?	
LADY MACBETH	I heard the owl scream and the crickets cry. Did you not speak?	15
MACBETH	When?	
LADY MACBETH	Now.	
MACBETH	As I descended?	
LADY MACBETH	Ay.	
MACBETH	Hark, who lies i'th'second chamber?	
LADY MACBETH	Donalbain,	
MACBETH	This is a sorry sight.	
LADY MACBETH	A foolish thought to say a sorry sight.	
MACBETH	There's one did laugh in's sleep, and one cried, 'Murder!' That they did wake each other; I stood and heard them, But they did say their prayers and addressed them Again to sleep.	20
LADY MACBETH	There are two lodged together.	
MACBETH	One cried, 'God bless us!' and 'Amen' the other, As they had seen me with these hangman's hands. List'ning their fear. I could not say, 'Amen' When they did say, 'God bless us.'	25
LADY MACBETH	Consider it not so deeply.	
MACBETH	But wherefore could not I pronounce 'Amen'? I had most need of blessing and 'Amen' Stuck in my throat.	30
LADY MACBETH	These deeds must not be thought After these ways; so it will make us mad.	

MACBETH	Methought I heard a voice cry, 'Sleep no more:	
	Macbeth does murder sleep' – the innocent sleep,	
	Sleep that knits up the ravelled sleeve of care,	35
	The death of each day's life, sore labour's bath,	
	Balm of hurt minds, great nature's second course,	
	Chief nourisher in life's feast.	

LADY MACBETH   What do you mean?

MACBETH	Still it cried, 'Sleep no more!' to all in the house;	
	'Glamis hath murdered sleep,' and therefore Cawdor	40
	Shall sleep no more: Macbeth shall sleep no more.	

LADY MACBETH	Who was it, that thus cried? Why, worthy thane,	
	You do unbend your noble strength to think	
	So brain-sickly of things. Go get some water	
	And wash this filthy witness from your hand.	45
	Why did you bring these daggers from the place?	
	They must lie there. Go carry them and smear	
	The sleepy grooms with blood.	

MACBETH	I'll go no more.	
	I am afraid to think what I have done;	
	Look on't again. I dare not.	

LADY MACBETH	Infirm of purpose!	50
	Give me the daggers. The sleeping and the dead	
	Are but as pictures. 'Tis the eye of childhood	
	That fears a painted devil. If he do bleed,	
	I'll gild the faces of the grooms withal,	
	For it must seem their guilt.	

Exit

Knock within

MACBETH	Whence is that knocking?	55
	How is't with me, when every noise appals me?	
	What hands are here? Ha: they pluck out mine eyes.	
	Will all great Neptune's ocean wash this blood	
	Clean from my hand? No: this my hand will rather	
	The multitudinous seas incarnadine,	60
	Making the green one red.	

Act 5, Scene 5, lines 1–50

In this extract, Macbeth is preparing to fight the armies of Malcolm and Macduff.

Enter MACBETH, SEYTON *and*
soldiers, with drum and colours

MACBETH   Hang out our banners on the outward walls;
The cry is still, 'They come'. Our castle's strength
Will laugh a siege to scorn; here let them lie
Till famine and the ague eat them up.
Were they not forced with those that should be ours,   5
We might as well have met them dareful, beard to beard,
And beat them backward home.

A cry within of women

What is that noise?

SEYTON   It is the cry of women, my good lord.

MACBETH   I have almost forgot the taste of fears;
The time has been, my senses would have cooled   10
To hear a night shriek and my fell of hair
Would at a dismal treatise rouse and stir
As life were in't. I have supped full with horrors;
Direness familiar to my slaughterous thoughts
Cannot once start me. Wherefore was that cry?   15

SEYTON   The queen, my lord, is dead.

MACBETH   She should have died hereafter.
There would have been a time for such a word.
Tomorrow, and tomorrow, and tomorrow
Creeps in this petty pace from day to day
To the last syllable of recorded time;   20
And all our yesterdays have lighted fools
The way to dusty death. Out, out, brief candle!
Life's but a walking shadow, a poor player
That struts and frets his hour upon the stage
And then is heard no more. It is a tale   25
Told by an idiot, full of sound and fury
Signifying nothing.

Enter a MESSENGER

Thou com'st to use thy tongue.
Thy story quickly.

MESSENGER   Gracious my lord,
                I should report that which I say I saw,
                But know not how to do't.

MACBETH   Well, say, sir.   30

MESSENGER   As I did stand my watch upon the hill
                I looked toward Birnam and anon methought
                The wood began to move.

MACBETH   Liar and slave!

MESSENGER   Let me endure your wrath if't be not so;
                Within this three mile may you see it coming.   35
                I say, a moving grove.

MACBETH   If thou speak'st false,
                Upon the next tree shall thou hang alive
                Till famine cling thee; if thy speech be sooth,
                I care not if thou dost for me as much.
                I pull in resolution and begin   40
                To doubt th'equivocation of the fiend
                That lies like truth. 'Fear not, till Birnam Wood
                Do come to Dunsinane', and now a wood
                Comes toward Dunsinane. Arm, arm, and out!
                If this which he avouches does appear,   45
                There is no flying hence nor tarrying here.
                I 'gin to be aweary of the sun
                And wish th'estate o'th'world were now undone.
                Ring the alarum-bell! Blow wind, come wrack;
                At least we'll die with harness on our back.   50

Set

A

KEY STAGE 3

Writing Test
Paper

English

Happy Acres

Writing Test Paper

Happy Acres

First name _____

Last name _____

Date _____

Instructions

- There are two writing tasks in this paper.

- The test is **1 hour and 15 minutes** long.

- You should spend: **45 minutes** on Section A (the longer writing task)
  30 minutes on Section B (the shorter writing task).

- You may spend the first 15 minutes planning your answer to Section A. Your plan will not be marked.

- Section A has 30 marks.

- Section B has 20 marks.

- Write your answer on lined paper.

- When you have finished, check your work carefully.

When you have completed the test, you can mark your answer using pages 123–128 of the Answers and Mark Scheme section of this book.

- Enter your marks below:

	Mark	Maximum mark
Section A		30
Section B		20
Total		50

Section A

Longer Writing Task

A Weekend at Happy Acres

You are a journalist working for a magazine aimed at people with families. Recently you received the following note from your manager:

> I would like you to spend the weekend, with your family, at the Happy Acres Holiday Park so that you can review it for our readers.
>
> All expenses are paid but this is not an advertisement. I want an honest account of your experience. Please include:
> - some factual information about the park
> - the positive aspects of your experience
> - the negative aspects of your experience
> - your judgement on whether this is a good place to spend a weekend with your family.

Write your report on your visit to Happy Acres.

Section B

Shorter Writing Task

Summer Job at Happy Acres

The Happy Acres Holiday Park has placed an advertisement in the local paper. This is the advertisement:

Outgoing, enthusiastic people wanted!

To meet increased demand during the summer holidays, Happy Acres Holiday Park is looking for temporary staff to work with children.

The job involves supervising children from 4 to 14 while they enjoy our facilities, organising games and creative play, and dealing with any situation that might arise!

Successful candidates will be:
- reliable
- enthusiastic
- creative
- patient
- flexible.

If you think you've got the right qualities and experience, please apply in writing to Ms A Caffley, Happy Acres Holiday Park, Springwood, Westby.

Write a letter applying for the job.

Reading Test Paper

Catching the Train

First name   _____

Last name   _____

Date   _____

Instructions

- Before you start to write, you have **15 minutes** to read the reading material (pages 42–47). There are three texts. Make sure you read all three.

- During this time you should not look at the questions on the following pages.

- You then have **1 hour** to answer all the questions on pages 48–54.

- Answer all the questions.

- Write your answers in the spaces provided.

- When you have finished, check your work carefully.

After you have completed the test, you can mark your answers using pages 110–112 of the Answers and Mark Scheme section of this book.

- Enter the marks for each answer in the small box next to your answer.

- At the bottom of each page put the total marks for that page.

- Enter your marks in the boxes below and add them up to get your total out of 32.

Page	48	49	50	51	52	53	54	Total mark	Maximum mark
Score									32

Catching the Train

Reading Material

Contents

Since Victorian times, trains and railways have been an important part of people's lives.

For some, they are just a way of getting from one place to another – sometimes quickly and efficiently, and sometimes not!

For others – whether they collect toy trains, 'spot' trains or like to takes trips and holidays to exotic places – they are a source of endless fascination and enjoyment.

In this page, from a website designed for school pupils, the writer explains how and why the railways grew in Victorian Britain, and how their growth changed people's lives. The Great Exhibition of 1851 was a huge exhibition of products from all over the world and attracted thousands of visitors.

The Railways of Victorian Britain

Most of the working people who came to the Great Exhibition arrived by rail, often from the north of England. King's Cross Station was opened in 1850 and there were nearly 7,000 miles of track linking London with the towns of the Midlands and the North.

Source 1: Great Exhibition, 1851

The most popular way of getting to the Great Exhibition was by buying a ticket that included a return rail journey and entry. These could cost 4, 5 or 6 shillings. Hundreds of thousands of people took advantage of these day trips, which were the idea of Thomas Cook.

He booked trains from all over Britain to take people to the Great Exhibition and charged them a fixed price for the return trip and the entry ticket. Overnight he had invented the 'day out'.

Source 2: Beach, Eastbourne

As Cook's business grew, he began to offer excursions to more and more places, including trips to other European countries. Soon the railway companies began to run their own excursions.

At first, railway companies tried to avoid dealing with the masses and preferred to run trains that only offered second- and first-class carriages. They also tried to avoid stopping their trains at every station. But in 1844 the Railways Act stated that at least one train a day must stop at every station, and include third-class carriages. Now large numbers of Victorians could afford to travel.

The railways were to make a huge difference to the leisure activities of the Victorians. Not only were opportunities for holidays and day trips increased, but sporting events also grew in popularity. Special trains and trips were run to take people to the races, cricket matches or the FA Cup Final, which was held for the first time in 1872. It was not only spectators that benefited: the football clubs that were being started in many of Britain's cities could now travel away to play against each other.

Source 3: Fun-fair

In 1888 the Football League was founded. It was made up of professional teams. It would have been impossible for the first teams to travel to play away matches without regular trains. So the railways were very important in the development of professional football in Britain.

But many of these developments only affected the better-off people in Britain. For most working people, the important changes were the cheap day returns that many railway companies started to offer.

Source 4: Cocoa advert

Source 5: Victorian country railway station

In 1871 bank holidays were introduced and so began the great British tradition of the day at the seaside, along with sticks of rock, candy-floss, walks along the pier, fun-fair rides and fish and chips. The first fish and chip shops appeared in the 1860s.

"Saviours of the Train"

from *The Railway Children* by E. Nesbit

Peter; his older sister, Bobbie; and his younger sister, Phyllis, live near a busy railway line. In this chapter they have gone to pick cherries near the line when they notice something strange and possibly very dangerous ...

They were almost at the gate when Bobbie said: 'Hush. Stop! What's that?'

'That' was a very odd noise indeed – a soft noise, but quite plainly to be heard through the sound of the wind in the tree branches, and the hum and whir of the telegraph wires. It was a sort of rustling, whispering sound. As they listened it stopped, and then it began again.

And this time it did not stop, but it grew louder and more rustling and rumbling.

'Look,' cried Peter suddenly, 'the tree over there!'

The tree he pointed at was one of those that have rough grey leaves and white flowers. The berries, when they come, are bright scarlet, but if you pick them, they disappoint you by turning black before you get them home. And, as Peter pointed, the tree was moving – not just the way trees ought to move when the wind blows through them, but all in one piece, as though it were a live creature and were walking down the side of the cutting.

'It's moving!' cried Bobbie. 'Oh, look! And so are the others. It's like the woods in *Macbeth*.'

'It's magic,' said Phyllis, breathlessly. 'I always knew the railway was enchanted.'

It really did seem a little like magic. For all the trees for about twenty yards of the opposite bank seemed to be slowly walking down towards the railway line, the tree with the grey leaves bringing up the rear like some old shepherd driving a flock of green sheep.

'What is it? Oh, what is it?' said Phyllis. 'It's much too magic for me. I don't like it. Let's go home.'

But Bobbie and Peter clung fast to the rail and watched breathlessly. And Phyllis made no movement towards going home by herself.

The trees moved on and on. Some stones and loose earth fell down and rattled on the railway metals far below.

'It's *all* coming down,' Peter tried to say, but he found there was hardly any voice to say it with. And, indeed, just as he spoke, the great rock, on the top of which the walking trees were, leaned slowly forward. The trees, ceasing to walk, stood still and shivered. Leaning with the rock, they seemed to hesitate a moment, and then rock and trees and grasses and bushes, with a rushing sound, slipped right away from the face of the cutting and fell on the line with a blundering crash that could have been heard half a mile off. And a cloud of dust rose up.

'Oh,' said Peter, in awestruck tones, 'isn't it exactly like when the coals come in? If there wasn't any roof to the cellar and you could see down.'

'Look what a great mound it's made!' said Bobbie.

'Yes, it's right across the down line,' said Phyllis.

'That'll take some sweeping up,' said Bobbie.

'Yes,' said Peter, slowly: he was still leaning on the fence. 'Yes,' he said again, still more slowly.

Then he stood upright.

'The 11.29 down hasn't gone by yet. We must let them know at the station, or there'll be a most frightful accident.'

'Let's run,' said Bobbie, and began.

But Peter cried, 'Come back!' and looked at Mother's watch. He was very prompt and businesslike, and his face looked whiter than they had ever seen it.

'No time,' he said, 'it's two miles away, and it's past eleven.'

'Couldn't we,' suggested Phyllis breathlessly, 'couldn't we climb up a telegraph post and do something to the wires?'

'We don't know how,' said Peter.

'They do it in war,' said Phyllis, 'I know I've heard of it.'

'They only cut them, silly,' said Peter, 'and that doesn't do any good. And we couldn't cut them if we got up, and we couldn't get up. If we had anything red, we could get down on the line and wave it.'

'But the train wouldn't see us till it got round the corner, and then it could see the mound just as well as us,' said Phyllis, 'better, because it's much bigger than us.'

'If we only had something red,' Peter repeated, 'we could go round the corner and wave to the train.'

'We might wave anyway.'

'They'd only think it was just *us*, as usual. We've waved so often before. Anyway, let's get down.'

They got down the steep stairs. Bobbie was pale and shivering. Peter's face looked thinner than usual. Phyllis was red-faced and damp with anxiety.

'Oh, how hot I am!' she said, 'and I thought it was going to be cold. I wish we hadn't put on our –' she stopped short, and then ended in quite a different tone – 'our flannel petticoats.'[1]

Bobbie turned at the bottom of the stairs.

'Oh, yes,' she cried; '*they're* red! Let's take them off.'

---

[1]*Petticoat – a sort of dress or skirt worn as underwear*

"Beijing to Shanghai Railway"
Diary of a 4h 48m Journey

New high-speed rail links are opening all over the world. These extracts are from a diary written by journalist Peter Foster on his journey between China's two biggest cities.

08.30: Our first glimpse into the future comes in the shape of the Beijing South Railway Station, a giant glass dome that's propped up on stilts. It looks like a flying saucer has just landed from outer space.

China has built more than 300 of its super-modern railway stations during the decade-long railway building boom, symbols of its growing power; much as the great London stations like Euston, Paddington and King's Cross were for the Victorians.

08.45: After putting the bags through an airport-style scanner, and submitting to a peremptory waft of a security guard's wand, we reach the 'Boarding Gate' for Train G1 – the 09.00 service to Shanghai.

A barrier opens with a wave of your ticket and the passengers are swept down to the platforms on banks of escalators. The number of each carriage is helpfully displayed on a moving digital display.

08.50: Settle into a First Class seat. The legroom on the plush, crimson corduroy seat is generous, and there's a footrest and plug for the laptop, with an airline-style tray table that folds out from the armrest. It's all neat, but not wildly flashy.

09.00: And we're off, gliding out of Beijing South behind a Chinese-built CRH-380BL locomotive. The platform is so clean I can see the guard's reflection in the polished granite as we pass. Within three minutes we're travelling at 180kmh; after five minutes the electronic speed readout shows 247kmh; and seven minutes after departure we've hit the top operating cruising speed of 300kmh (186mph). At this rate, with a brief stop in Nanjing, we'll reach Shanghai in 4 hours, 48 minutes.

09.30: Even after 30 minutes the sensation of speed is remarkable. It feels like we're in an airliner, blasting down the runway, just moments away from getting airborne. (Obviously hoping that's not the case today.) A hostess sets a refreshing cup of green tea down on my table. Even at this speed, the surface barely ripples.

09.50: Another train comes blasting down the line in the opposite direction. This must be one of the test bunnies. There have been some rumblings recently that China's railways might have been built too fast, cutting corners on safety. Engineers deny this. By the time this line opens on Friday the service will have already have been running flat-out (but empty) for a month, with 1,500 trains clocking up 2 million kilometres of dry runs.

10.30: Go for a stroll up the train and, having been quite pleased to have been allocated a seat in first class, now find myself suffering from serious seat envy issues. First class is not, as I had fondly imagined, the best seat in the house. That title indisputably belongs to the 'executive sight-seeing class' right at the front of the train. There are six flat-bed pods – like an airline business class seat – which look straight out over the driver's head and down the tracks. (Cost £170, one way.)

11.09: Time to test the 'facilities'. Happy to report they are very clean and comfortable, with a full-length dress mirror behind the door. (A major advance on the hole-over-the-tracks toilet I last used on a local train from Chengde to Beijing a few weeks back.) The modern vacuum flush is a little startling, but highly efficient.

11.40: Rural China is flashing by outside the window. We're flying through the countryside at about 40ft (nearly 80 per cent of the track is built on raised concrete pylons) while straw-hatted farmers till fields dotted with the tombs of their ancestors, which they work around like an English farmer might circumvent an old oak tree. Some trudge behind mechanical rotavators, others have mules to plough the land, while the majority hoe manually between their lines of crops. Two hours ago it was fields of maize common to north China, but now the fields have morphed into the rice paddies of the warmer, wetter south . . .

12.00: Lunch time. There is a great deal to praise about this train, but the food isn't among its plus points. The carriage fills with the sickly smell of steamed cabbage as fellow passengers open their VIP lunch trays – steamed rice, bok choi,[1] sweetcorn, a chicken leg and some beef and vegetables. It's the Chinese equivalent of a school dinner.

12.32: Arrive Nanjing. We're on the fast train today, only making one stop to Shanghai. The longer version, taking in all 24 stations on the line, takes five-and-a-half hours.

---

[1] Bok choi – a vegetable, sometimes called 'Chinese cabbage'

Questions 1–5: *The Railways of Victorian Britain* (page 43 of the reading material).

1 mark

1. Give two ways in which the Railways Act made sure more people (especially poorer people) could use the railways.

_____

_____

_____

2 marks

2. How, according to the writer, did Thomas Cook invent the 'day out'?

_____

_____

_____

1 mark

3. The writer mentions a number of important events in the development of the railways. Put the following events in order by putting a number in the box (1–5). The first answer has been done for you.

The Football League was founded	
The Railway Act was passed	1
The first FA Cup Final was held	
Bank holidays were introduced	
King's Cross Station was opened	

4. On either side of the text there are small illustrations, labelled as 'Sources 1–5'. Give **two** reasons why these have been included on the page.

2 marks

_____

_____

_____

_____

_____

5. How, according to the writer, did the railways have a 'huge' impact on the lives of Victorians?

3 marks

_____

_____

_____

_____

_____

SUBTOTAL

Questions 6–11 are about "Saviours of the Train" (pages 44–45 of the reading material).

6. What do the children hear that is unusual?

_____

_____

7. Pick out two phrases which make it seem as though the tree is moving deliberately.

_____

_____

_____

_____

8. How does the writer show us that Peter knows a lot about the railway?

_____

_____

_____

_____

_____

_____

9. The children consider several ways of stopping the train. Explain why they decide that each of these would not work:

a) Running to the station to warn the stationmaster.

1 mark

_____

_____

_____

b) Climbing up the telegraph post and 'doing something' to the wires.

1 mark

_____

_____

_____

c) Waving at the train.

1 mark

_____

_____

_____

10. How will the girls' flannel petticoats help them to stop the train?

3 marks

_____

_____

_____

_____

_____

SUBTOTAL

11. What impression do you get of the three 'railway children' from the extract?

Think about:
- how they react when they see the tree and earth moving
- what they do when they realise the train in danger
- how they relate to each other.

Write about all three children.

Use evidence from the text to support your ideas.

_____

_____

_____

_____

_____

_____

_____

_____

_____

_____

_____

_____

_____

Questions 12–16 are about "Beijing to Shanghai Railway" (pages 46–47 of the reading material).

12. Write down the phrase from the first diary entry that backs up the writer's statement that the new train represents the future.

_____

_____

1 mark

13. How does the writer show that the platform is very clean?

_____

_____

_____

1 mark

14. What do you infer from the fact that the surface of his tea 'barely ripples'?

_____

_____

_____

1 mark

15. Which of the following aspects make the reader feel that the article has been written during the train journey?

Tick two of the statements below. If you tick more than two statements, you will receive no marks.

The article is about a train journey.	
Each section starts with a time.	
The writer describes what he sees.	
There is a lot of information in the article.	
The article is written in the present tense.	

1 mark

16. How does the writer use his diary to reflect on the contrast between the modern railway and a more traditional way of life?

_____

_____

_____

_____

_____

_____

_____

Shakespeare Test Paper

Romeo and Juliet, As You Like It and *Macbeth*

Set

B

KEY STAGE 3

Shakespeare
Test Paper

English

Romeo and Juliet, As You Like It and Macbeth

First name _____

Last name _____

Date _____

Instructions

In the following pages you will find three questions which assess your reading and understanding of Shakespeare. Each is on a different play:

Romeo and Juliet	page 56
As You Like It	page 61
Macbeth	page 66

- **Only** answer the question on the play you have studied.

- Read the question carefully.

- Write your answer on lined paper.

- You have **45 minutes** to complete the task.

- When you have completed the test, you can mark your answer using page 115 and pages 118–120 of the Answers and Mark Scheme section of this book.

- Enter your mark below:

MAXIMUM MARK	18		ACTUAL MARK	

Romeo and Juliet

Romeo and Juliet

Act 1, Scene 1, lines 156–220
Act 2, Scene 2, lines 1–69

In the first extract, Romeo tells Benvolio about his love for Rosaline. In the second, after meeting Juliet at the Capulets' ball, he waits under her window to declare his love for her.

In these extracts, how does Shakespeare use language to explore ideas about love?

Support your ideas by referring to both of the extracts printed on the following pages.

Romeo and Juliet

Act 1, Scene 1, lines 156–220

In this extract, Benvolio questions his cousin Romeo about his mood and feelings.

ROMEO	Ay me! Sad hours seem long.
	Was that my father that went hence so fast?
BENVOLIO	It was. What sadness lengthens Romeo's hours?
ROMEO	Not having that, which, having, makes them short.
BENVOLIO	In love?
ROMEO	Out.
BENVOLIO	Of love?
ROMEO	Out of her favour, where I am in love.
BENVOLIO	Alas, that love, so gentle in his view,
	Should be so tyrannous and rough in proof.
ROMEO	Alas, that love, whose view is muffled still,
	Should, without eyes, see pathways to his will!
	Where shall we dine? O me! What fray was here?
	Yet tell me not, for I have heard it all.
	Here's much to do with hate, but more with love.
	Why, then, O brawling love, O loving hate,
	O any thing, of nothing first create!
	O heavy lightness, serious vanity!
	Mis-shapen chaos of well-seeming forms!
	Feather of lead, bright smoke, cold fire, sick health,
	Still-waking sleep, that is not what it is!
	This love feel I that feel no love in this.
	Dost thou not laugh?
BENVOLIO	No, coz, I rather weep.
ROMEO	Good heart, at what?
BENVOLIO	At thy good heart's oppression.
ROMEO	Why, such is love's transgression.
	Griefs of mine own lie heavy in my breast,
	Which thou wilt propagate, to have it prest
	With more of thine: this love that thou hast shown
	Doth add more grief to too much of mine own.
	Love is a smoke raised with the fume of sighs;

160

165

170

175

180

185

Being purged, a fire sparkling in lovers' eyes;
Being vex'd a sea nourish'd with lovers' tears.
What is it else? A madness most discreet,
A choking gall and a preserving sweet.
Farewell, my coz.

BENVOLIO   Soft! I will go along;   190
And if you leave me so, you do me wrong.

ROMEO   Tut, I have lost myself; I am not here.
This is not Romeo, he's some other where.

BENVOLIO   Tell me in sadness, who is that you love.

ROMEO   What, shall I groan and tell thee?   195

BENVOLIO   Groan? Why, no, but sadly tell me who.

ROMEO   Bid a sick man in sadness make his will:
Ah, word ill urged to one that is so ill!
In sadness, cousin, I do love a woman.

BENVOLIO   I aim'd so near, when I supposed you loved.   200

ROMEO   A right good mark-man! And she's fair I love.

BENVOLIO   A right fair mark, fair coz, is soonest hit.

ROMEO   Well, in that hit you miss: she'll not be hit
With Cupid's arrow; she hath Dian's wit;
And, in strong proof of chastity well arm'd,   205
From love's weak childish bow she lives unharm'd.
She will not stay the siege of loving terms,
Nor bide the encounter of assailing eyes,
Nor ope her lap to saint-seducing gold;
O, she is rich in beauty, only poor,   210
That when she dies with beauty dies her store.

BENVOLIO   Then she hath sworn that she will still live chaste?

ROMEO   She hath, and in that sparing makes huge waste,
For beauty starved with her severity
Cuts beauty off from all posterity.   215
She is too fair, too wise, wisely too fair,
To merit bliss by making me despair:
She hath forsworn to love, and in that vow
Do I live dead that live to tell it now.

BENVOLIO   Be ruled by me, forget to think of her.   220

Act 2, Scene 2, lines 1–69

In this extract from the 'balcony scene', Romeo and Juliet declare their love for each other.

ROMEO   He jests at scars that never felt a wound.

                               JULIET *appears above at a window*

But, soft, what light through yonder window breaks?
It is the east, and Juliet is the sun.
Arise, fair sun, and kill the envious moon,
Who is already sick and pale with grief,   5
That thou her maid art far more fair than she:
Be not her maid, since she is envious;
Her vestal livery is but sick and green
And none but fools do wear it. Cast it off.
It is my lady, O, it is my love!   10
O that she knew she were!
She speaks yet she says nothing. What of that?
Her eye discourses; I will answer it.
I am too bold. 'Tis not to me she speak.
Two of the fairest stars in all the heaven,   15
Having some business, do entreat her eyes
To twinkle in their spheres till they return.
What if her eyes were there, they in her head?
The brightness of her cheek would shame those stars,
As daylight doth a lamp; her eyes in heaven   20
Would through the airy region stream so bright
That birds would sing and think it were not night.
See, how she leans her cheek upon her hand!
O, that I were a glove upon that hand,
That I might touch that cheek!

JULIET   Ay me!

ROMEO   She speaks.   25
O, speak again, bright angel! for thou art
As glorious to this night, being o'er my head
As is a winged messenger of heaven
Unto the white-upturned wondering eyes
Of mortals that fall back to gaze on him   30
When he bestrides the lazy-pacing clouds
And sails upon the bosom of the air.

JULIET	O Romeo, Romeo! Wherefore art thou Romeo?	
	Deny thy father and refuse thy name.	
	Or, if thou wilt not, be but sworn my love,	35
	And I'll no longer be a Capulet.	
ROMEO	[Aside] Shall I hear more, or shall I speak at this?	
JULIET	'Tis but thy name that is my enemy;	
	Thou art thyself, though not a Montague.	
	What's Montague? It is nor hand, nor foot,	40
	Nor arm, nor face, nor any other part	
	Belonging to a man. O, be some other name!	
	What's in a name? That which we call a rose	
	By any other name would smell as sweet;	
	So Romeo would, were he not Romeo call'd,	45
	Retain that dear perfection which he owes	
	Without that title. Romeo, doff thy name,	
	And for that name which is no part of thee	
	Take all myself.	
ROMEO	I take thee at thy word:	
	Call me but love, and I'll be new baptized.	50
	Henceforth I never will be Romeo.	
JULIET	What man art thou that thus bescreen'd in night	
	So stumblest on my counsel?	
ROMEO	By a name	
	I know not how to tell thee who I am:	
	My name, dear saint, is hateful to myself,	55
	Because it is an enemy to thee.	
	Had I it written, I would tear the word.	
JULIET	My ears have not yet drunk a hundred words	
	Of that tongue's utterance, yet I know the sound:	
	Art thou not Romeo and a Montague?	60
ROMEO	Neither, fair saint, if either thee dislike.	
JULIET	How camest thou hither, tell me, and wherefore?	
	The orchard walls are high and hard to climb,	
	And the place death, considering who thou art,	
	If any of my kinsmen find thee here.	65
ROMEO	With love's light wings did I o'er-perch these walls;	
	For stony limits cannot hold love out,	
	And what love can do that dares love attempt;	
	Therefore thy kinsmen are no let to me.	

As You Like It

As You Like It

Act 1, Scene 2, lines 190–240
Act 2, Scene 4, lines 1–58

In the first extract, Rosalind and Celia watch the wrestling match, and Rosalind falls in love with Orlando. In the second extract, Rosalind, Celia and Touchstone arrive in the Forest of Arden, where they see the shepherd Silvius talking of his love of Phoebe to Corin.

What different aspects of love do we see in these extracts?

Support your ideas by referring to both of the extracts printed on the following pages.

As You Like It

Act 1, Scene 2, lines 190–240

In this extract, Rosalind falls in love with Orlando as she watches him wrestling with Charles.

CHARLES	Come, where is this young gallant that is so desirous to lie with his mother earth?	
ORLANDO	Ready, sir; but his will hath in it a more modest working.	
DUKE FREDERICK	You shall try but one fall.	
CHARLES	No, I warrant your grace, you shall not entreat him to a second, that have so mightily persuaded him from a first.	195
ORLANDO	You mean to mock me after, you should not have mocked me before: but come your ways.	
ROSALIND	Now Hercules be thy speed, young man!	
CELIA	I would I were invisible, to catch the strong fellow by the leg.	
		They wrestle
ROSALIND	O excellent young man!	200
CELIA	If I had a thunderbolt in mine eye, I can tell who should down.	
		Shout. CHARLES *is thrown*
DUKE FREDERICK	No more, no more.	
ORLANDO	Yes, I beseech your grace. I am not yet well breathed.	
DUKE FREDERICK	How dost thou, Charles?	
LE BEAU	He cannot speak, my lord.	205
DUKE FREDERICK	Bear him away. What is thy name, young man?	
ORLANDO	Orlando, my liege, the youngest son of Sir Rowland de Boys.	
DUKE FREDERICK	I would thou hadst been son to some man else: The world esteem'd thy father honourable, But I did find him still mine enemy:	210
	Thou shouldst have better pleased me with this deed, Hadst thou descended from another house.	

But fare thee well; thou art a gallant youth.
I would thou hadst told me of another father.

Exeunt DUKE FREDERICK, *train, and* LE BEAU

CELIA	Were I my father, coz, would I do this?	215
ORLANDO	I am more proud to be Sir Rowland's son,	
	His youngest son; and would not change that calling,	
	To be adopted heir to Frederick.	
ROSALIND	My father loved Sir Rowland as his soul,	
	And all the world was of my father's mind.	220
	Had I before known this young man his son,	
	I should have given him tears unto entreaties,	
	Ere he should thus have ventured.	
CELIA	Gentle cousin,	
	Let us go thank him and encourage him.	
	My father's rough and envious disposition	225
	Sticks me at heart. Sir, you have well deserved.	
	If you do keep your promises in love	
	But justly, as you have exceeded all promise,	
	Your mistress shall be happy.	
ROSALIND	Gentleman,	

Giving him a chain from her neck

	Wear this for me, one out of suits with fortune,	230
	That could give more, but that her hand lacks means.	
	Shall we go, coz?	
CELIA	Ay. Fare you well, fair gentleman.	
ORLANDO	Can I not say, I thank you? My better parts	
	Are all thrown down, and that which here stands up	
	Is but a quintain, a mere lifeless block.	235
ROSALIND	He calls us back: my pride fell with my fortunes;	
	I'll ask him what he would. Did you call, sir?	
	Sir, you have wrestled well and overthrown	
	More than your enemies.	
CELIA	Will you go, coz?	
ROSALIND	Have with you. Fare you well.	240

Exeunt ROSALIND *and* CELIA

Act 2, Scene 4, lines 1–58

In this extract, Rosalind – disguised as a boy – and Celia and Touchstone arrive in the forest.

Enter ROSALIND, *dressed as a boy,* CELIA, *dressed like a shepherdess, and* TOUCHSTONE

ROSALIND	O Jupiter, how weary are my spirits!
TOUCHSTONE	I care not for my spirits, if my legs were not weary.
ROSALIND	I could find in my heart to disgrace my man's

ROSALIND I could find in my heart to disgrace my man's
apparel and to cry like a woman; but I must comfort
the weaker vessel, as doublet and hose ought to show   5
itself courageous to petticoat. Therefore courage, good Aliena!

CELIA I pray you, bear with me. I cannot go no further.

TOUCHSTONE For my part, I had rather bear with you than bear
you; yet I should bear no cross if I did bear you,
for I think you have no money in your purse.   10

ROSALIND Well, this is the Forest of Arden.

TOUCHSTONE Ay, now am I in Arden; the more fool I; when I was
at home, I was in a better place: but travellers must be content.

ROSALIND Ay, be so, good Touchstone. Look you, who comes here; a
young man and an old in solemn talk.   15

Enter CORIN *and* SILVIUS

CORIN That is the way to make her scorn you still.

SILVIUS O Corin, that thou knew'st how I do love her!

CORIN I partly guess; for I have loved ere now.

SILVIUS No, Corin, being old, thou canst not guess,
Though in thy youth thou wast as true a lover   20
As ever sigh'd upon a midnight pillow.
But if thy love were ever like to mine –
As sure I think did never man love so –
How many actions most ridiculous
Hast thou been drawn to by thy fantasy?   25

CORIN	Into a thousand that I have forgotten.
SILVIUS	O, thou didst then ne'er love so heartily!
	If thou remember'st not the slightest folly
	That ever love did make thee run into,
	Thou hast not loved. 30
	Or if thou hast not sat as I do now,
	Wearying thy hearer in thy mistress' praise,
	Thou hast not loved.
	Or if thou hast not broke from company
	Abruptly, as my passion now makes me, 35
	Thou hast not loved.
	O Phoebe, Phoebe, Phoebe!

Exit

ROSALIND	Alas, poor shepherd! Searching of thy wound,
	I have by hard adventure found mine own.
TOUCHSTONE	And I mine. I remember, when I was in love I broke 40
	my sword upon a stone and bid him take that for
	coming a-night to Jane Smile; and I remember the
	kissing of her batlet and the cow's dugs that her
	pretty chopt hands had milked; and I remember the
	wooing of a peascod instead of her, from whom I took 45
	two cods and, giving her them again, said with
	weeping tears, 'Wear these for my sake.' We that are
	true lovers run into strange capers; but as all is
	mortal in nature, so is all nature in love mortal in folly.
ROSALIND	Thou speakest wiser than thou art ware of. 50
TOUCHSTONE	Nay, I shall ne'er be ware of mine own wit till I
	break my shins against it.
ROSALIND	Jove, Jove! This shepherd's passion
	is much upon my fashion.
TOUCHSTONE	And mine; but it grows something stale with me. 55
CELIA	I pray you, one of you question yond man
	if he for gold will give us any food.
	I faint almost to death.

Macbeth

Macbeth

Act 3, Scene 1, lines 73 to the end
Act 3, Scene 4, lines 83 to the end

In the first extract, Macbeth orders the murder of Banquo and his son, Fleance. In the second, he has just seen Banquo's ghost.

What advice would you give an actor playing Macbeth in these scenes?

Support your ideas by referring to both of the extracts printed on the following pages.

Macbeth

Act 3, Scene 1, lines 73 to the end

In this extract, Macbeth orders the murders of Banquo and his son, Fleance.

MACBETH   Have you consider'd of my speeches? Know
That it was he in the times past which held you
So under fortune, which you thought had been   75
Our innocent self: this I made good to you
In our last conference, pass'd in probation with you,
How you were borne in hand, how cross'd, the instruments,
Who wrought with them, and all things else that might
To half a soul and to a notion crazed   80
Say 'Thus did Banquo.'

First Murderer   You made it known to us.

MACBETH   I did so, and went further, which is now
Our point of second meeting. Do you find
Your patience so predominant in your nature
That you can let this go? Are you so gospell'd   85
To pray for this good man and for his issue,
Whose heavy hand hath bow'd you to the grave
And beggar'd yours for ever?

First Murderer   We are men, my liege.

MACBETH   Ay, in the catalogue ye go for men;
As hounds and greyhounds, mongrels, spaniels, curs,   90
Shoughs, water-rugs and demi-wolves, are clept
All by the name of dogs: the valued file
Distinguishes the swift, the slow, the subtle,
The housekeeper, the hunter, every one
According to the gift which bounteous nature   95
Hath in him closed; whereby he does receive
Particular addition from the bill
That writes them all alike: and so of men.
Now, if you have a station in the file,
Not i'the worst rank of manhood, say't;   100
And I will put that business in your bosoms,
Whose execution takes your enemy off,
Grapples you to the heart and love of us,
Who wear our health but sickly in his life,
Which in his death were perfect.

Second Murderer   I am one, my liege,   105
Whom the vile blows and buffets of the world
Have so incensed that I am reckless what
I do to spite the world.

First Murderer	And I another	
	So weary with disasters, tugg'd with fortune,	
	That I would set my lie on any chance,	110
	To mend it, or be rid on't.	
MACBETH	Both of you	
	Know Banquo was your enemy.	
Both Murderers	True, my lord.	
MACBETH	So is he mine; and in such bloody distance,	
	That every minute of his being thrusts	
	Against my near'st of life: and though I could	115
	With barefaced power sweep him from my sight	
	And bid my will avouch it, yet I must not,	
	For certain friends that are both his and mine,	
	Whose loves I may not drop, but wail his fall	
	Who I myself struck down; and thence it is,	120
	That I to your assistance do make love,	
	Masking the business from the common eye	
	For sundry weighty reasons.	
Second Murderer	We shall, my lord,	
	Perform what you command us.	
First Murderer	Though our lives—	
MACBETH	Your spirits shine through you. Within this hour at most	125
	I will advise you where to plant yourselves;	
	Acquaint you with the perfect spy o'the time,	
	The moment on't; for't must be done to-night,	
	And something from the palace; always thought	
	That I require a clearness: and with him –	130
	To leave no rubs nor botches in the work –	
	Fleance his son, that keeps him company,	
	Whose absence is no less material to me	
	Than is his father's, must embrace the fate	
	Of that dark hour. Resolve yourselves apart:	135
	I'll come to you anon.	
Both Murderers	We are resolved, my lord.	
MACBETH	I'll call upon you straight: abide within.	

Exeunt Murderers

It is concluded. Banquo, thy soul's flight,
If it find heaven, must find it out to-night.

Exit

Act 3, Scene 4, lines 83 to the end

In this extract, Macbeth has seen the ghost of Banquo at a great feast he is holding after becoming king.

LADY MACBETH	My worthy lord, Your noble friends do lack you.
MACBETH	I do forget.

MACBETH   I do forget.
Do not muse at me, my most worthy friends.   85
I have a strange infirmity, which is nothing
To those that know me. Come, love and health to all;
Then I'll sit down. Give me some wine; fill full.
I drink to the general joy o' the whole table,
And to our dear friend Banquo, whom we miss;   90
Would he were here! To all, and him, we thirst,
And all to all.

Lords   Our duties, and the pledge.

Re-enter GHOST OF BANQUO

MACBETH Avaunt! And quit my sight! Let the earth hide thee!
Thy bones are marrowless, thy blood is cold;
Thou hast no speculation in those eyes
Which thou dost glare with!

LADY MACBETH   Think of this, good peers,   95
But as a thing of custom: 'tis no other;
Only it spoils the pleasure of the time.

MACBETH What man dare, I dare:
Approach thou like the rugged Russian bear,
The arm'd rhinoceros, or the Hyrcan tiger.   100
Take any shape but that, and my firm nerves
Shall never tremble: or be alive again,
And dare me to the desert with thy sword.
If trembling I inhabit then, protest me
The baby of a girl. Hence, horrible shadow!   105
Unreal mockery, hence!

GHOST OF BANQUO *vanishes*

Why, so: being gone,
I am a man again. Pray you, sit still.

LADY MACBETH	You have displaced the mirth, broke the good meeting, With most admired disorder.	
MACBETH	Can such things be, And overcome us like a summer's cloud, Without our special wonder? You make me strange Even to the disposition that I owe, When now I think you can behold such sights, And keep the natural ruby of your cheeks, When mine is blanched with fear.	110
ROSS	What sights, my lord?	115
LADY MACBETH	I pray you, speak not; he grows worse and worse; Question enrages him. At once, good night: Stand not upon the order of your going, But go at once.	
LENNOX	Good night; and better health Attend his majesty!	
LADY MACBETH	A kind good night to all!	120

Exeunt all but MACBETH *and* LADY MACBETH

MACBETH	It will have blood; they say, blood will have blood. Stones have been known to move and trees to speak. Augurs and understood relations have By magot-pies and choughs and rooks brought forth The secret'st man of blood. What is the night?	125
LADY MACBETH	Almost at odds with morning, which is which.	
MACBETH	How say'st thou, that Macduff denies his person At our great bidding?	
LADY MACBETH	Did you send to him, sir?	
MACBETH	I hear it by the way; but I will send: There's not a one of them but in his house I keep a servant fee'd. I will to-morrow, And betimes I will, to the weird sisters. More shall they speak; for now I am bent to know, By the worst means, the worst. For mine own good, All causes shall give way: I am in blood Stepp'd in so far that, should I wade no more, Returning were as tedious as go o'er: Strange things I have in head, that will to hand; Which must be acted ere they may be scann'd.	130 135
LADY MACBETH	You lack the season of all natures, sleep.	140
MACBETH	Come, we'll to sleep. My strange and self-abuse Is the initiate fear that wants hard use: We are yet but young in deed.	

Exeunt

Set
B
KEY STAGE 3

Writing Test
Paper

English

Days Out

Writing Test Paper

Days Out

First name _____

Last name _____

Date _____

Instructions

- There are two writing tasks in this paper.

- The test is **1 hour** and **15 minutes** long.

- You should spend: **45 minutes** on Section A (the longer writing task)
  30 minutes on Section B (the shorter writing task).

- You may spend the first 15 minutes planning your answer to Section A. Your plan will not be marked.

- Section 1 has 30 marks.

- Section B has 20 marks.

- Write your answer on lined paper.

- When you have finished, check your work carefully.

When you have completed the test, you can mark your answer using pages 123–128 of the Answers and Mark Scheme section of this book.

- Enter your marks below:

	Mark	Maximum mark
Section A		30
Section B		20
Total		50

Section A

Longer Writing Task

A New Railway

It has been proposed that a new high-speed railway will be built close to where you live. The local council is interested in hearing the views of young people about this and have asked you to hold a meeting at school to discuss the issue. You have been chosen to write the report for them. This is your brief:

The government has proposed that a new high-speed rail link will pass through the outskirts of our town. Before we give our view, we would like to gather together the views of all sections of our community.

We would like you to hold a meeting at your school and report back to us. Please include:
- arguments given in favour of the rail link
- arguments against the rail link
- any conclusions the meeting was able to come to, whether for or against the rail link
- any other ideas/proposals you might have.

Write your report on the meeting's views about the proposed rail link.

Section B

Shorter Writing Task

A Great Day Out!

A competition to design a leaflet advertising tourist attractions in your local area has been announced.

Here are the instructions:

A Great Day Out!

Our area is already very popular with tourists, but we want to attract more – especially young people.

We want you to come up with a new leaflet advertising one of our local attractions or the whole area.

The winning entry will:
- include lots of information
- appeal to children and young people
- tell them what's so great about our area
- persuade them to come here and enjoy themselves.

You don't need to include illustrations, though you can indicate where they would be. It's what you have to say – and how you say it – that we're interested in.

Write your leaflet.

SUBTOTAL

Set **C**

English

Young and Old

Reading Test Paper

Young and Old

First name _____

Last name _____

Date _____

Instructions

- Before you start to write you have **15 minutes** to read the reading material (pages 75–80). There are three texts. Make sure you read all three.

- During this time you should not look at the questions on the following pages.

- You will then have **1 hour** to answer all the questions on pages 81–87.

- Answer all the questions.

- Write your answers in the spaces provided.

- When you have finished, check your work carefully.

After you have completed the test, you can mark your answers using pages 113–115 of the Answers and Mark Scheme section of this book.

Enter the marks for each answer in the small box next to your answer.

At the bottom of each page put the total marks for that page.

Enter your marks in the boxes below and add them up to get your total out of 32.

Page	81	82	83	84	85	86	87	Total mark	Maximum mark
Score									32

Reading Material

Contents

When young people meet older people they can have very different reactions. They can gain a lot from the experience, as suggested by our first extract. But sometimes, as when Pip meets Miss Havisham in the second extract, the experience can be disturbing.

When people get older they often look back on their youth. They can be full of regrets and stuck in the past, like Miss Havisham; or, like Thomas Goodman, they can enjoy both their memories and their life today.

"Adopt a Granny" scheme

This article describes a scheme to get young and old people together to make friends and help each other . . .

Traditionally, in Britain and all over the world, grandparents have played a huge role in their grandchildren's lives, looking after them when their parents are busy, playing with them, teaching them useful skills or just lending a sympathetic ear. But recent reports show that more and more children are growing up not knowing their grandparents.

Sometimes, sadly, this is because they have died. More often it is because they simply live too far away. The days of spending your life in the same village or town, living down the street from, or even next door to, members of the extended family, are gone for most of us. Grandparents are more likely to be on the other side of the country or even the other side of the world.

This means grandparents, parents and children are all missing out. We're always hearing about the difficulties young parents have in bringing up their children – perhaps a lot of these problems could be solved by a little bit of timely advice from Nan, Gran or Grandma. Young children, too, miss a lot when they don't get the chance to interact with older people. Grandparents often have more time to play with them and to listen to them, while the benefits of the company of young people for older folk are many. Lots of senior citizens will tell you that being with their grandchildren 'keeps them young'.

That's why we've set up an 'Adopt a Granny' scheme here in Puddington.

The idea is simple. If you're a senior citizen who has something to offer to the young – and perhaps you have no grandchildren of your own – or if you're a parent who thinks your children would benefit from contact with the older generation, get in touch with us now. We'll try to match you up with someone who lives close to you. You can meet, see how you get along – and take it from there!

Stan and Vera have been part of the scheme for two years now and, according to Stan, they've had a 'smashing time' getting to know Alfie and Rhianna, who live just around the corner from them in Bigelow village.

'Our own grandchildren live in Australia,' says Vera. 'We're lucky if we get to see them once a year and Skype just isn't the same. Frankly, we were beginning to find life a bit boring until we joined "Adopt a Granny". It's as if a little bit of sunshine has come into our lives. We always look forward to seeing the children and we feel part of the world again. It's like a new lease of life!'

Of course, there are certain rules we have to keep to for everyone's safety and comfort and certain checks that have to be made. We're a registered charity, working closely with the District Council, and we can assure you that we will make sure everything's properly organised and supervised.

So what can you do once you've been matched with someone? There are countless activities you can do together: going on days out; baking cakes together (Vera's speciality); playing football in the park; helping with homework – basically, anything you might do with your own children or grandparents. In addition, we will be organising fun days from time to time so you can meet other people who are taking part in the scheme, swap notes and just have fun together.

So, why not give it a go? Pop into your local library or village hall to pick up a leaflet and application form, or ring us now on 0799 687 9313.

"Miss Havisham"

from *Great Expectations* by Charles Dickens

In this extract, Pip, who lives with his older sister, has been sent for by Miss Havisham: the mysterious and very rich lady who lives nearby. His uncle, Mr Pumblechook, has left him at the door and a young girl, Estella, is taking him into the house.

We went into the house by a side door – the great front entrance had two chains across it outside – and the first thing I noticed was, that the passages were all dark, and that she had left a candle burning there. She took it up, and we went through more passages and up a staircase, and still it was all dark, and only the candle lighted us.

At last we came to the door of a room, and she said, 'Go in.'

I answered, more in shyness than politeness, 'After you, miss.'

To this she returned: 'Don't be ridiculous, boy; I am not going in.' And scornfully walked away, and – what was worse – took the candle with her.

This was very uncomfortable, and I was half afraid. However, the only thing to be done being to knock at the door, I knocked, and was told from within to enter. I entered, therefore, and found myself in a pretty large room, well lighted with wax candles. No glimpse of daylight was to be seen in it. It was a dressing-room, as I supposed from the furniture, though much of it was of forms and uses then quite unknown to me. But prominent in it was a draped table with a gilded looking-glass, and that I made out at first sight to be a fine lady's dressing-table.

Whether I should have made out this object so soon if there had been no fine lady sitting at it, I cannot say. In an arm-chair, with an elbow resting on the table and her head leaning on that hand, sat the strangest lady I have ever seen, or shall ever see.

She was dressed in rich materials – satins, and lace, and silks – all of white. Her shoes were white. And she had a long white veil dependent from her hair, and she had bridal flowers in her hair, but her hair was white. Some bright jewels sparkled on her neck and on her hands, and some other jewels lay sparkling on the table. Dresses, less splendid than the dress she wore, and half-packed trunks, were scattered about. She had not quite finished dressing, for she had but one shoe on – the other was on the table near her hand – her veil was but half arranged, her watch and chain were not put on, and some lace for her bosom lay with those trinkets, and with her handkerchief, and gloves, and some flowers, and a prayer-book all confusedly heaped about the looking-glass.

It was not in the first few moments that I saw all these things, though I saw more of them in the first moments than might be supposed. But I saw that everything within my view which ought to be white, had been white long ago, and had lost its lustre and was faded and yellow. I saw that the bride within the bridal dress had withered like the dress, and like the flowers, and had no brightness left but the brightness of her sunken eyes. I saw that the dress had been put upon the rounded figure of a young woman, and that the figure upon which it now hung loose had shrunk to skin and bone. Once, I had been taken to see some ghastly waxwork at the fair, representing I know not what impossible personage lying in state. Once, I had been taken to one of our old marsh churches to see a skeleton in the ashes of a rich dress that had been dug out of a vault under the church pavement. Now, waxwork and skeleton seemed to have dark eyes that moved and looked at me. I should have cried out, if I could.

'Who is it?' said the lady at the table.

'Pip, ma'am.'

'Pip?'

'Mr. Pumblechook's boy, ma'am. Come – to play.'

'Come nearer; let me look at you. Come close.'

It was when I stood before her, avoiding her eyes, that I took note of the surrounding objects in detail, and saw that her watch had stopped at twenty minutes to nine, and that a clock in the room had stopped at twenty minutes to nine.

'Look at me,' said Miss Havisham. 'You are not afraid of a woman who has never seen the sun since you were born?'

I regret to state that I was not afraid of telling the enormous lie comprehended in the answer 'No.'

'Do you know what I touch here?' she said, laying her hands, one upon the other, on her left side.

'Yes, ma'am.' (It made me think of the young man.)

'What do I touch?'

'Your heart.'

'Broken!'

She uttered the word with an eager look, and with strong emphasis, and with a weird smile that had a kind of boast in it. Afterwards she kept her hands there for a little while, and slowly took them away as if they were heavy.

'I am tired,' said Miss Havisham. 'I want diversion, and I have done with men and women. Play.'

I think it will be conceded by my most disputatious reader, that she could hardly have directed an unfortunate boy to do anything in the wide world more difficult to be done under the circumstances.

'I sometimes have sick fancies,' she went on, 'and I have a sick fancy that I want to see some play. There, there!' with an impatient movement of the fingers of her right hand; 'play, play, play!'

Remembering Schooldays

Writing in 1871, Thomas Goodman, then an elderly man, remembers his schooldays at Oundle. The head teacher, Mr Bullen, is referred to as 'the master' and the other teachers as 'ushers'.

The cane was very generally used in the school. Indeed the ushers (of whom there were four) were allowed to use it, but the birch was reserved for special occasions only. I remember once, when Mr Bullen was caning a boy who seemed terribly frightened at the punishment, he exclaimed, "Oh pray, Sir, don't because you are in a passion," to which he replied by an interrogation, "Am I in a passion?" When the boy immediately answered, "Oh no, Sir, you are not in a passion," the master then rejoined, with a sharper cut of the cane than ever, "but I am in a passion."

Oundle had a very convenient river for bathing and occasionally, I believe more to save the trouble of feet-washing than anything else, we were taken down to the river, in one part of which those who were unable to swim might venture to bathe with safety. But when the art had been acquired, they were allowed to go into deeper water, and the elder Mr Dix sometimes, for fun's sake, used to take hold of a boy with one hand at the wrist, and another at the ankle, and throw him several yards into deep water – a feat which seemed to gratify the swimmer as an evidence of his skill and courage. I remember a boy once coming behind me when I was swimming and seizing me by the neck, sent me down several feet under the water, and I believe I am right in the assumption that my eyes were open, and able to see the fish as they swam along.

We had no other playground than the churchyard. There were many walnut trees planted in the churchyard; two of which, in the north-west corner, a retired spot, served capitally for a swing, which was also a favorite pastime with the boys, and many became skilful either at swinging themselves standing upon the rope, or, putting one leg above the rope and the other under it, turning themselves over repeatedly while they were at full swing. … There was considerable danger in boys jumping from one gravestone to another and sometimes in jumping over the tombstones. I was once attempting to go over one which was very easy on the one side but difficult on the other, as the slab at the top was far from being level… I caught my toe against the edge of the stone and my body went upon the ground with such violence that I began to think I should never get my breath again and I naturally abstained from making a second effort.

We were very irregular in our walks. Indeed, according to my recollections, we scarcely ever took them except on Sunday evenings, but I think we must have done so occasionally on other days, as I know it was a great treat to hear Mr Dix tell a story as we clustered round him at the river side, which he composed as he walked along with a pipe or cigar in his mouth – the smoking of which gave him time to recollect himself.

The punishments at Oundle School were very badly and unjustly regulated, in consequence of which the ushers were much more severe than the master, especially in their tasks. The latter would occasionally order a boy to write a sheet of paper, which, being foolscap, would of course, if properly filled, take up a considerable time, but the ushers would more frequently set half a dozen sheets. Again the amount depended upon what they were to write, the usual custom being to state the offence which had been committed as, for example, "I must not jump over the desks" or "I must get up when the bell rings". It often happened that a boy would get his companions to help him in writing these tasks, and it was thought to be done more expeditiously[1] if one boy wrote the letter "I" from the top to the bottom of the sheet and another undertook to write the next word "must" in the same way, and so on to the end, until the whole of the sheets were filled. This practice, of course, was discovered and in its place a boy was desired to fill his paper by copying from some book, which would take him twice as long, if not more.

---

[1]*expeditiously* – quickly

The classical usher, named Hinde, while a boy was repeating his lesson, if he found him defective,[2] was accustomed to make him stand by his side and, taking hold of one of his ears, used to give it a pull for every mistake he made. This, I think, was always done in the absence of the master, for I don't believe Mr Bullen would have allowed such a cruel mode of torturing a boy, as with all the master's gusts of passion, he had his periods of patience and forbearance, and I do not think that upon the whole he was disliked by the pupils.

[2]*defective* – inadequate, not good enough

Questions 1–5 are about the "Adopt a Granny" scheme (on page 76 of the reading material).

1. From the second paragraph, give two reasons why children might not see their own grandparents.

_____

_____

_____

_____

2. How, according to the writer, would each of the following benefit from the "Adopt a Granny" scheme?

Older people	
Parents	
Children	

3. What two reasons do Vera and Stan give for joining the scheme?

_____

_____

_____

_____

_____

4. How does the writer reassure readers that the "Adopt a Granny" scheme is safe and genuine?

_____

_____

_____

_____

_____

_____

_____

5. This text has more than one purpose. Tick the boxes to show which **three** of the following statements accurately describe the writer's purpose. If you tick more than three statements, you will receive no marks.

The writer wants to persuade people to join the "Adopt a Granny" scheme.	
The writer wants to persuade readers to visit the Puddington area.	
The writer is informing us about the "Adopt a Granny" scheme.	
The writer argues that children do not need grandparents.	
The writer argues that children's lives are improved by knowing older people.	

Questions 6–11 are about the 'Miss Havisham' extract from *Great Expectations* (pages 77–78 of the reading material).

6. Pick out two details from the first paragraph which make the house seem unwelcoming.

_____

_____

_____

7. How would you describe the girl's attitude to Pip? Use evidence from the text to back up your opinion.

_____

_____

_____

_____

8. Pip describes Miss Havisham as 'the strangest lady I have ever seen, or shall ever see'. Explain in your own words what is strange about her appearance.

_____

_____

_____

_____

9. **(a)** Of which two things does Miss Havisham remind Pip?

1 mark

_____

_____

_____

_____

(b) What do these comparisons tell us about the effect her appearance has on Pip?

2 marks

_____

_____

_____

10. When Miss Havisham puts her hands on her heart, it makes Pip 'think of the young man'. Who do you think 'the young man' might be?

2 marks

_____

_____

_____

_____

_____

11. How does Dickens create an air of mystery about Miss Havisham?

Think about:
- Pip's role as the narrator and his character
- the way the house and Pip's entry into it are described
- the way Miss Havisham is described
- what Miss Havisham says and does.

Use evidence from the text to support your ideas.

_____

_____

_____

_____

_____

_____

_____

_____

_____

_____

_____

_____

_____

Questions 12–16 are about *Remembering Schooldays* (pages 79–80 of the reading material).

12. What does the boy mean when he says that Mr Bullen is 'in a passion'?

_____

_____

13. Why would a boy be pleased if Mr Dix picked him up and threw him into the deep water?

_____

_____

_____

14. Give two games played by the boys in the churchyard:

_____

_____

1 mark

1 mark

1 mark

15. Which of the following statements reflect Thomas Goodman's feelings about his schooldays?

Tick **three** of the statements below. If you tick more than three statements, you will receive no marks.

He hated everything about Oundle.	
He thinks punishments were inconsistent and sometimes cruel.	
On the whole, he respects Mr Bullen.	
He had some enjoyable times at Oundle.	
He thinks all the ushers were very caring.	
He never thinks about his schooldays.	

16. In this text, Goodman describes the discipline at his school. What do you think would be the reaction of modern readers to this? Explain as fully as you can.

_____

_____

_____

_____

_____

_____

_____

Set
C

KEY STAGE 3

Shakespeare Test Paper

English

Romeo and Juliet, As
You Like It and Macbeth

Shakespeare Test Paper

Romeo and Juliet, As You Like It and Macbeth

First name _____

Last name _____

Date _____

Instructions

In the following pages you will find three questions which assess your reading and understanding of Shakespeare. Each is on a different play:

Romeo and Juliet	page 89
As You Like It	page 94
Macbeth	page 99

- **Only** answer the question on the play you have studied.

- Read the question carefully.

- Write your answer on lined paper.

- You have **45 minutes** to complete the task.

- When you have completed the test, you can mark your answer using pages 115 and 120–122 of the Answers and Mark Scheme section of this book.

- Enter your mark below:

MAXIMUM MARK	18		ACTUAL MARK	

Romeo and Juliet

Romeo and Juliet

Act 3, Scene 2, lines 36–96
Act 3, Scene 5, lines 168–242

In the first extract, the nurse tells Juliet that Romeo has killed her cousin Tybalt and has been banished from Verona. In the second, after the secret marriage of Romeo and Juliet, Juliet's father tells her that he will force her to marry Paris.

What do we learn from these extracts about the relationship between Juliet and her nurse?

Support your ideas by referring to both of the extracts printed on the following pages.

Romeo and Juliet

Act 3, Scene 2, lines 36–96

In this extract, after Friar Lawrence has married them, Juliet is waiting for news of Romeo, not knowing that he has killed Tybalt and has been banished from Verona.

JULIET	Ay me! What news? Why dost thou wring thy hands?
NURSE	Ah, well-a-day! He's dead, he's dead, he's dead!
	We are undone, lady, we are undone!
	Alack the day! He's gone, he's kill'd, he's dead!
JULIET	Can heaven be so envious?
NURSE	Romeo can,

    40

Though heaven cannot. O Romeo, Romeo,
Whoever would have thought it? Romeo!

JULIET   What devil art thou, that dost torment me thus?
This torture should be roar'd in dismal hell.
Hath Romeo slain himself? Say thou but 'Ay,'   45
And that bare vowel 'I' shall poison more
Than the death-darting eye of cockatrice:
I am not I, if there be such an 'Ay',
Or those eyes shut, that make thee answer 'Ay'.
If he be slain, say 'Ay'; or if not, 'No':   50
Brief sounds determine of my weal or woe.

NURSE   I saw the wound, I saw it with mine eyes –
God save the mark – here on his manly breast.
A piteous corse, a bloody piteous corse;
Pale, pale as ashes, all bedaub'd in blood –   55
All in gore-blood; I swounded at the sight.

JULIET   O, break, my heart! Poor bankrupt, break at once!
To prison, eyes, ne'er look on liberty!
Vile earth, to earth resign. End motion here;
And thou and Romeo press one heavy bier!   60

NURSE   O Tybalt, Tybalt, the best friend I had!
O courteous Tybalt! Honest gentleman!
That ever I should live to see thee dead!

JULIET   What storm is this that blows so contrary?
Is Romeo slaughter'd, and is Tybalt dead?   65
My dear-loved cousin, and my dearer lord?

	Then, dreadful trumpet sound the general doom!	
	For who is living, if those two are gone?	
NURSE	Tybalt is gone and Romeo banished;	
	Romeo that kill'd him, he is banished.	70
JULIET	O God! Did Romeo's hand shed Tybalt's blood?	
NURSE	It did, it did. Alas the day, it did!	
JULIET	O serpent heart, hid with a flowering face!	
	Did ever dragon keep so fair a cave?	
	Beautiful tyrant! Fiend angelical!	75
	Dove-feather'd raven! Wolvish-ravening lamb!	
	Despised substance of divinest show!	
	Just opposite to what thou justly seem'st,	
	A damned saint, an honourable villain!	
	O nature, what hadst thou to do in hell,	80
	When thou didst bower the spirit of a fiend	
	In moral paradise of such sweet flesh?	
	Was ever book containing such vile matter	
	So fairly bound? O that deceit should dwell	
	In such a gorgeous palace!	
NURSE	There's no trust,	85
	No faith, no honesty in men; all perjured,	
	All forsworn, all naught, all dissemblers.	
	Ah, where's my man? Give me some aqua vitae:	
	These griefs, these woes, these sorrows make me old.	
	Shame come to Romeo!	
JULIET	Blister'd be thy tongue	90
	For such a wish! He was not born to shame:	
	Upon his brow shame is ashamed to sit;	
	For 'tis a throne where honour may be crown'd	
	Sole monarch of the universal earth.	
	O, what a beast was I to chide at him!	95
NURSE	Will you speak well of him that kill'd your cousin?	

Act 3, Scene 5, lines 168–242

In this extract, Juliet has just said goodbye to Romeo after their first night together. However, her father tells her that he will force her to marry Paris.

NURSE	God in heaven bless her!	
	You are to blame, my lord, to rate her so.	
CAPULET	And why, my lady wisdom? Hold your tongue,	170
	Good prudence. Smatter with your gossips, go.	
NURSE	I speak no treason.	
CAPULET	O, God 'I' good e'en.	
NURSE	May not one speak?	
CAPULET	Peace, you mumbling fool!	
	Utter your gravity o'er a gossip's bowl;	
	For here we need it not.	
LADY CAPULET	You are too hot.	175
CAPULET	God's bread! It makes me mad: day, night, work, play,	
	Alone, in company, still my care hath been	
	To have her match'd: and having now provided	
	A gentleman of noble parentage,	
	Of fair demesnes, youthful, and nobly lined,	180
	Stuff'd, as they say, with honourable parts,	
	Proportion'd as one's thought would wish a man;	
	And then to have a wretched puling fool,	
	A whining mammet, in her fortune's tender,	
	To answer 'I'll not wed; I cannot love,	185
	I am too young; I pray you, pardon me.'	
	But, as you will not wed, I'll pardon you.	
	Graze where you will you shall not house with me.	
	Look to't, think on't, I do not use to jest.	
	Thursday is near; lay hand on heart. Advise.	190
	And you be mine, I'll give you to my friend;	
	And you be not, hang, beg, starve, die streets,	
	For, by my soul, I'll ne'er acknowledge thee,	
	Nor what is mine shall never do thee good.	
	Trust to't, bethink you. I'll not be forsworn.	195
		Exit
JULIET	Is there no pity sitting in the clouds,	
	That sees into the bottom of my grief?	
	O, sweet my mother, cast me not away!	
	Delay this marriage for a month, a week;	
	Or, if you do not, make the bridal bed	200
	In that dim monument where Tybalt lies.	

| LADY CAPULET | Talk not to me, for I'll not speak a word: |
| | Do as thou wilt, for I have done with thee. |

Exit

JULIET	O God! O nurse, how shall this be prevented?	205
	My husband is on earth, my faith in heaven.	
	How shall that faith return again to earth,	
	Unless that husband send it me from heaven	
	By leaving earth? Comfort me, counsel me.	
	Alack, alack, that heaven should practise stratagems	
	Upon so soft a subject as myself!	210
	What say'st thou? Hast thou not a word of joy?	
	Some comfort, nurse.	
NURSE	Faith, here it is.	
	Romeo is banish'd; and all the world to nothing,	
	That he dares ne'er come back to challenge you;	
	Or, if he do, it needs must be by stealth.	215
	Then, since the case so stands as now it doth,	
	I think it best you married with the county.	
	O, he's a lovely gentleman!	
	Romeo's a dishclout to him: an eagle, madam,	
	Hath not so green, so quick, so fair an eye	220
	As Paris hath. Beshrew my very heart,	
	I think you are happy in this second match,	
	For it excels your first: or if it did not,	
	Your first is dead; or 'twere as good he were,	
	As living here and you no use of him.	225
JULIET	Speakest thou from thy heart?	
NURSE	And from my soul too;	
	Or else beshrew them both.	
JULIET	Amen!	
NURSE	What?	
JULIET	Well, thou hast comforted me marvellous much.	230
	Go in: and tell my lady I am gone,	
	Having displeased my father, to Laurence's cell,	
	To make confession and to be absolved.	
NURSE	Marry, I will; and this is wisely done.	

Exit

JULIET	Ancient damnation! O most wicked fiend!	235
	Is it more sin to wish me thus forsworn,	
	Or to dispraise my lord with that same tongue	
	Which she hath praised him with above compare	
	So many thousand times? Go, counsellor!	
	Thou and my bosom henceforth shall be twain.	240
	I'll to the friar, to know his remedy:	
	If all else fail, myself have power to die.	

Exit

As You Like It

As You Like It

Act 1, Scene 1, lines 26–82
Act 2, Scene 3, lines 1–77

In the first extract, Orlando confronts his brother, Oliver, about the way he has treated him since their father's death. In the second, Adam warns him not to return home as his life is in danger.

What impressions might an audience get of Orlando from these extracts?

Support your ideas by referring to both of the extracts printed on the following pages.

As You Like It

Act 1, Scene 1, lines 26–82

In this extract, Orlando argues with his brother, Oliver, about the way he has been treated since their father's death.

ADAM	Yonder comes my master, your brother.
ORLANDO	Go apart, Adam, and thou shalt hear how he will shake me up.

Enter OLIVER

OLIVER	Now, sir! What make you here?	
ORLANDO	Nothing. I am not taught to make anything.	30
OLIVER	What mar you then, sir?	
ORLANDO	Marry, sir, I am helping you to mar that which God made, a poor unworthy brother of yours, with idleness.	
OLIVER	Marry, sir, be better employed, and be naught awhile.	
ORLANDO	Shall I keep your hogs and eat husks with them? What prodigal portion have I spent, that I should come to such penury?	35
OLIVER	Know you where you are, sir?	
ORLANDO	O, sir, very well; here in your orchard.	
OLIVER	Know you before whom, sir?	40
ORLANDO	Ay, better than him I am before knows me. I know you are my eldest brother; and, in the gentle condition of blood, you should so know me. The courtesy of nations allows you my better, in that you are the first-born; but the same tradition takes not away my blood, were there twenty brothers betwixt us. I have as much of my father in me as you; albeit, I confess, your coming before me is nearer to his reverence.	45
OLIVER	What, boy! (*strikes him*)	50
ORLANDO	Come, come, elder brother, you are too young in this. (*seizes him*)	
OLIVER	Wilt thou lay hands on me, villain?	

ORLANDO	I am no villain. I am the youngest son of Sir Rowland de Boys. He was my father, and he is thrice a villain that says such a father begot villains. Wert thou not my brother, I would not take this hand from thy throat till this other had pulled out thy tongue for saying so. Thou hast railed on thyself.	55
ADAM	Sweet masters, be patient. For your father's remembrance, be at accord.	60
OLIVER	Let me go, I say.	
ORLANDO	I will not, till I please. You shall hear me. My father charged you in his will to give me good education. You have trained me like a peasant, obscuring and hiding from me all gentleman-like qualities. The spirit of my father grows strong in me, and I will no longer endure it. Therefore allow me such exercises as may become a gentleman, or give me the poor allottery my father left me by testament; with that I will go buy my fortunes.	65
		70
OLIVER	And what wilt thou do? Beg, when that is spent? Well, sir, get you in. I will not long be troubled with you. You shall have some part of your will. I pray you, leave me.	
ORLANDO	I will no further offend you than becomes me for my good.	75
OLIVER	Get you with him, you old dog.	
ADAM	Is 'old dog' my reward? Most true, I have lost my teeth in your service. God be with my old master! He would not have spoke such a word.	

Exeunt ORLANDO and ADAM

| OLIVER | Is it even so? Begin you to grow upon me? I will physic your rankness, and yet give no thousand crowns neither. | 80 |

Act 2, Scene 3, lines 1–77

In this extract, Orlando returns home after the wrestling match and is warned by Adam that he is danger from his brother.

Enter ORLANDO *and* ADAM, *meeting*

ORLANDO	Who's there?
ADAM	What, my young master? O, my gentle master!
	O my sweet master! O you memory
	Of old Sir Rowland! Why, what make you here?
	Why are you virtuous? Why do people love you?
	And wherefore are you gentle, strong and valiant?
	Why would you be so fond to overcome
	The bonny priser of the humorous duke?
	Your praise is come too swiftly home before you.
	Know you not, master, to some kind of men
	Their graces serve them but as enemies?
	No more do yours. Your virtues, gentle master,
	Are sanctified and holy traitors to you.
	O, what a world is this, when what is comely
	Envenoms him that bears it!
ORLANDO	Why, what's the matter?
ADAM	O unhappy youth!
	Come not within these doors. Within this roof
	The enemy of all your graces lives,
	Your brother – no, no brother, yet the son –
	Yet not the son, I will not call him son
	Of him I was about to call his father –
	Hath heard your praises, and this night he means
	To burn the lodging where you use to lie
	And you within it. If he fail of that,
	He will have other means to cut you off.
	I overheard him and his practices.
	This is no place. This house is but a butchery:
	Abhor it, fear it, do not enter it.
ORLANDO	Why, whither, Adam, wouldst thou have me go?
ADAM	No matter whither, so you come not here.
ORLANDO	What? Wouldst thou have me go and beg my food?
	Or with a base and boisterous sword enforce
	A thievish living on the common road?

Line numbers: 5, 10, 15, 20, 25, 30

	This I must do, or know not what to do.	35
	Yet this I will not do, do how I can.	
	I rather will subject me to the malice	
	Of a diverted blood and bloody brother.	
ADAM	But do not so. I have five hundred crowns,	
	The thrifty hire I saved under your father,	40
	Which I did store to be my foster-nurse	
	When service should in my old limbs lie lame	
	And unregarded age in corners thrown.	
	Take that, and He that doth the ravens feed,	
	Yea, providently caters for the sparrow,	45
	Be comfort to my age! Here is the gold.	
	And all this I give you. Let me be your servant.	
	Though I look old, yet I am strong and lusty;	
	For in my youth I never did apply	
	Hot and rebellious liquors in my blood,	50
	Nor did not with unbashful forehead woo	
	The means of weakness and debility.	
	Therefore my age is as a lusty winter,	
	Frosty, but kindly. Let me go with you.	
	I'll do the service of a younger man	55
	In all your business and necessities.	
ORLANDO	O good old man, how well in thee appears	
	The constant service of the antique world,	
	When service sweat for duty, not for meed!	
	Thou art not for the fashion of these times,	60
	Where none will sweat but for promotion,	
	And having that, do choke their service up	
	Even with the having. It is not so with thee.	
	But, poor old man, thou prunest a rotten tree	
	That cannot so much as a blossom yield	65
	In lieu of all thy pains and husbandry.	
	But come thy ways. We'll go along together,	
	And ere we have thy youthful wages spent,	
	We'll light upon some settled low content.	
ADAM	Master, go on, and I will follow thee	70
	To the last gasp, with truth and loyalty.	
	From seventeen years till now almost fourscore	
	Here lived I, but now live here no more.	
	At seventeen years many their fortunes seek,	
	But at fourscore it is too late a week.	75
	Yet fortune cannot recompense me better	
	Than to die well, and not my master's debtor.	

Exeunt

Macbeth

Macbeth

Act 1, Scene 7, lines 28 to the end
Act 5, Scene 1, lines 18–61

In the first extract, Lady Macbeth persuades her husband to go through with the murder of Duncan. In the second, she is seen walking and talking in her sleep.

What do we learn about the character of Lady Macbeth from these extracts?

Support your ideas by referring to both of the extracts printed on the following pages.

Macbeth

Act 1, Scene 7, lines 28 to the end

In this extract, Lady Macbeth tries to persuade Macbeth to kill King Duncan.

Enter LADY MACBETH

MACBETH	How now? What news?	
LADY MACBETH	He has almost supped. Why have you left the chamber?	
MACBETH	Has he asked for me?	
LADY MACBETH	Know you not he has?	30

MACBETH
We will proceed no further in this business.
He hath honoured me of late, and I have bought
Golden opinions from all sorts of people,
Which would be worn now in their newest gloss,
Not cast aside so soon.

LADY MACBETH   Was the hope drunk   35
Wherein you dressed yourself? Hath it slept since?
And wakes it now to look so green and pale
At what it did so freely? From this time,
Such I account thy love. Art thou afeard
To be the same in thine own act and valour,   40
As thou art in desire? Wouldst thou have that
Which thou esteem'st the ornament of life,
And live a coward in thine own esteem,
Letting I dare not wait upon I would,
Like the poor cat i'th'adage?

MACBETH   Prithee, peace.   45
I dare do all that may become a man.
Who dares do more is none.

LADY MACBETH   What beast was't then
That made you break this enterprise to me?
When you durst do it, then you were a man.
And to be more then what you were, you would   50
Be so much more the man. Nor time, nor place
Did then adhere, and yet you would make both.
They have made themselves and that their fitness now
Does unmake you. I have given suck and know
How tender 'tis to love the babe that milks me: 55
I would, while it was smiling in my face,
Have plucked my nipple from his boneless gums
And dashed the brains out, had I so sworn
As you have done to this.

MACBETH   If we should fail?

LADY MACBETH   We fail!
　　　　　　　　But screw your courage to the sticking place   60
　　　　　　　　And we'll not fail. When Duncan is asleep,
　　　　　　　　Whereto the rather shall his day's hard journey
　　　　　　　　Soundly invite him, his two chamberlains
　　　　　　　　Will I with wine and wassail so convince
　　　　　　　　That memory, the warder of the brain,   65
　　　　　　　　Shall be a fume, and the receipt of reason
　　　　　　　　A limbeck only. When in swinish sleep
　　　　　　　　Their drenched natures lie as in death,
　　　　　　　　What cannot you and I perform upon
　　　　　　　　Th'unguarded Duncan? What not put upon   70
　　　　　　　　His spongy officers, who shall bear the guilt
　　　　　　　　Of our great quell?

MACBETH   Bring forth men-children only,
　　　　　　　　For thy undaunted mettle should compose
　　　　　　　　Nothing but males. Will it not be received,
　　　　　　　　When we have marked with blood those sleepy two   75
　　　　　　　　Of his own chamber and used their very daggers,
　　　　　　　　That they have done't?

LADY MACBETH   Who dares receive it other,
　　　　　　　　As we shall make our griefs and clamour roar
　　　　　　　　Upon his death?

MACBETH   I am settled and bend up
　　　　　　　　Each corporal agent to this terrible feat.   80
　　　　　　　　Away, and mock the time with fairest show,
　　　　　　　　False face must hide what the false heart doth know.

                                                                    Exeunt

Act 5, Scene 1, lines 18–61

In this extract, the doctor and Lady Macbeth's gentlewoman watch her as she sleep walks.

Enter LADY MACBETH *with a taper*

GENTLEWOMAN Lo you, here she comes. This is her very guise, and,
Upon my life, fast asleep. Observe her. Stand close.

DOCTOR How came she by that light?

GENTLEWOMAN Why, it stood by her. She has light by her continually.
'Tis her command.

DOCTOR You see her eyes are open.

GENTLEWOMAN Ay, but their sense is shut.

DOCTOR What is it she does now? Look how she rubs her hands.

GENTLEWOMAN It is an accustomed action with her, to seem thus washing her hands; I have known her to continue in this a quarter of an hour.

LADY MACBETH Yet here's a spot.

DOCTOR Hark, she speaks. I will set down what comes from her to satisfy my remembrance the more strongly.

LADY MACBETH Out damned spot! Out, I say! One, two. Why then 'tis time to do't. Hell is murky. Fie, my lord, fie, a soldier, and afeard? What need we fear? Who knows it, when none can call our power to account? Yet who would have thought the old man to have had so much blood in him?

DOCTOR Do you mark that?

LADY MACBETH	The Thane of Fife had a wife. Where is she now? What, will these hands ne'er be clean? No more o'that, my lord, no more o'that. You mar all this with starting.
DOCTOR	Go to, go to; you have known what you should not.
GENTLEWOMAN	She has spoke what she should not, I am sure of that. Heaven knows what she has known.
LADY MACBETH	Here's the smell of blood still. All the perfumes of Arabia will not sweeten this little hand. O, O, O!
DOCTOR	What a sigh is there? The heart is sorely charged.
GENTLEWOMAN	I would not have such a heart in my bosom for the dignity of the whole body.
DOCTOR	Well, well, well –
GENTLEWOMAN	Pray God it be, sir.
DOCTOR	This disease is beyond my practice. Yet I have known those which have walked in their sleep who have died holily in their beds.
LADY MACBETH	Wash your hands, put on your nightgown, look not so pale. I tell you again, Banquo's buried. He cannot come out on's grave.
DOCTOR	Even so?
LADY MACBETH	To bed, to bed; there's knocking at the gate. Come, come, come, come, give me your hand. What's done cannot be undone. To bed, to bed, to bed.

Exit

40

45

50

55

60

Set

C

KEY STAGE 3

Writing Test
Paper

English

Making an Impression

Writing Test Paper

Making an Impression

First name _____

Last name _____

Date _____

Instructions

- There are two writing tasks in this paper.

- The test is **1 hour and 15 minutes** long.

- You should spend: **45 minutes** on Section A (the longer writing task)
  30 minutes on Section B (the shorter writing task).

- You may spend the first 15 minutes planning your answer to Section A. Your plan will not be marked.

- Section A has 30 marks.

- Section B has 20 marks.

- Write your answer on lined paper.

- When you have finished, check your work carefully.

When you have completed the test, you can mark your answer using pages 123–128 of the Answers and Mark Scheme section of this book.

- Enter your marks below:

	Mark	Maximum mark
Section A		30
Section B		20
Total		50

Section A

Longer Writing Task

If I could meet . . .

A television programme has launched a competition for young people, asking them to write an essay about a person they look up to but have never met. The winners will get the opportunity to present a programme about their heroes.

Here is the competition brief:

> We all have people we look up to in our lives – heroes or role models. Some of them are people close to us; but others are well-known people we have never met, perhaps even figures from history.
>
> We want you to write about the person you would most like to meet. It can be anyone well-known (alive or dead) – a writer, a musician, a politician, an actor – anyone you find inspiring.
>
> You should include:
> - some background information about the person
> - the reasons you find him/her inspirational
> - the influence he/she has had on you and other people
> - anything you would to ask him/her if you did meet.

Write your essay.

Section B

Shorter Writing Task

Thanks for the present

Your grandmother is having a long holiday with some other relatives in Australia. She missed your birthday but sent you a present. She does not like using computers so you have decided to write a letter, thanking her for the present and telling her your news.

Here's the note enclosed with her present:

Sorry I couldn't be there for your birthday. I hope you had a wonderful time.

I'm enclosing a little something for you – hope the colour suits and I got your size right!

I've decided to stay on here with Joe, Marlene and the children for another month. I'm having a great time but missing you all.

I'd love to hear all about what you've been up to while I've been gone.

Write your letter.

Answers and Mark Scheme

The following pages include answers and mark schemes for all the practice papers.

Use them to mark your papers and when you have arrived at a total mark for each test, keep a note of them to use them to keep track of your progress as you complete all three sets.

Reading Test Answers

Set A – 'Into the Woods!'

'The Way Through the Woods'

1. They have shut/closed the road through the woods.
   They have planted trees.
   *(1 mark for **both** answers. 0 marks for one only)*

2. **(a)** anemone
   (b) ring-dove
   (c) badger
   *(1 mark for **all 3** correct)*

3. Give yourself a mark for any of the following up to maximum of two: *(Maximum 2 marks)*
   - He is the only person who still goes into the woods.
   - He knows the woods better than anyone else does.
   - Because of his job, he knows a lot about nature and the woods.

4. Give yourself a mark for any **one** of the following: *(1 mark)*
   - It makes the reader pause and think about what has gone before.
   - It makes you wonder what has been left out.
   - It tells you that the poet has something else to say.

5. Look at the statements below and give yourself the number of marks (maximum 5) for the one which most closely describes your answer.

   You have made one or two simple points about the language and content of the passage, e.g. *Nobody goes in the woods* or *You can hear strange things in the woods.*
   (1 mark)

   You have shown that you are aware of how the language helps to create the atmosphere, answering at least two bullet points, e.g. pointing out how it is described as being very quiet because nobody goes there before something is heard, or commenting on repetition.
   (2 marks)

   You have shown that you understand how the language and content create an impression of mystery and the supernatural. You have answered all three bullet points briefly, quoting from the text. You might have commented on the focus on nature taking over the path, on the description of natural sounds, and on the effects of repetition.
   (3 marks)

You have explored how the language and content create the atmosphere. You have answered all three bullet points, supporting your points with quotations. You might have commented on the peaceful atmosphere created in the first stanza, the way the poet chooses to describe sounds rather than sights in the second stanza, and the slight changes to the repeated phrase about the way through the woods. *(4 marks)*

Your answer is full and focused, addressing all three bullet points fully and using short quotations to back up your points effectively. You have shown a high level of awareness of the writer's techniques (e.g. use of refrain; onomatopoeia) and their effect on the reader. You might have included a personal response. *(5 marks)*

'Westerly Woods Adventure Park '

6. '…covered in a blanket of deep snow'. *(1 mark)*

7. They might prefer to have company/be with other people. *(1 mark for **both** answers. 0 for one)*
They might like the help/guidance of a guide/expert.

8.

People being appealed to	Phrase from the text
People who feel they need a good rest	*Comfortable and stress-free*
People who like to meet new people on holiday	*A whole village*
People who like to feel they're close to nature	*Clustered round the tranquil natural lake which lies at the centre of the woods* (either 'clustered round the tranquil natural lake' or 'at the centre of the woods' would be enough)

(1 mark for two correct answers. 2 marks for three correct answers – maximum 2)

9. Give yourself 1 mark for each of the following (or similar) points: *(Maximum 2 marks)*
   - They accommodate large numbers and young people often like to stay together.
   - As the facilities are described as 'basic' they are probably quite cheap so young people could afford to stay there.

10. Look at the statements below and give yourself the number of marks (maximum 3) for the one which most closely describes your answer.

   You have made one or two simple points. You might have picked out one word or phrase, e.g. *'thrill-seekers' sounds like they want people who like excitement.* *(1 mark)*

   You have picked out at least two phrases, explaining them, and mentioning both 'fun' and 'excitement', e.g. *the writer gives examples of activities a lot of people find fun, like climbing ropes or going down slides and the use of the word 'challenge' suggests it might not be easy and so is more exciting.* *(2 marks)*

   Your answer is focused. You have picked out at least three phrases, explaining them and relating them to the idea that the trails are exciting and fun. You might have mentioned all the examples given above and perhaps 'with a difference' or 'physical and mental skills through fun'. *(3 marks)*

'The Wild Wood' from *The Wild in the Willows*

11. 'with great cheerfulness of spirit' *(1 mark)*

12. Give yourself a mark for any **two** of the following: *(1 mark. 0 marks if only one given)*
- 'logs tripped him'
- 'trees crowded nearer and nearer'
- 'holes made ugly mouths'

13. The answers below are suggestions. Give yourself a mark for any other reasonable interpretation (but not paraphrasing of the quotations).

And then – yes! – no! – yes!	Mole is not sure whether the faces are real or not. At the end he thinks they are.
Certainly a little narrow face, with hard eyes, had flashed up	He is sure that he has really seen something and it was not attractive.
...all fixing on him with evil glances of malice and hatred	He now sees so many of them that he knows he cannot be mistaken. He is also sure that they are dangerous/evil.

(1 mark for two correct answers, 2 marks for three)

14. (a) The use of the phrase 'at first' suggests that Mole will soon realise that his first thought was wrong. Give yourself a mark for any similar answer – but the phrase 'at first' must be mentioned. *(1 mark)*

(b) Give yourself a mark for any of the following: *(1 mark)*
- another animal, which might attack mole;
- the animals with the evil faces;
- whatever was hiding in the woods;
- a human being;
- something evil and dangerous.

15.

Mole imagines the faces.	False
The faces and noises are all made by the rabbit.	False
At the end of the extract we do not know whose faces they are.	True
At the end of the extract Mole is safe.	False
At the end of the extract the rabbit is safe.	True

(1 mark if three or four answers are correct. 2 marks if all answers are correct)

16. Look at the statements below and give yourself the number of marks (maximum 5) for the one which most closely describes your answer.

You have made one or two simple points about the language and content of the passage, e.g. *The mole is scared* or *There are strange things in the woods.* *(1 mark)*

You have shown that you are aware of how the language helps create the atmosphere, answering at least two bullet points, e.g. pointing out that Mole starts off happy and confident in spite of not knowing the woods, or saying that lots of little things happen to make him more frightened. *(2 marks)*

You have shown that you understand how the language and content create an impression of mystery and the supernatural. You have answered at least three bullet points briefly, quoting from the text. You might have commented on the short sentences ending in 'began' and the way Mole's mood changes as he realises he is not imagining things. *(3 marks)*

You have explored how the language and content create the atmosphere. You have answered all four bullet points, supporting your points with quotations. You might have commented on the way Mole's cheerfulness contrasts with the descriptions of the woods, the way the darkness closes in and the mystery of what is making the faces and noises. *(4 marks)*

Your answer is full and focused, addressing all three bullet points fully and using short quotations to back up your points effectively. You have shown a high level of awareness of the writer's techniques (e.g. the way in which we see it from Mole's point of view; the imagery of the forest; the contrast between the small vulnerable animal and the huge unknown woods) and their effect on the reader. You might have shown a personal response. *(5 marks)*

Reading Test Answers

Set B – 'Catching the Train'

'The Railways of Victorian Britain.'

1. A train (at least one train) had to stop at each station every day.
    Trains had to include third class carriages. *(1 mark for **both** answers. 0 marks if only one given)*

2. He booked trains from all over the country and charged people a fixed price to include return travel and entrance to the Great Exhibition. *(1 mark for part of the above. 2 marks for all of the above)*

3.
The Football league was founded	5
The Railway act was passed	1
The first FA cup final was held	4
Bank holidays were introduced	3
King's Cross station was opened	2

(All answers must be correct – 1 mark)

4. Give yourself a mark for any two of the following (or similar) answers, up to a maximum of two marks:
    *   They show how many different activities/the variety of activities the Victorians could enjoy because of the railways.
    *   They illustrate some of the things mentioned so we can get a better idea of what it was like.
    *   They are icons that we can click to lead us to more information. *(Maximum 2 marks)*

5. Give yourself a mark for any of the following points, up to a maximum of three:
- They allowed people to travel greater distances.
- They made travel more affordable/cheaper so that poorer people could travel.
- They gave people the opportunity to go to new places and events.
- They helped to make sporting events more popular.
- They helped to create the idea of the 'day trip' or excursion.

(Maximum of 3)

'Saviours of the Train' from *The Railway Children*

6. A rustling, whispering sound.

(1 mark)

7. 'as though it were a living creature and were walking down the side of the cutting'; 'bringing up the rear like some old shepherd…'

(1 mark for each – maximum 2 marks)

8. He knows when the train is due (11.29).
He knows how fast it goes (there is not enough time to get to the station).
He knows that cutting the telegraph wires would not help.

(1 mark for two of these points; 2 marks for all three points)

9. **(a)** The station is too far away and they would not get there in time.

(1 mark)

(b) They could only cut the wires, which would not help/they would not be able to get up there (give yourself a mark for either of these).

(1 mark)

(c) As they often wave to the trains, nobody would take any notice.

(1 mark)

10. Look at the answers below to see which is closest to yours and give yourself the appropriate number of marks:
- If the children wave something the driver is more likely to notice them: they usually just wave their hands.

(1 mark)

- The petticoats are red and would attract attention because of their colour.

(2 marks)

- Red is associated with/symbolises danger and so the driver would realise it was a warning/the train was in danger.

(3 marks)

11. Look at the statements below and give yourself the number of marks (maximum 5) for the one which most closely describes your answer.

You have made one or two simple points about the children in general or just one of the children, e.g. *The children are brave* or *Peter knows a lot about the trains.*

(1 mark)

You have shown that you are aware of the children's characters, answering at least two bullet points, e.g. mentioning that they are confused at first and a bit frightened but soon try to find a solution to the problem, or noticing that Phyllis is the most frightened of the three.

(2 marks)

You have shown that you understand how the language and content create an impression of the children's characters. You have answered all three bullet points briefly or two in greater detail, quoting from the text. You have mentioned all three of the children, distinguishing between their characters.

(3 marks)

You have explored aspects of all three characters as well as how they get on and act together. You have answered all three bullet points in some detail, supporting your points with quotations. You might have commented on the different ways the excitement and fear affects them. You might have mentioned how each one takes a different role (Bobbie being the oldest, Peter the boy and Phyllis the youngest) as well as how they discuss the situation and come up with a solution together.

(4 marks)

Your answer is full and focused, addressing all three bullet points and using short quotations to back up your points effectively. You have shown a high level of awareness of the writer's techniques and their effect on the reader. You might have commented on the use of dialogue and the way they speak to each other and/or the contrast between their wonder at the 'magical' happenings and their practical common sense when they realise what is actually happening. You might have given a personal response. A good answer could deal with each bullet point in turn or write about each child in turn before commenting on them as a group.

(5 marks)

'Beijing to Shanghai Railway'

12. '…like a flying saucer has just landed from outer space.' *(1 mark)*

13. He says that it is so clean he can see the guard's reflection in the polished granite. *(1 mark)*

14. It must be a very smooth ride/it is not a rough or bumpy journey. *(1 mark)*

15.

The article is about a train journey.	
Each section starts with a time.	✓
The writer describes what he sees.	
There is a lot of information in the article.	
The article is written in the present tense.	✓

*(1 mark for **both** correct answers. 0 marks if more than two boxes ticked.)*

16. Give yourself a mark for any of the following (or similar) answers, up to a maximum of 3 marks:
- He writes a lot about how modern the train is before mentioning more traditional aspects of Chinese life.
- He says how quickly the train goes past the people working in the fields.
- He looks out and sees people still working the same way they have done for centuries, with very little technology, while he is on a very advanced train.
- He mentions the tombs of people's ancestors in the fields, which reminds us of how things have been the same for centuries (until now).
- He notices how different the north and south are, and always have been, yet they are now connected by the high speed train. *(Maximum 3 marks)*

Reading Test Answers

Set C Answers – 'Young and Old'

'Adopt a Granny'

1. Their grandparents could be dead.
They might live a long way away (in this country or abroad). *(1 mark for **both**)*

2.

Older people	*Contact with young people makes them feel younger.*
Parents	*They could get help with, and advice about, bringing up children.*
Children	*Older people have more time to play with them and listen to them.*

(1 mark for two correct answers; 2 marks for three)

3. They were missing their own grandchildren.
They were bored/finding life a bit boring. *(1 mark for **both**)*

4. Give yourself a mark for any of the following answers, up to maximum of 3 marks:
- S/he mentions that it is a registered charity.
- S/he says they work closely with the local authority.
- S/he mentions that checks have to be made before people can join.
- S/he says that everything they do is properly organised and supervised. *(Maximum 3 marks)*

5.

The writer wants to persuade people to join the "Adopt a Granny" scheme.	✓
The writer wants to persuade readers to visit the Puddington area.	
The writer is informing us about the "Adopt a Granny" scheme.	✓
The writer argues that children do not need grandparents.	
The writer argues that children's lives are improved by knowing older people.	✓

(1 mark for two correct, 2 for three – 0 marks if more than three boxes ticked)

'Miss Havisham'

6. There are two chains across the entrance.
The passages are all dark. *(1 mark for **both** answers)*

7. Give yourself a mark for any of the following:
Points: She looks down on him/she is unfriendly/she appears to be snobbish or distant.
Evidence: She tells him what to do ('go on')/she addresses him as 'boy'/she is described as walking away
'scornfully.' *(1 mark for the point and one mark for supporting quotation – maximum of 2 marks)*

8. Give yourself a mark for any of the following (or similar) answers, up to a maximum of 2 marks:
- She is dressed as a bride and her clothes and jewels are very expensive, but the clothes are faded and yellowish.
- She is old and thin, so the clothes do not fit her.
- It seems very strange for such an old woman to be dressed as a bride. *(Maximum 2 marks)*

9. (a) A waxwork (of someone lying in state) at the fair.
A skeleton (dug up from the vaults of the church). *(1 mark for **both**)*

(b) Give yourself a mark for any of the following (or similar) answers, up to a maximum of 2 marks:
- She seems to him to be more dead than alive/like a dead person or thing come to life.
- She is a bit frightening but at the same time fascinating.
- He finds her appearance unpleasant/repulsive but has to look at her.
- He is shocked/horrified by what he sees.
- He does not really think of her as a living person. *(Maximum 2 marks)*

10. Look at the answers below, decide which is closest to your answer, and give yourself the appropriate mark:
It is a young man from her past who let her down. *(1 mark)*
It is a young man who promised to marry her and then left her/died (on her wedding day). *(2 marks)*

11. Look at the statements below and give yourself the number of marks (maximum 5) for the one which most closely describes your answer.

You have made one or two simple/ general points, e.g. *Pip thinks she is very strange* or *It is dark in the house.* *(1 mark)*

You have shown some awareness of the atmosphere created, addressing at least two bullet points, e.g. mentioning that Pip is brought to the house not knowing what to expect, or that the house is described as if no-one lives there. *(2 marks)*

You have shown that you understand how the language and content create an air of mystery. You have answered at least three bullet points briefly or two in greater detail, quoting from the text. You might have mentioned how the reader only sees what Pip sees or that we are made to wonder what the explanation is for Miss Havisham's odd appearance. *(3 marks)*

You have answered all three bullet points in some detail and have supported your points with quotations. You might have commented on how nothing is explained to Pip before he meets her, the gloomy atmosphere, the almost ghost-like appearance of Miss Havisham and the oddness of her request at the end of the extract. *(4 marks)*

Your answer is full and focused, addressing all four bullet points and using short quotations to back up points effectively. You have shown a high level of awareness of the writer's techniques and their effect on the reader. You might have commented on the language used to describe both the room and Miss Havisham, the way the different characters speak and the comparisons Pip makes. You might have given a personal response. *(5 marks)*

'Remembering Schooldays'

12. He was in a bad temper/he was angry. *(1 mark)*

13. It showed that he considered them good enough swimmers to go in the deep water. *(1 mark)*

14. Swinging on a rope.
Jumping over tombstones. *(1 mark for both)*

15.

He hated everything about Oundle.	
He thinks punishments were inconsistent and sometimes cruel.	✓
On the whole, he respected Mr Bullen.	✓
He had some enjoyable times at Oundle.	✓
He thinks all the ushers were very caring.	
He never thinks about his schooldays.	

(1 mark for two correct answers, 2 marks for three. 0 marks if more than four boxes ticked)

16. Any of the following (or similar) points:
- They would be shocked/horrified/outraged.
- They would be surprised *or* they would not be surprised because they knew how different it was.
- They would think that it was wrong.
- They would think it was very different from now.
- They would find it funny/be amused because of the way Goodman describes it.
- They would be glad it is not like that now.
- They would not understand why people put up with it. *(1 mark for each valid point up to maximum of 3)*

Shakespeare Test Answers

When you are marking your Shakespeare answer, first decide which description your answer most closely resembles. Then give it a mark depending on whether it matches 1, 2 or 3 of the statements given.

Mark Scheme

1–3 marks
- You have given a few simple facts and opinions about the extracts.
- There may be some misunderstanding/answers may not always be relevant.
- You have retold the 'story' of the extracts or copied out sections of it.

4–6 marks
- You have given a little explanation, showing some awareness of the needs of the question.
- Your comments are relevant but mostly about the plot.
- You have made some broad references to how the characters speak.

7–9 marks
- You have shown some general understanding of the question, although some points might not be developed.
- You have made some comments on the language the characters use.
- Some of your points are backed up with reference to the text.

10–12 marks
- You have discussed how the extracts relate to the question, even though all the ideas might not be of equal quality.
- You have shown awareness of the characters' use of language and its effects.
- Most of your points are backed up with reference to the text.

13–15 marks
- There is a clear focus on how the extracts relate to the question.
- You have made good, consistent comments on the characters' language and its effect on the audience.
- You have chosen quotations well and linked them together to present an overall argument.

16–18 marks
- You have analysed every quotation in depth in relation to the question and there is evaluation.
- You have commented on every quotation in terms of the language that the characters use.
- You have picked out individual words from quotations and linked them into the overall argument.

Shakespeare Tests: Examples of Possible Content

On the following pages, you will find examples of the kind of comments pupils might make when answering each of the questions in the practice papers.

They do not represent 'correct' answers or points that you must make, but they will help you to relate the mark scheme to the particular question you have answered.

Some of these suggested comments cover only one extract; others focus on a few lines. You will be expected to cover **both extracts** in detail in order to gain good marks. Your answers, especially those gaining higher marks will, of course, be much longer. They should be written in complete sentences with points developed and connected.

Shakespeare Tests – Set A

Romeo and Juliet

1–3 marks
Juliet is in love with Romeo and cannot wait to see him. Juliet does not want Romeo to leave.

4–6 marks
Juliet's feelings are confused because she loves Romeo but he has killed her cousin. Juliet pretends to Romeo that it is still night so that he will not leave her.

7–9 marks
The strength of her love is shown by her emotional reaction to the nurse's news and by the risks she takes. In the first extract she wants it to be night but in the second she wants it to be day ('it is the nightingale and not the lark'.)

10–12 marks
The audience might be a bit confused by her reactions in the first extract and might think they show how young she is. A lot of her language relates to death and makes us feel she has no hope ('dreadful trumpet sound the general doom').

13–15 marks
Juliet's opening soliloquy establishes her mood. She uses imagery to express her impatience: 'gallop apace, you fiery footed steeds'. Her mood changes when the nurse enters. Convinced that Romeo is dead, she thinks of her own death: 'and thou and Romeo press one heavy bier'. At the start of the second extract she wants the moment to last for ever but, even though she is in love, she dwells on death: 'I have an ill–divining soul!'

16–18 marks

In her opening soliloquy, Juliet expresses the strength of her feelings and her desire for Romeo to the audience. She longs for 'love-performing night' to help her consummate her love. These scenes both take place in the dark, reflecting the secret and forbidden nature of her love. In the second extract she wants Romeo to stay, because she loves him, and to go, because he is in danger. Her deliberate confusion of the lark and the nightingale reflects this dilemma. She ends with a terrible premonition of Romeo 'dead in the bottom of a tomb', as he will be at the end of the play.

As You Like It

1–3 marks

Orlando and his brother do not get on. Adam, Orlando's servant, goes to the forest with him.

4–6 marks

Orlando fights with his older brother, who treats him like a servant. They do not act as brothers should. Adam shows more loyalty to Orlando and offers to help him escape to the forest.

7–9 marks

Orlando tells the story of how he has been treated by his brother – like the 'animals on his dunghill.' He picks a quarrel with Oliver, who calls him 'boy' and 'villain'. There is no brotherly love between them. Adam shows he is on Orlando's side by saying he will follow him and help him. This shows love and loyalty.

10–12 marks

Orlando's speech is about a lack of family love. Oliver has not treated Orlando as a brother should: 'his horses are bred better'. Orlando provokes Oliver so we can see what he is really like. Adam tries to make them behave like brothers but Oliver turns on him. He has served the family loyally but is called an 'old dog'. Orlando, on the other hand, says Adam shows 'the constant service of the antique world', suggesting that this is how people should behave but things have changed for the worse.

13–15 marks

Orlando's first speech introduces the theme of family love and loyalty, and of families breaking up. He is angry with his brother for treating him like 'his animals on the dunghill'. This image reminds us of the story of the prodigal son and Orlando asks 'what prodigal portion have I spent', implying that, unlike the prodigal son, he has done nothing to deserve ill-treatment. Oliver's cruelty is contrasted with the love and loyalty of Adam, who is willing to serve and help Orlando 'to the last gasp.'

16–18 marks

Orlando tells Oliver that 'in the gentle condition of blood, you should know me.' This means that he is Oliver's equal in birth. It also reflects the idea that brothers should look after each other and that what Oliver is doing is unnatural. Oliver also treats Adam as an 'old dog'. While Orlando deserves better treatment because of his 'blood', Adam deserves it because of his 'service'. The values 'of the antique world' are being destroyed by Oliver, as they are by Duke Frederick, who has also turned against his brother.

Macbeth

1–3 marks

Macbeth murders Duncan but is not sure and says he is afraid. At the end he is worried about the battle.

4–6 marks

Macbeth has killed Duncan but is worried about all the noises and something saying 'sleep no more' but Lady Macbeth tells him not to be stupid. He is brave when he is preparing for the battle and is ready to die.

7–9 marks

Macbeth seems nervous, asking questions and talking about noises. He is worried about not being able to say 'amen'. This is because he has done such an evil deed. He is full of guilt. At the end he is in a different mood and seems not to care about anything, even Lady Macbeth's death because he says 'she should have died hereafter'. He is angry with the messenger but knows the prophecies are coming true. This seems to make him determined and brave.

10–12 marks

At first Macbeth and Lady Macbeth speak in short sentences because it is very tense and they are nervous. When he describes what is worrying him she does not seem to understand: 'a foolish thing to say a sorry sight'. Hearing someone say 'Macbeth does murder sleep' is a sign of his guilty conscience. He changes as the play goes on and in the second scene he says, 'I have almost forgot the taste of fears'. Now he is brave and reckless.

13–15 marks

Because Macbeth has committed such a terrible sin he will 'sleep no more.' He feels he cannot ever get rid of the guilt. His mood is different in the second extract and he says Lady Macbeth 'should have died hereafter.' Perhaps he is saying she died too young or perhaps that she would have died anyway. He is philosophical and resigned to his fate: 'Life's but a walking shadow'. He knows the prophecies are coming true. This seems to make him determined and brave.

16–18 marks

At the beginning Macbeth is nervous and worried, shown by his choppy speech and questions. Lady Macbeth does not understand, telling him to 'consider it not so deeply'. But Macbeth's guilt is overwhelming. He keeps repeating that 'I could not say Amen'. This is important because it is as if he is cut off from God, so he cannot pray. Sleep is also very significant in the play. It is 'innocent' and he is guilty so he will 'sleep no more.' In the second extract he reflects on life, which he sees as 'full of sound and fury, signifying nothing' but at the end he is defiant and impressive as he vows to 'die with harness on our back.'

Shakespeare Tests – Set B

Romeo and Juliet

1–3 marks

Romeo is in love with a girl who does not love him. He stays behind after the party to tell Juliet he loves her.

4–6 marks

In the first scene Romeo thinks he loves Rosaline and talks all about love. After that he falls in love with Juliet. This is true love and in the balcony scene they tell each other how much they are in love.

7–9 marks

Romeo has been acting oddly and he tells his cousin that he is love. He talks a lot about love and how it does not make sense: 'feather of lead, bright smoke'. He seems to enjoy being miserable. In the second extract he looks up to Juliet, who is on her balcony, and compares her to the sun. He uses a lot of language about the sun, the stars and the moon to show how great his love is.

10–12 marks

Romeo talks in the first scene all about love rather than about the girl he loves, using oxymoron, e.g. 'cold fire' and 'sick health' to express how it makes him feel. She will never have him because she has sworn to 'live chaste'. His love is pointless. In contrast, when he falls in love with Juliet she falls in love with him. In the second extract she is placed above him and his language ('bright angel') suggests he almost worships her. We know she returns his love because she talks about it in a soliloquy, which she does not know he can hear.

13–15 marks

In the first extract Romeo is 'playing with words', trying to express the contradictions of love, 'a madness most discreet'. The fact that his love will never be returned seems to add to its attraction. The second extract shows how his love for Juliet is returned equally. Romeo uses a series of images to describe Juliet: the moon is 'envious' of her and her beauty would 'shame those stars'. Juliet returns his feelings, as she shows in her speech, so this love is quite different but it is doomed in another way.

16–18 marks

In the first scene Romeo might be playing a part – the part of the 'melancholy lover' – which would be familiar to Shakespeare's audience. He enjoys 'the fume of sighs' as well as the 'fire sparkling in a lover's eyes' and his language is clever and entertaining. The fact that Rosaline will never return his love only adds to his enjoyment. When he falls in love with Juliet so quickly we might think it is the same again – so in the second scene he has to convince us as well as her of his sincerity.

As You Like It

1–3 marks

Rosalind falls in love with Orlando at the wrestling match. The shepherd is in love with Phoebe.

4–6 marks

At the wrestling match, Rosalind falls in love with Orlando because he was a friend of her father, the old Duke. We also see how she and her cousin Celia love each other in spite of their fathers. When she hears Silvius talking about Phoebe, she sympathises.

7–9 marks

After Orlando wins the wrestling match, Rosalind gives him a chain to wear for her. It is not clear whether she has fallen in love with him. Silvius's love is not returned he does not believe anyone can love like him ('thou hast not loved') and Rosalind feels sorry for him as she is also in love ('this shepherd's passion/is much upon my fashion').

10–12 marks

After Orlando reveals his identity, Rosalind recalls that her father loved his father 'as his soul'. Her father has been overthrown by the new Duke, Frederick, who says, 'I wouldst thou hadst been son to some man else'. In spite of this Rosalind loves his daughter, Celia. She gives Orlando a token, showing she is falling in love with him. She goes to the forest not knowing whether he loves her. Her love might be unrequited like Silvius's love for Phoebe: 'Alas, poor shepherd! Searching of thy wound, I have by hard adventure found mine own,'

13–15 marks

As Rosalind and Celia watch the wrestling match, they seem amused, excited and attracted to him, Rosalind crying out 'O excellent young man!' When she finds out who his father is, and that her father loved his 'as his soul,' it makes her love him, just as it makes Frederick hate him. She does not openly say she loves him but drops hints ('overthrown more than your enemies') and the giving of the chain is a symbolic gesture. In the second extract we see an exaggerated portrayal of unrequited love in Silvius, whose speeches, spoken in verse with a repeated 'thou hast not loved', might seem funny.

16–18 marks

The wrestling match brings family relationships into focus: Rosalind and Celia are close in spite of their fathers' enmity and Orlando is effectively fighting his brother. Rosalind seems to fall in love with Orlando almost because of his father's loyalty to hers – as if love can be inherited. Silvius is a figure out of the pastoral tradition – a romantic idea of a shepherd – almost a parody, with his miserable verse and the refrain of 'thou hadst not loved'. Touchstone responds with a crude tale of being in love with Jane Smile, showing us another extreme of love, but Rosalind empathises, seeing his love as 'mush upon my fashion.'

Macbeth

1–3 marks

Macbeth tells the murderers to kill Banquo. He is scared when he sees the ghost.

4–6 marks

Macbeth has to persuade the murderers to kill Banquo. He tells them he was their enemy. He is pleased that he will get rid of Banquo. When he sees the ghost no-one else sees it so he has to act terrified and as if he really believes he sees it.

7–9 marks

Macbeth is now the king and he needs to show that he is strong and confident. He goes on about how Banquo is their enemy and how low they are: 'in the catalogue ye go for men' making them think they will be manlier if they kill Banquo. At the end of the scene he should be happy because he has got what he wants. At the start of the second extract he has seen the ghost and is recovering. He should be a bit scared but trying to hide it from the guests.

10–12 marks

Macbeth should seem sincere because he is relying on the murderers. Even though he is the king he has to flatter them a bit. When they agree he says 'your spirits shine through you' so he must be very pleased and relieved, smiling and maybe shaking their hands. When he has seen the ghost he moves away from the table and tries to put a brave face on, toasting 'our dear friend Banquo' but when the ghost comes back his fear shows as he shouts out 'Avaunt! And quit my sight!

13–15 marks

In the first extract his speech is calm and confident. He should be aware that he is the king now and in command, confidently lying to the murderers ('Know that it was…') and asking them long questions to get a reaction (Do you find…?' Are you so gospell'd…?'). His speeches should seem rehearsed as this is all planned. By contrast, the ghost of Banquo is totally unexpected and he has to show real fear and horror, jumping up, shouting 'Avaunt!' He reacts to Lady Macbeth by saying he is as brave as any man but this makes him show fear, his mood frightening everyone else.

16–18 marks

Macbeth is the only person who can see Banquo's ghost. Whether he is looking at another actor or an empty space he has to convince the audience that he really sees it and express his horror and his guilt. At the start of the extract he makes a huge effort to be calm and says he has 'a strange infirmity'. He could say this slowly as if he is thinking hard of an excuse and calming himself. When he toasts Banquo ('Would he were here!') his gestures might be a bit too big and his voice too loud.

Shakespeare Tests – Set C

Romeo and Juliet

1–3 marks

Juliet is upset because of Romeo and Tybalt. The nurse looks after Juliet.

4–6 marks

Juliet is upset because she thinks the nurse is telling her that Romeo is dead but it is Tybalt who is dead. The nurse has brought her up and has been her best friend but she takes her father's side.

7–9 marks

Juliet is confused by what the nurse tells her and turns on her, calling her a 'devil'. When Juliet attacks Romeo, the nurse agrees with her but this makes Juliet attack the nurse ('blister'd be thy tongue'). In the second extract the nurse at first supports Juliet but later tells her to marry Paris. Juliet realises she now has no-one to turn to but the Friar.

10–12 marks

The nurse has been Juliet's close confidante and Juliet relies on her to help her and to take messages so she only knows what the nurse tells her and when the nurse cries 'he's dead!' she thinks it is Romeo. When she realises it is Tybalt who is dead she is angry and impatient with the nurse. Juliet's emotions change so quickly in this scene the nurse cannot keep up. Although she knows Juliet loves Romeo she still asks: 'Will you speak well of him that kill'd your cousin?'

13–15 marks

In the second extract, Juliet's relationship with the nurse changes completely. At first, the nurse steps in to defend her, bravely standing up to Capulet: 'You are to blame, my lord, to rate her so.' This shows her closeness to Juliet and would make the audience think that she will try to help Juliet. However, when Juliet's parents leave she seems to take their side. According to her, Romeo is 'dead: or ''twere as good he were'. She seems to want to help Juliet but not to understand her feelings.

16–18 marks

The first extract shows a comic misunderstanding as the nurse, in vivid, melodramatic language ('a piteous corse, a bloody piteous corse'), gives the news of Tybalt's death and Juliet thinks she is talking about Romeo. This lack of understanding becomes more serious in the next extract as the pragmatic nurse, choosing to ignore the couple's marriage, tells Juliet to treat the 'dishclout' Romeo as if he were dead and marry Paris. Juliet's reaction is cool and controlled as she fools the nurse into thinking she agrees, telling her with heavy irony, 'thou hast comforted me marvellous much'.

As You Like It

1–3 marks

Orlando is a good character. His brother wants to kill him so he goes to the forest.

4–6 marks

Orlando has been badly treated by his brother and treated as a servant so he is angry and wants his rights. He does not want to run away but Adam persuades him and he shows that he appreciates Adam.

7–9 marks

Orlando stands up to Oliver and confronts him with the bad treatment he has received. He is in the right and does not deserve to be called 'villain'. He deserves better because of 'the gentle condition of blood'. Adam respects Orlando and wants to help him, so he thinks he is a good man. Orlando also respects Adam, who is a good servant.

10–12 marks

Orlando's speech about his treatment gains the audience's sympathy. Oliver has not treated Orlando as a brother should and Orlando ironically calls himself 'a poor unworthy brother'. He provokes Oliver so Adam (and the audience) can see what he is really like. Orlando is quite aggressive and tries to 'lay hands' on Oliver. He is also proud and insulted by being called 'villain'. Adam shows that he believes in Orlando by offering to help him and Orlando returns his love and respect, saying that Adam shows 'the constant service of the antique world'.

13–15 marks

Orlando is angry with his brother for treating him badly since their father's death. He refers to the story of the prodigal son, asking if he should 'keep your hogs', as the son in the story did, but, unlike the prodigal son he has done nothing wrong and has had no 'prodigal portion' to waste. The audience might see him as proud – and aggressive when he physically attacks his brother – but they are likely to sympathise with his position, especially when Oliver threatens to have him killed. Oliver's cruelty is contrasted with the love and loyalty of Adam, who is willing to serve and help Orlando 'to the last gasp.'

16–18 marks

Orlando tells Oliver that 'in the gentle condition of blood, you should know me.' This means that he is Oliver's equal in birth. This might give some people the impression he is too keen on his status as a nobleman but most would think he has been unjustly deprived of his rights. It also reflects the idea that brothers should look after each other and that what Oliver is doing is unnatural. The values 'of the antique world' are being destroyed by Oliver, as they are by Duke Frederick, who has also turned against his brother.

Macbeth

1–3 marks

Macbeth is worried about murdering Duncan but Lady Macbeth tells him he has to. Then she goes mad and sleep walks.

4–6 marks

Lady Macbeth is a lot stronger than Macbeth. He thinks it is wrong to kill the king but she says he is a coward and she will help him. In the second extract she has changed and keeps washing her hands, showing she has a guilty conscience.

7–9 marks

Lady Macbeth is annoyed with Macbeth when he says 'we will proceed no further in this business.' This means he does not want to kill Duncan. She says if he does not do it he will be a 'coward'. She says some very shocking things, even that she would kill her own child rather than not kill Duncan. This shows her cruelty and her determination. In the sleep-walking scene she is very different. She relives the murder of Duncan and wants to get rid of the guilt: 'Out damned spot'.

10–12 marks

In the first extract Lady Macbeth shows how strong and ruthless she is. Although it was Macbeth who first thought of the murder, she is at least as ambitious and she bullies him into doing it, saying she will not love him if he does not do it ('Such I account thy love' and questioning his manhood 'When you durst do it, then you were a man.') She has no sense of right and wrong and shows this in the horrible image of dashing out her baby's brains. Macbeth seems to love and admire her for this, telling her to 'bring forth men-children only.'

13–15 marks

In contrast with the ambitious, determined woman who thought her husband a coward because he had a conscience, in the second extract Lady Macbeth finally shows some weakness. Trying to wash out the 'damned spot' reminds us of how earlier she said a little water would clear them of the deed. Now she says 'Hell is murky' as if she feels she will go there and, like Macbeth did after the murder, she now cannot see how she can get rid of the guilt: 'All the perfumes of Arabia will not sweeten this little hand.'

16–18 marks

Lady Macbeth's questions and her mocking tone seem designed to provoke a reaction from Macbeth. His reply ('…who dares do more is none') sounds like it should be the last word, but she turns it against him, shockingly suggesting that the murder of an old man in his sleep is a 'manly' thing to do. She seems to want to prove she is more of a man than he is but her idea of what makes a man in perverse and grotesque. She says she knows 'how tender 'tis to love the babe', perhaps making the audience momentarily see a softer, 'womanly' side to her, but then she chillingly describes how she would dash out its brains.

Writing Test Answers

The two writing tests are marked for different elements of writing and each attracts a different number of marks. Make sure you use the right mark scheme for the task you are marking.

When you look at the mark schemes you will see that different descriptions have different numbers of marks for them.

When you are marking your writing test answers, decide which description your answer most closely resembles. Give it a mark according to how closely it matches the statements given.

Longer Writing Task: Mark Scheme

This mark scheme applies to the Longer Writing Tasks in Sets A, B and C. There are three parts to the mark scheme. The first two ('Sentence Structure and Punctuation' and 'Text structure and Organisation') are exactly the same for all three practice papers. The third section ('Composition and Effect') includes guidance on how you might gain marks in each of the practice papers.

The total number of marks available is 30.

Sentence Structure and Punctuation

0 marks
- You may have used some simple connectives, such as 'and' and 'but', but sentences are usually simple.
- You have used some full stops, capital letters, question marks and exclamation marks.

1–2 marks
- You have used connectives such as 'if' and 'because', and the relative pronouns 'who' and 'which' to form some complex sentences.
- You have used full stops, question marks and exclamation marks accurately. You have used commas in sentences, usually correctly, and speech marks if needed.

3–4 marks
- You have used a wide range of connectives to make clear relationships between ideas, e.g. 'although', 'meanwhile' or 'on the other hand'. Your sentences vary in length and structure.
- You have used a variety of punctuation, mostly accurately, e.g. commas to mark subordinate clauses and correct punctuation of speech, if needed.

5–6 marks
- You have used a variety of sentence structures to create effect, e.g. starting sentences with subordinate clauses ('After a short period, they...' 'Despite her feelings, she...') or using short sentences. You might have used modal verbs such as 'could' or 'may'.
- You have used a range of punctuation, e.g. brackets for asides, commas to mark subordinate clause, semi-colons and colons – with few errors.

7 marks

- You have varied your sentence lengths to create interesting effects, with appropriate connectives used. You have used a range of sentences structures and techniques to create effects, e.g. repetition, contrast, fragments. The passive voice might be used, e.g. 'it was thought that…'
- You have used a full range of punctuation accurately and skilfully to assist the meaning and create a pleasing effect.

8 marks

- You have used a wide range of sentence types with skill and accuracy to clarify meaning and interest the reader. There might be some unusual or creative use of sentence structure.
- You have used a full range of punctuation correctly, adding to the effect of the writing.

Text Structure and Organisation

0 marks

- You have made some attempt to organise writing, putting connected ideas together.
- You might have used paragraphs, but without much logic.

1–2 marks

- You have used paragraphs starting with the main topic.
- The piece has a recognisable beginning and end.

3–4 marks

- You have used paragraphs of different lengths, arranged in a logical order.
- There are a clear introduction and conclusion.

5–6 marks

- You have arranged detailed content well within and between paragraphs.
- Your paragraphs are connected, using phrases such as 'on the other hand' and 'as a result of this'.

7 marks

- Your paragraphs are varied in length to suit the content. They are linked with a range of appropriate words and phrases.
- Your paragraphs are arranged in a controlled way to interest the reader, e.g. flashbacks in a narrative or argument and counter-argument.

8 marks

- You have organised and shaped your writing in a controlled way, designed to involve the reader.
- You have used paragraphing or other organisational devices imaginatively.

Composition and Effect

0 marks

- You have a general idea of the purpose and audience.
- There is some relevant content.
  Practice Paper A – You have given some information about the park and an opinion.
  Practice Paper B – You have written about the railway and have given one or two arguments.
  Practice Paper C – You have written about a person and have given a reason for your choice.

1–3 marks

- Your purpose is clear.
- You try to interest the reader.
- You have developed some ideas in detail.

Practice Paper A – You have given more detailed information. You have mentioned both positive and negative aspects, e.g. that there is plenty to do but it is very expensive.

Practice Paper B – You show understanding of the problem. You have reported arguments on both sides e.g. it will spoil the views but it might bring business to the area.

Practice Paper C – You have explained reasons for your choice. You have tried to make the person sound interesting to the reader.

4–6 marks

- Your writing engages the reader's interest.
- You have explored a range of relevant ideas in some detail.
- Your viewpoint is clear.

Practice Paper A – You have given a range of information. You have considered negative and positive aspects and have made clear judgement, e.g. that, on balance, you would recommend it for families with young children but not for older people.

Practice Paper B – You have set out arguments for and against in more detail and have ended with some thoughtful proposals, e.g. that the council look more closely at the compensation available to people who might suffer because of the railway.

Practice Paper C – You have written convincingly about the qualities of the person described and conveyed your enthusiasm for her/him, e.g. saying that s/he has shown bravery and determination in achieving their fame.

7–9 marks

- You have used a range of techniques to achieve your purpose.
- You have taken into account the reader's viewpoint.
- Your view is well-argued and consistent.

Practice Paper A – Your writing is entertaining as well as informative. You arrive at a convincing conclusion, e.g. that although you did not enjoy many aspects of the experience, your children had a great time and want to return, so you would recommend that parents give it a try.

Practice Paper B – Your writing has an impersonal tone. You have given several arguments for and against, a succinct summary of the debate and some clear proposals/ideas e.g. that your meeting felt that the government had not set out a convincing case for the new railway and you would like the council to come up with alternatives.

Practice Paper C – You have given a detailed and enthusiastic description of the chosen person. You have written convincingly about what makes him/her a good role model, and have included interesting/entertaining ideas about the meeting, e.g. saying that the qualities s/he has shown in their career have inspired you to aim higher and that if you met them, you would ask them what advice s/he would give to their younger self.

10–12 marks

- Your style is well-judged, using a wide range of techniques.
- Your tone is appropriate for both purpose and audience.
- All the content is relevant and used to support the argument.

Practice Paper A – You have given a sense of your personality and viewpoint with enough detailed information to allow the reader to form an opinion, e.g. describing various attractions, reporting the views of different groups of people and giving clear information about pricing, accessibility etc.

Practice Paper B – Your writing reads like an official report. You have summarised a range of arguments and have offered well-judged proposals and ideas e.g. giving brief accounts of all the arguments put, and who put them, grouping similar ideas together and making a judgment about the feelings of the majority.

Practice Paper C – Your writing is imaginative and creative, putting forward convincing arguments and successfully engaging the reader, e.g. giving some amusing anecdotes about your subject (and maybe about yourself) and saying what this tells you about them or coming up with some questions for them which are different from those usually asked of celebrities.

13–14 marks

- You have shown complete understanding and control of purpose and audience.
- There is a strong individual style, created by the use of a range of techniques.
  Practice Paper A – You have written a sophisticated and creative review. It does everything asked for above but from an original, individual viewpoint.
  Practice Paper B – Your report is thorough and balanced, and is professionally presented. It does everything asked for above but from an original, individual viewpoint.
  Practice Paper C – Your writing is original, entertaining and possibly moving. It does everything asked for above but from an original, individual viewpoint.

Shorter Writing Task: Mark Scheme

This mark scheme applies to the Shorter Writing Tasks in Sets A, B and C. There are three part to the mark scheme. The first two ('Spelling' and 'Sentence Structure, Punctuation and Paragraphing') are exactly the same for all three practice papers. The third part ('Composition and Effect') includes guidance on how the bullet points might be achieved in each of the practice papers.

The total number of marks available is 20.

Spelling

0 marks

- You have spelt simple (mostly one syllable) words correctly.
  Down/grass/young/chair/eat/pencil/finger

1 mark

- You have spelt simple words, including more common words with more than one syllable, correctly, e.g. adverbs ending in 'ly', verbs ending in 'ed' and 'ing', and most plurals.
  Crowded/ smiling/ sincerely/slowly/reason/honest/donkeys/flies/women

2 marks

- You have spelt more complex words that fit regular patterns correctly, e.g. words with prefixes such as 'dis', 'un' or 'pre'; suffixes such as 'tion' or 'ful'; common homophones.
  Beautiful/disappoint/unnatural/knowledge/frequently/education/whose/whether

3 marks

- Most spelling, including that of irregular words, is correct.
  Initials/mischievous/vicious/principle/efficient/seize/aggressive/definitely

4 marks

- Almost all spelling, including that of complex irregular words, is correct.
  Colossal/precocious/accommodation/occasionally/occurred/chronological

Sentence Structure, Punctuation and Paragraphing

0 marks

- You use simple sentences; you might use linking words such as 'and' and 'but'. You have used full stops and capital letters.
- You might have used paragraphs.

1–2 marks

- You have used sentences of different lengths. You have used a variety of connectives, including relative pronouns. You have used commas, full stops and question marks, usually correctly.
- You have used paragraphs, mainly in a logical order, containing some detail.

3–4 marks

- You have used a variety of sentence lengths and types, and a range of connectives. You have correctly used a range of punctuation, including commas for subordination. If needed, you have correctly used punctuation for speech.
- You have developed your ideas within paragraphs, which are linked to achieve a logical whole.

5 marks

- Your sentences are varied in length and type to achieve appropriate effects. You have used a wide range of punctuation – brackets, dashes, colons and semicolons – usually correctly.
- You have used paragraphs of different lengths, appropriate to their content, within a well-structured piece. Your ideas are developed in an interesting way within them.

6 marks

- You have used a wide range of sentence structures to achieve particular effects. You have used a wide range of punctuation correctly to make meaning clear.
- Your paragraphs are linked effectively to create a pleasing whole. The ideas within them are linked and developed in a sophisticated way.

Composition and Effect

0 marks

- You have a general idea of the purpose and audience.
- There is some relevant content.
  Practice Paper A – Your writing looks like a letter. In it, you apply for a job.
  Practice Paper B – You have given some information about an attraction.
  Practice paper C – Your writing looks like a letter. In it, you say 'thank you'.

1–3 marks

- Your purpose is clear.
- You have tried to interest the reader.
- Your ideas are developed in detail.
  Practice Paper A – You have clearly written a letter, with the proper opening and closing. You have given relevant information, e.g. about your qualifications. You have attempted a formal tone.
  Practice Paper B – You have set out your writing like a leaflet, perhaps using headlines and bullet points. You have given relevant, positive information, e.g. describing all the things you can do at a leisure park.
  Practice Paper C – You have clearly written a letter, using an informal tone. You have given news and have shown an interest in the reader, e.g. telling her about your school trip and asking if she's planning any trips in Australia.

4–6 marks

- Your writing engages the reader's interest.
- The tone of your writing is consistent.
- Your viewpoint is clear.
  Practice Paper A – You have used an appropriate formal tone. You have expressed enthusiasm and have given interesting information, perhaps picking out details from your experience and saying why they would make you good at the job.
  Practice Paper B – You have given a range of information, e.g. about cinemas, leisure parks and places to eat. You have used a persuasive tone. Your writing is clearly aimed at young people.
  Practice Paper C – You have written an entertaining, chatty letter, clearly intended for an older family member, e.g. by focusing on things that have happened locally that might interest her and by not using text language etc.

7–9 marks

- You have used a range of techniques to achieve your purpose.
- Your tone is appropriate for both purpose and audience.
- Your view is well-argued and consistent.

  Practice Paper A – You have addressed all the requirements of the advertisement, 'selling' yourself convincingly, e.g. by saying how you have demonstrated various qualities in the past and how these would be useful in the future. You have written your letter in the correct form.

  Practice Paper B – You have addressed all the requirements of the competition in an entertaining, persuasive and creative way, e.g. organising the information in an attractive way, using quotations from happy visitors or giving a personal, quirky reaction to the place.

  Practice Paper C – You have given a detailed and enthusiastic account of your news, perhaps telling funny stories about what your family has been up to. You have engaged with the interests and concerns of the older recipient, e.g. discussing what's happening on her favourite TV programmes. You have used an appropriate form for an informal letter.

10 marks

- You show complete understanding and control of purpose and audience. There is a strong individual style, created by the use of a range of techniques.

  Practice Paper A – You have written a mature and convincing letter of application. It reads like the real thing.

  Practice Paper B – You have written an original, informative, persuasive and creative leaflet. Anyone reading it would want to visit your area.

  Practice Paper C – You have written an original, entertaining and possibly moving letter. Your own grandmother would love to receive it.

KS3 Success

Science

Practice Test Papers

Age 11-14

John Beeby

Contents

Introduction

Sets
ABC

KEY STAGE 3

Introduction

Science

Introduction

How to Use
the Practice Test Papers

About these Practice Test Papers

At the end of Key Stage 3, tests will be used by your teachers to determine your level of achievement in science.

In this book, you have three sets of test papers that will allow you to track your progress in Key Stage 3 Science. They will help you to identify your strengths and weaknesses in the subject. By sitting all three papers, you will be able to monitor your rate of progress.

The test papers will:
- test your knowledge and understanding of scientific facts and ideas, and how you use these to answer questions
- provide practice questions in all science topics
- help to familiarise you with the different question styles that appear in test papers
- highlight opportunities for further study and skills practice that will lead to improvement
- record results to track progress.

How to Use the Test Papers

The questions in these test papers have been written in the style that you will see in actual tests.

While you should try to complete the different sections in each set in the same week, you should complete sets A, B and C **at intervals** through Key Stage 3, or Year 9.

Make sure you leave a reasonable amount of time between each assessment – it is unrealistic to expect to see much improvement in just a few weeks. Spreading out the sets will mean you have an opportunity to develop and practise any areas you need to focus on. You will feel much more motivated if you wait for a while, because your progress will be much more obvious.

If you want to re-use the papers, write in pencil and then rub out the answers. However, don't repeat the set too soon or you will remember the answers and the results won't be a true reflection of your abilities.

How to Prepare for the Tests

Revision: After covering the necessary science topics, read through your notes from school, or course notes. Perhaps use a revision guide to recap the key points. You can also add notes and diagrams to a mind map.

Equipment you will need:
- pen(s), pencil and rubber
- ruler
- protractor
- pair of compasses
- calculator
- a watch or clock to keep track of the pace at which you are answering questions.

When you feel that you're properly prepared, take the first set of test papers.

Taking the Tests

1. Each set of tests is made up of **two** test papers. Each paper is worth **75 marks**. You should spend **75 minutes (one and a quarter hours)** on **each** paper.
2. Choose a time to take the first paper when you can work through it in one go. Make sure you have an appropriate place to sit and take the test, and where you will be uninterrupted.
3. Answer **all** the questions in the test. If you are stuck on one question, move on and come back to it later. Tests often start with easier questions. These become more complex, and cover more than one topic, as you work through the test papers.
4. Read the questions **carefully**, so that you understand exactly what you need to do. Don't spend too long on any one question.
5. Write the answers in the spaces provided. The space provided for you to write your answer will also give you an indication of how detailed your answer needs to be. It will depend on the size of your writing, but if you need to use a lot more space, you're writing too much!
6. The number of marks allocated to each question is shown. This will tell you how many key points are needed in the answer.
7. Remember that marks may be awarded for key points or working out even if your final answer isn't correct, so **always show your working**, and keep it neat. It may be that if you get the answer wrong, you could still be awarded one mark for showing your working. Sometimes, the second mark for a calculation could be for the units of measurement, so make sure you include these.
8. Stay calm! Don't be fazed by questions. You may see some, for instance, that are based on topics that you haven't covered. When you do, it could be that the information you need to answer the question is provided in the question itself; or the question may be looking to see how you can apply your understanding to a new situation. Some questions will also test your understanding of how science works. You will not be able to revise for these, but practising doing this type of question will help.

How to Use the Mark Scheme

When you've sat the test, you, or a parent or guardian, should use the mark scheme to mark it. You could mark the test together. It's often helpful for you to discuss the answers with someone as you go through the mark scheme.

The answers and mark scheme will:
- give you an answer to the question **in full**. Any words shown in brackets aren't necessary to obtain the full marks, but should help your understanding of the question
- tell you where alternative answers are acceptable. If it's possible to use different words or terms in an answer, these will be separated by a forward slash, e.g. / . Sometimes when an answer isn't fully correct, certain alternatives may be acceptable
- provide Helpful Hints on answering particular questions.

When you've gone through the test paper, add up the marks to give you your total.

Tips for the Top

After sitting a test paper:
1. Try to analyse your performance. For questions that were incorrect, identify where you went wrong. Are there gaps in your knowledge and understanding? Were there topics where you were under-prepared? Have you misunderstood some of the science?
2. Pay attention to the Helpful Hints in the answers and mark scheme. These will give you revision tips, and important information about answering a question on a topic. They will also help you to avoid errors made by many students sitting tests.
3. Look for instructions in the question and the **command words**, as they will tell you exactly what kind of response is required, and the level of detail required in your answer.

For questions beginning:
- **Give, name** and **state** – you need to write down an answer that's short and concise. The answer could be from knowledge you have, or from information in the question.
- **Describe** – you need to write down a *more detailed* answer that gives the *key features* of something.
- **Explain** – you need to *give reasons* to answer how or why something happens.
- **Suggest** – you need to *apply* your knowledge to a new situation. This could be where you cannot give a conclusive answer or where you may not have enough evidence to draw a firm conclusion. Or, there may be more than one answer. Your suggestion could be based on your own scientific knowledge and understanding and/or information in the question.

When you've assessed your performance in the first test paper, do any additional work you need to. When you sit the second, and finally the third test, check to see how your performance is improving by comparing marks.

y7content. → in more detail in y9

Test Paper 1

Science

First name _____

Last name _____

Date _____

Instructions:

- The test is **75 minutes** long.

- Find a quiet place where you can sit down and complete the test paper undisturbed.

- You will need a pen, pencil, rubber and ruler. You may find a protractor and a calculator useful.

- The test starts with easier questions.

- Try to answer all of the questions.

- The number of marks available for each question is given in the margin.

- Show any rough working on this paper.

- Check your work carefully.

- Check how you have done using pages 101–112 of the Answers and Mark Scheme.

MAXIMUM MARK	75	ACTUAL MARK	

1. The diagram shows the structure of an atom.

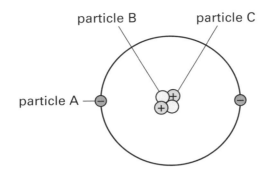

(a) (i) What is the name of subatomic particle A? Tick the correct box.

Electron ✓   Neutron ☐

Positron ☐   Proton ☐

(ii) What is the name of subatomic particle B? Tick the correct box.

Electron ☐   Neutron ✓

Positron ☐   Proton ☐

(iii) What is the name of subatomic particle C? Tick the correct box.

Electron ☐   Neutron ☐

Positron ☐   Proton ✓

(b) Complete the table below.

Particle	Relative mass
Electron	1/1800
Neutron	1

1 mark

1 mark

1 mark

1 mark

SUBTOTAL

7

2. We all look different. We show variation.

Human characteristics are a combination of genetic and environmental variation.

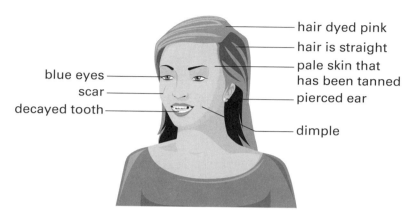

blue eyes
scar
decayed tooth

hair dyed pink
hair is straight
pale skin that has been tanned
pierced ear
dimple

(a) From the picture of Jade, above:

(i) Give **two** characteristics that are controlled by her genes.

* Blue eyes

* dimple

(ii) Give **two** characteristics that are the result of her environment.

* Pale skin that has been tanned pink hair

* Decayed tooth

(b) Give **two** characteristics that are controlled by genes but are affected by the environment.

* Decayed tooth Hair colour

* skin colour

(c) A study investigated certain characteristics of the men in a town.

The table shows the percentage of men with different blood groups.

Blood group	% of men with blood group
A	42
B	10
AB	4
O	44

(i) Label and plot a graph of the results.

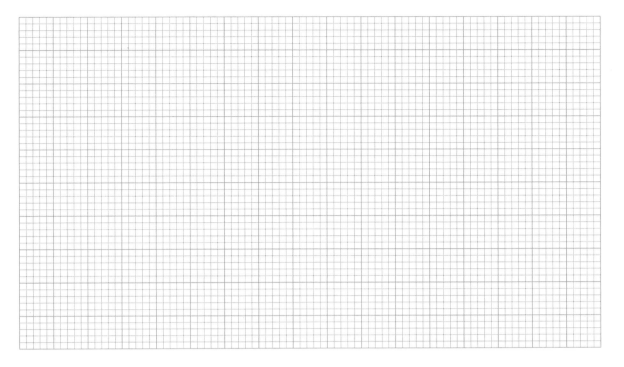

(ii) Here is a graph that shows the number of men of different height ranges in the town.

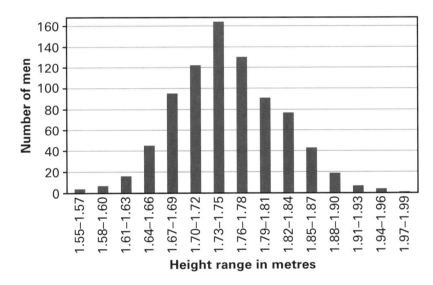

Use information from both graphs.

What type of variation is shown by:

Blood groups? _____

Height? _____

3. Complete the table below on energy transfers.

Process	Type of energy at the start	Final energy forms	
		Wanted forms	Wasted forms
Switching on a torch		light	
Lighting a Bunsen burner			light
Releasing a stretched spring	elastic potential		
Releasing a toy car at the top of a ramp		kinetic	

4. These diagrams show the male and female reproductive systems of humans.

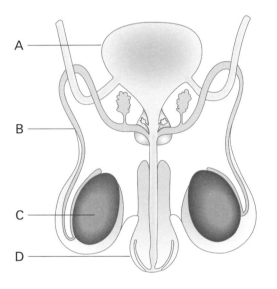
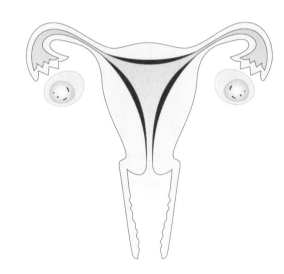

(a) In the male reproductive system:

(i) Which letter shows the testis? Tick the correct box.

A ☐   B ☐

C ☐   D ☐

(ii) Which letter shows the sperm duct? Tick the correct box.

A ☐   B ☐

C ☐   D ☐

(b) On the diagram of the female reproductive system, label the:

    (i) ovary

    (ii) vagina

(c) In which organs are the sex cells produced?

_____

(d) Where does fertilisation occur?

_____

5.   Iron is extracted from its ore in a blast furnace.

  (a) The ore used in the blast furnace is haematite. It has the formula Fe_2O_3.

    (i) How many atoms are present in the formula of haematite?

    _____

    (ii) The word equation for one of the chemical reactions in the blast furnace is:

    iron oxide   **+**   **carbon**   →   **iron**   **+**   **carbon dioxide**

    What is happening to the carbon in this reaction?

    _____

  (b) One ore of aluminium is bauxite, which is aluminium oxide. Explain why aluminium cannot be extracted from aluminium oxide using carbon.

_____

_____

_____

  (c) In nature, the elements gold and silver are usually found as the metals themselves and not compounds. Sodium is never found as sodium, but always as sodium compounds. Explain why.

_____

_____

_____

6. Kayleigh is a lighting technician in a theatre.

She puts filters over the theatre lights.

stage lighting white light	stage lighting white light	stage lighting white light

blue filter ⬤ green filter ⬤ red filter ⬤

coloured light A   coloured light B   coloured light C

(a) What colour is:

Coloured light A? _____

Coloured light B? _____

Coloured light C? _____

1 mark

(b) The actors' costumes absorb and reflect different colours.

(i) What colour will a red shirt appear under red light? Tick the correct box.

Black	Blue	Red	White	Yellow

1 mark

(ii) What colour will a blue dress appear under red light? Tick the correct box.

Black	Blue	Red	White	Yellow

1 mark

(iii) What colour will a yellow tie appear under red light? Tick the correct box.

Black	Blue	Red	White	Yellow

1 mark

7. This is a diagram of the carbon cycle.

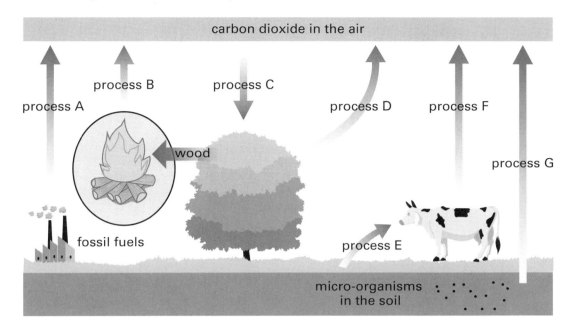

(a) Give the letters of the processes that release carbon dioxide into the air?

_____

_____

2 marks

(b) Give the letters of the processes where oxidation reactions?

_____

_____

2 marks

(c) Which process is photosynthesis?

_____

1 mark

(d) What is the name of processes A and B?

_____

1 mark

SUBTOTAL

8. An astronaut is testing a new space suit.

2 marks

(a) Give **one** reason why the astronaut would need to wear a space suit when in space. Explain your answer.

_____

_____

2 marks

(b) The space suit has four jet packs to move the astronaut.

In one test, the forces produced by the jet packs are shown below.

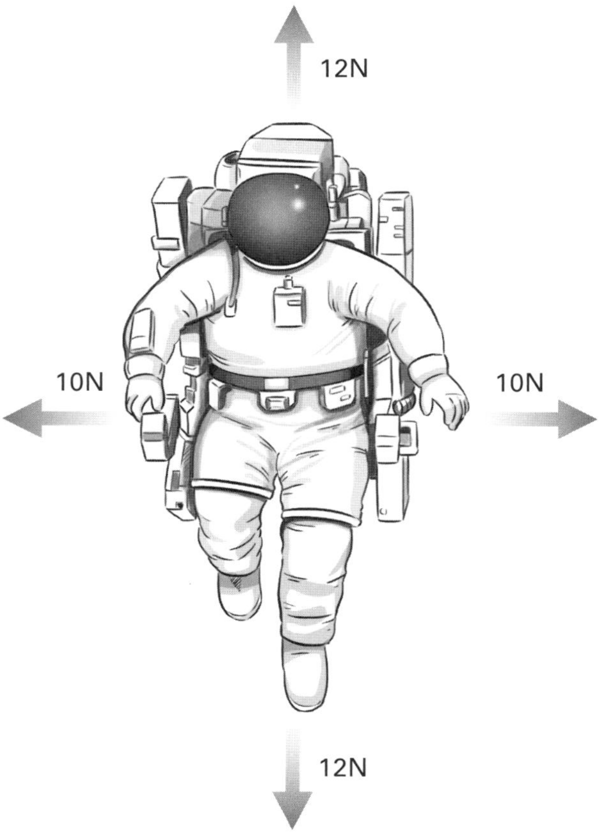

In which direction will the astronaut move? Explain your answer.

_____

_____

_____

1 mark

(c) The astronaut is on the Moon.

He has a mass of 100kg.

The gravitational field strength on the Moon is 1.6N/kg.

How much will he weigh?

_____ N

9. This picture shows an important biological molecule.

(a) What is the name of this biological molecule?

_____

(b) Name the **four** scientists whose work led to finding out the structure of this molecule.

_____

_____

_____

(c) Where is this molecule found in our cells?

_____

(d) Explain why this molecule is so important in forensic science investigations.

_____

_____

_____

_____

_____

10. The current Periodic Table is shown below.

| 1 | 2 | | | | | | | | | | | | | | 3 | 4 | 5 | 6 | 7 | 0 |

| | | | Key | | | | | 1
H
hydrogen
1 | | | | | | | | | | | | 4
He
helium
2 |

Key:
relative atomic mass
atomic symbol
name
atomic (proton) number

7 **Li** lithium 3	9 **Be** beryllium 4														11 **B** boron 5	12 **C** carbon 6	14 **N** nitrogen 7	16 **O** oxygen 8	19 **F** fluorine 9	20 **Ne** neon 10
23 **Na** sodium 11	24 **Mg** magnesium 12														27 **Al** aluminium 13	28 **Si** silicon 14	31 **P** phosphorus 15	32 **S** sulfur 16	35.5 **Cl** chlorine 17	40 **Ar** argon 18
39 **K** potassium 19	40 **Ca** calcium 20	45 **Sc** scandium 21	48 **Ti** titanium 22	51 **V** vanadium 23	52 **Cr** chromium 24	55 **Mn** manganese 25	56 **Fe** iron 26	59 **Co** cobalt 27	59 **Ni** nickel 28	63.5 **Cu** copper 29	65 **Zn** zinc 30	70 **Ga** gallium 31	73 **Ge** germanium 32	75 **As** arsenic 33	79 **Se** selenium 34	80 **Br** bromine 35	84 **Kr** krypton 36
85 **Rb** rubidium 37	88 **Sr** strontium 38	89 **Y** yttrium 39	91 **Zr** zirconium 40	93 **Nb** niobium 41	96 **Mo** molybdenum 42	98 **Tc** technetium 43	101 **Ru** ruthenium 44	103 **Rh** rhodium 45	106 **Pd** palladium 46	108 **Ag** silver 47	112 **Cd** cadmium 48	115 **In** indium 49	119 **Sn** tin 50	122 **Sb** antimony 51	128 **Te** tellurium 52	127 **I** iodine 53	131 **Xe** xenon 54
133 **Cs** caesium 55	137 **Ba** barium 56	139 **La*** lanthanum 57	178 **Hf** hafnium 72	181 **Ta** tantalum 73	184 **W** tungsten 74	186 **Re** rhenium 75	190 **Os** osmium 76	192 **Ir** iridium 77	195 **Pt** platinum 78	197 **Au** gold 79	201 **Hg** mercury 80	204 **Tl** thallium 81	207 **Pb** lead 82	209 **Bi** bismuth 83	209 **Po** polonium 84	210 **At** astatine 85	222 **Rn** radon 86
223 **Fr** francium 87	226 **Ra** radium 88	227 **Ac*** actinium 89	261 **Rf** rutherfordium 104	262 **Db** dubnium 105	266 **Sg** seaborgium 106	264 **Bh** bohrium 107	277 **Hs** hassium 108	268 **Mt** meitnerium 109	271 **Ds** darmstadtium 110	272 **Rg** roentgenium 111							

Elements with atomic numbers 112–116 have been reported but not fully authenticated

(a) Which scientist published the first true Periodic Table?

_____

(b) What principles did he use to arrange the elements in the Periodic Table?

_____

_____

(c) How would scientists describe the elements that are bordered on the far right of the table?

_____

(d) What term would scientists use to describe one of the columns of the Periodic Table?

_____

11. Zainab is a food analyst. She is investigating the quality of a sample of octadecanoic acid.

She puts a sample of solid octadecanoic acid into a test tube and heats it.

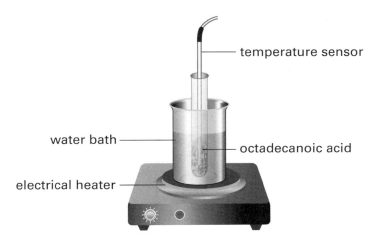

(a) Zainab uses a datalogger to measure the temperature of her sample every two minutes. Here are her results:

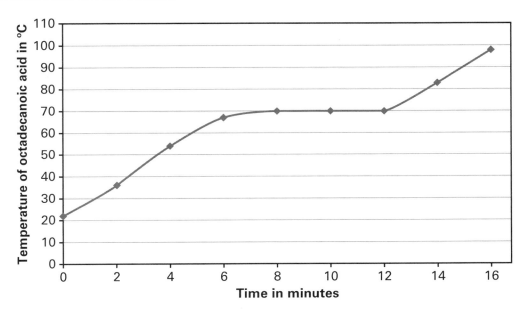

Explain what is happening between 8 and 12 minutes.

3 marks

_____

_____

_____

(b) From the graph, Zainab can tell that the octadecanoic acid is pure. Explain how she knows.

2 marks

_____

_____

_____

12. Scarlett is learning about how sound travels.

Her teacher sets up an experiment with an electric bell in a glass bell jar.

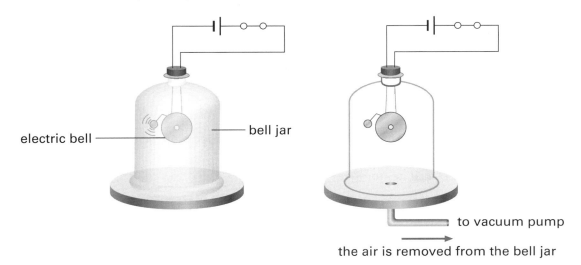

electric bell

bell jar

to vacuum pump

the air is removed from the bell jar

(a) Explain why she could not hear the bell when all the air was removed from the bell jar.

_____

_____

1 mark

(b) The table below gives the speed of sound as it travels through different media.

Medium	Speed of sound in m/s
Air	330
Alcohol	1160
Brick	4200
Steel	6100
Water, distilled	1490
Wood (hardwood)	4000

(i) Draw a bar chart to display the data.

3 marks

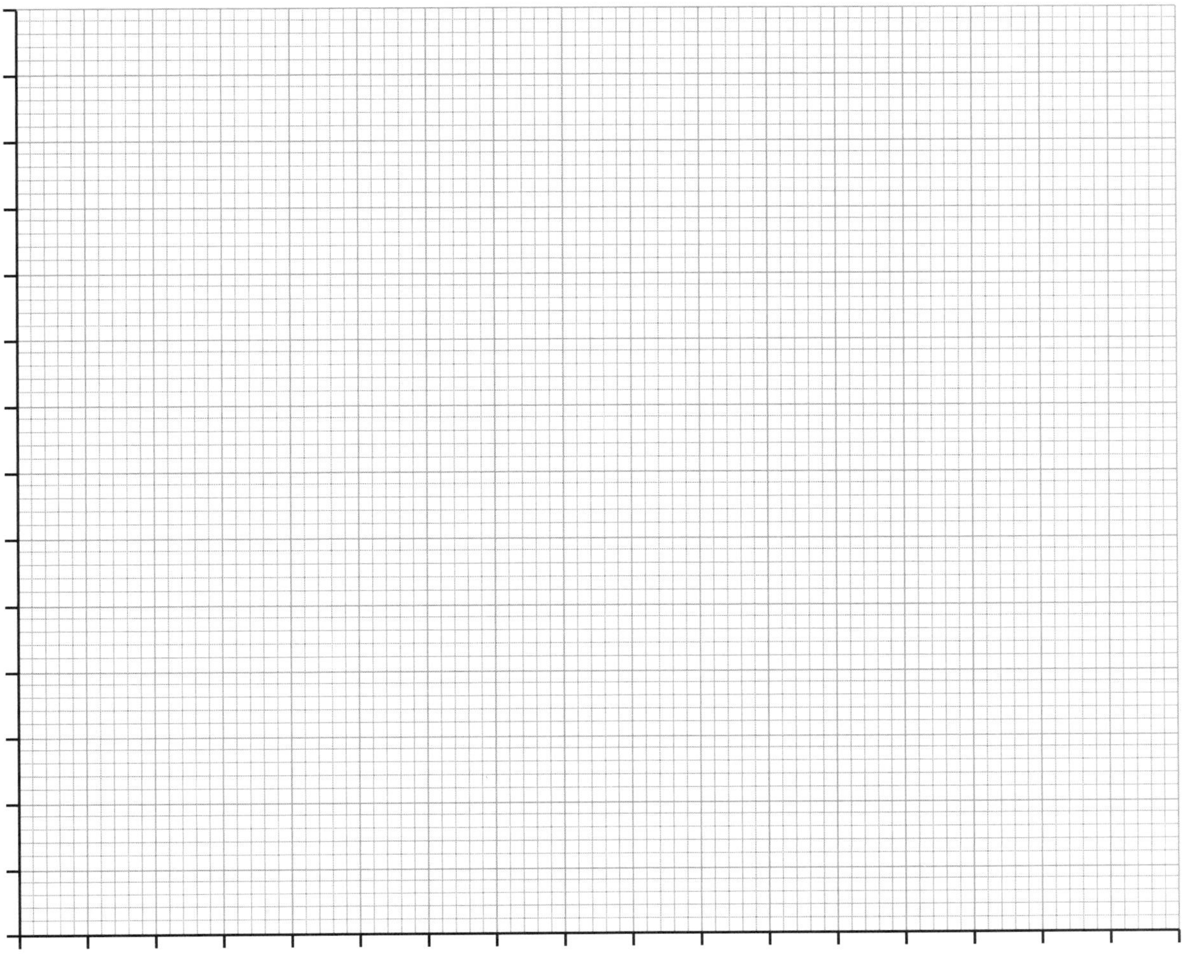

(ii) Compare the speed of sound in the listed solids, liquids and the gas. Suggest an explanation as to the differences.

2 marks

_____

_____

_____

(c) Explain how sound is used by ships to work out the depth of water.

3 marks

_____

_____

_____

_____

SUBTOTAL

13. Josh sets up the electrical circuit shown below.

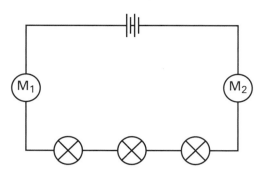

(a) Josh wants to measure the current in the circuit.

    (i) What type of meter should he use?

_____

    (ii) The reading of the current is 0.5A on meter M_1.

    What is the meter reading on meter M_2?

_____

(b) Josh sets up a different type of circuit, shown here.

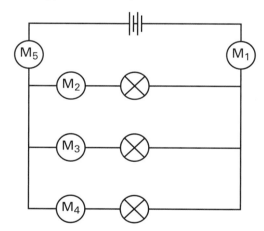

The circuit has two cells and three light bulbs – the same as the previous circuit.

(i) What is the name of this type of circuit?

_____

(ii) The reading on meter M_1 is 0.6A, and on meters M_2 and M_3 it is 0.2A.

What is the reading on:

Meter M_4? _____

Meter M_5? _____

14. A toxic insecticide is sprayed on farmland to control insect pests. Some of the insecticide ends up in the sea.

(a) Here is a food web diagram of some of the organisms affected.

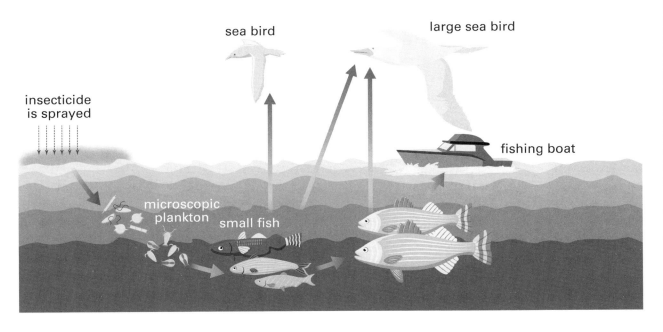

(i) Suggest why the sea birds start to die but the microscopic plankton and the fish are not killed.

_____

_____

_____

3 marks

(ii) Explain how, after some time, the insecticide begins to appear in humans.

1 mark

_____

SUBTOTAL

year7

Test Paper 2

First name _____

Last name _____

Date _____

Instructions:

- The test is **75 minutes** long.

- Find a quiet place where you can sit down and complete the test paper undisturbed.

- You will need a pen, pencil, rubber and ruler. You may find a protractor and a calculator useful.

- The test starts with easier questions.

- Try to answer all of the questions.

- The number of marks available for each question is given in the margin.

- Show any rough working on this paper.

- Check your work carefully.

- Check how you have done using pages 101–112 of the Answers and Mark Scheme.

MAXIMUM MARK	75		ACTUAL MARK	

1. Jasmine is eating a cereal bar. She looks at the nutritional information on the pack.

Nutritional information		
Typical values	**Per 100 g**	**Per bar**
Energy kJ kCal	1900 452	760 181
Protein	6.0	2.4
Carbohydrate	52.0	20.8
Fat (lipids)	24.5	9.8
Fibre	4.7	1.9

(a) Why does the information refer to 'Typical values' per 100 g and per bar?

1 mark

_____

_____

(b) Calculate the mass of the cereal bar that Jasmine is eating. Show your working out.

2 marks

_____ **g**

(c) Write down one function of each of the following:

3 marks

Protein

_____

Carbohydrate

_____

Fat (lipids)

_____

SUBTOTAL

(d) Which nutrients essential for health are missing from the nutritional information?

_____

_____

(e) Jasmine reads in a magazine that teenage girls should eat no more than 20g of saturated fat every day.

Each cereal bar contains 4g.

If all her saturated fat came from cereal bars, what would be the maximum number of bars she should eat in a day?

_____

2. The photographs show some ways of generating electricity.

Nuclear

Coal

Solar

Wind

(a) Which of these ways of producing electricity:

(i) depends on fossil fuel?

_____

(ii) are based on renewable energy sources?

_____

(iii) produce no carbon dioxide during electricity production?

_____

(iv) can be used at home to produce electricity?

_____

(b) The diagram shows how hydroelectric power is produced.

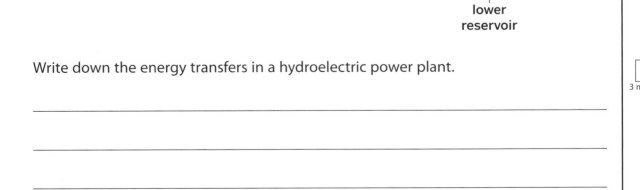

Write down the energy transfers in a hydroelectric power plant.

_____

_____

_____

3. The graph below shows the physical states of carbon dioxide at different temperatures and pressures.

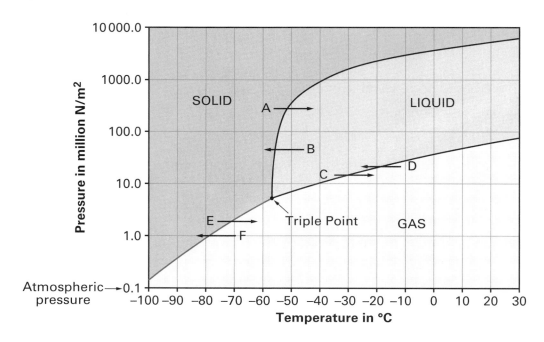

(a) At which of the following temperatures and pressures is carbon dioxide a liquid? Use the graph to help you.

Tick the correct box in the table below.

Temperature in °C	Pressure in million N/m²	Liquid?
30	10.0	
20	1000.0	
0	10 000.0	
−60	1.0	

(b) At what temperature does carbon dioxide boil at a pressure of 10 million N/m²?

_____

(c) What happens to the melting point of carbon dioxide as the pressure is increased?

_____

(d) The arrows on the graph show state changes of carbon dioxide.

(i) Which one of the arrows shows carbon dioxide freezing? Tick the correct box.

A   B   C   D   E

1 mark

(ii) Which one of the arrows shows carbon dioxide boiling? Tick the correct box.

A   B   C   D   E

1 mark

(iii) Sublimation is a process where a solid changes to a gas without going through a liquid state.

Which one of the arrows shows sublimation? Tick the correct box.

A   B   C   D   E

1 mark

(e) A point called the Triple Point is marked on the graph.

(i) Suggest what the Triple Point is.

_____

1 mark

(ii) At what temperature does the Triple Point occur?

_____

1 mark

SUBTOTAL

4. The diagrams below show the structure of the tissues that form the lining of the mouth and the trachea (windpipe).

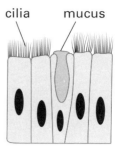

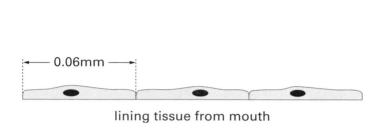

lining tissue from mouth   lining tissue from trachea

(a) Give two differences in the structure of the tissue lining the mouth and the tissue lining the trachea.

_____

_____

_____

_____

(b) The actual width of the cell shown is 0.06mm.

Calculate the magnification of the diagram. Show your working.

$$\text{Magnification} = \frac{\text{size on diagram}}{\text{actual size}}$$

Magnification = x ————————————

5. Megan sits on a see-saw.

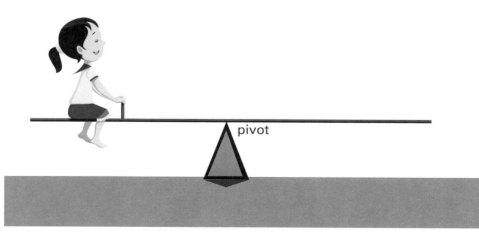

(a) What type of turning moment does Megan produce?

1 mark

____

(b) Megan weighs 350N. She sits 2m away from the pivot of the see-saw.
Calculate the turning moment produced by Megan. Show your working-out.

2 marks

____ Nm

(c) Thomas joins Megan on the see-saw.

2 marks

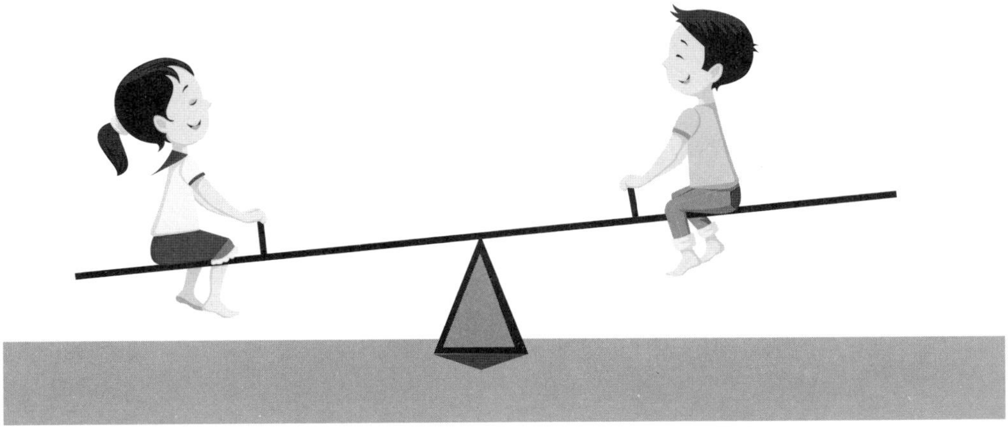

Thomas moves about until the see-saw is balanced. He is now sitting 1.75m from the pivot. Calculate Thomas's weight.

____ N

(d) Megan's dog sits on the see-saw with her.
The dog weighs 20N and sits 1.5m away from the pivot.
Calculate the turning moment that is now on the left-hand side of the see-saw.

2 marks

____ Nm

SUBTOTAL

6. James is investigating the chemical reaction between zinc and copper sulfate.

He measures out some copper sulfate solution into a beaker and records its temperature.

He then weighs out some zinc powder and adds it to the copper sulfate solution.

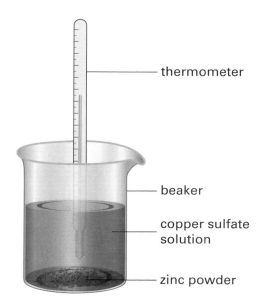

James records the temperature rise.

He then repeats the investigation with different masses of zinc powder.

Here are his results:

Mass of zinc powder in g	Temperature rise in °C
0	0.0
1	4.5
2	10.0
3	14.5
4	20.0
5	25.0
6	29.5

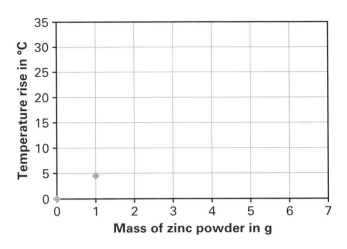

(a) (i) Plot a graph of James's results.
The first two points have been done for you.

(ii) Draw the best line through the points.

(b) Jess carries out a similar investigation.
She uses a polystyrene coffee cup instead of a beaker.
She also covers the cup with a lid.
Whose experiment will produce more reliable results?
Explain why.

_____

_____

_____

_____

_____

(c) A chemical reaction has taken place between the zinc and copper sulfate.
Give a word equation for this chemical reaction.

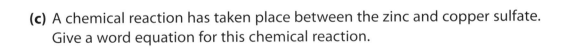

31

(d) Jess repeats the experiment with magnesium instead of zinc.
Look at the reactivity series below and suggest why the temperature rise is greater.

Sodium
Calcium
Magnesium
Aluminium   Decreasing
Zinc   reactivity
Copper
Silver

_____

_____

_____

7. Agnieszka is brewing some beer.

(a) Which micro-organism is used to brew beer?

_____

(b) This organism can respire with or without oxygen.

(i) Write a full symbol equation for **aerobic** respiration. The formula for glucose is $C_6H_{12}O_6$.

_____ + _____ $\rightarrow$ _____ + _____ (+ ENERGY)

(ii) Write a word equation for **anaerobic** respiration.

_____ $\rightarrow$ _____ + _____ (+ ENERGY)

(c) Agnieszka took some measurements to find the density of her beer.

Use the formula:

$$\text{density in g per cm}^3 = \frac{\text{mass in g}}{\text{volume in cm}^3}$$

The mass of her sample of beer = 525g

The volume of her sample of beer = 500cm^3

_____ g per cm^3

8. The Earth rotates on its axis and orbits the Sun.

This diagram shows the Earth's orbit around the Sun.

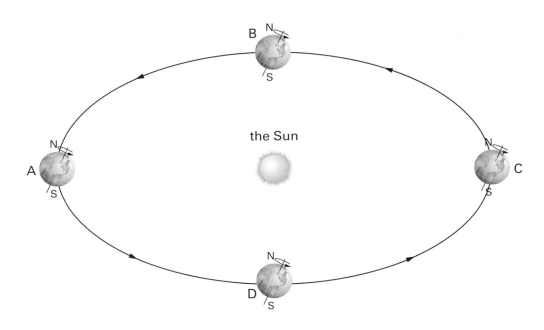

(a) (i) Which position shows the Earth when it is winter in the Northern Hemisphere?

1 mark

Tick the correct box.

Position A ☐   Position B ☐

Position C ☐   Position D ☐

(ii) Explain why, when it is winter in the Northern Hemisphere, it is summer in the Southern Hemisphere.

2 marks

_____

_____

_____

_____

(b) (i) How long does the Earth take to orbit around the Sun?

1 mark

_____

SUBTOTAL

(ii) How long does it take the Earth to do a complete rotation on its axis?

_____

9. Alex is making some fertiliser in the lab.

He reacts nitric acid with the alkali potassium hydroxide in the correct quantities.

(a) Acids react with alkalis to form a salt and water.
Summarise this reaction using a word equation.

_____ + _____ → _____ + _____

(b) (i) How will the pH of the mixture change as the alkali is added to the acid?

_____

_____

_____

(ii) What could he use to check that he has added the correct volumes of acid and alkali?

_____

(c) The formula of potassium hydroxide is KOH.
The formula of nitric acid is HNO_3.
Write a symbol equation for the reaction between potassium hydroxide and nitric acid.

_____ + _____ → _____ + _____

(d) The reaction produces a solution of the fertiliser.
How can Alex produce solid fertiliser?

_____

_____

_____

10. In her PE lesson, Olivia breathes into a spirometer to measure the volume of air in her lungs.

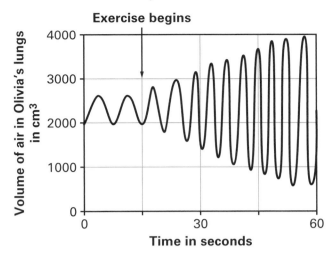

(a) How long after breathing into the spirometer does Olivia begin her exercise?

_____

(b) As she begins to exercise, her breathing changes.

(i) Write down two ways in which Olivia's breathing changes.

1 _____

_____

2 _____

_____

(ii) Explain why these changes in her breathing occur.

_____

_____

_____

_____

_____

11. William gets on a bus and makes a journey of 1500 metres.

His journey is shown in the distance–time graph below.

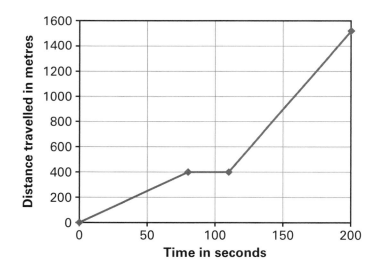

(a) How long does William's bus journey take?

_____

(b) Calculate the average speed of the bus over the journey.

_____

(c) When did the bus stop to pick up passengers?

_____

(d) (i) During which period was the bus travelling fastest?

_____

(ii) Calculate the speed of the bus during this part of the journey.

_____

1 mark

1 mark

1 mark

1 mark

3 marks

year8

Test Paper 1

First name _____

Last name _____

Date _____

Instructions:

- The test is **75 minutes** long.

- Find a quiet place where you can sit down and complete the test paper undisturbed.

- You will need a pen, pencil, rubber and ruler. You may find a protractor and a calculator useful.

- The test starts with easier questions.

- Try to answer all of the questions.

- The number of marks available for each question is given in the margin.

- Show any rough working on this paper.

- Check your work carefully.

- Check how you have done using pages 101–112 of the Answers and Mark Scheme.

MAXIMUM MARK	75		ACTUAL MARK	

1. Huw put some copper wire into a test tube of silver nitrate solution and left the test tube undisturbed for one day.

Here are his results.

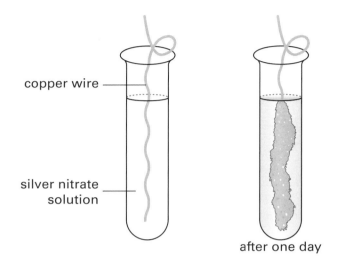

copper wire

silver nitrate solution

after one day

(a) A chemical reaction has taken place.

    (i) What is the name of this type of chemical reaction?

_____

    (ii) Write a word equation for the chemical reaction that has taken place.

_____   +   →   +   _____

_____   _____   _____   _____

(b) Huw repeats the experiment with different metals.

He adds different metal nitrate solutions to the metals.

His results are shown in the table below.

Solution	Metal			
	Copper	**Iron**	**Lead**	**Tin**
Copper nitrate	no reaction	reaction	reaction	reaction
Iron nitrate	no reaction	no reaction	no reaction	no reaction
Lead nitrate	no reaction	reaction	no reaction	reaction
Tin nitrate	no reaction	reaction	no reaction	no reaction

(i) Use these results to put the metals in order of their reactivity.

Most reactive

_____

_____

_____

_____

Least reactive

(ii) Where does silver fit into this reactivity series? Explain why.

_____

_____

_____

2.   This question is about lenses and mirrors.

(a) (i) Complete the sentences below by choosing the correct words from the box.

| reflection | refraction | slows down | speeds up |

Light entering the lens _____ and changes direction. This is called

_____.

As light leaves the lens, moving from glass to air, it _____,
so light rays are bent the other way.

(ii) Give **two** examples of where lenses are used.

1 _____

2 _____

1 mark

(b) The following diagram shows a mirror.

Which **two** statements about mirrors are correct?

Tick the correct boxes.

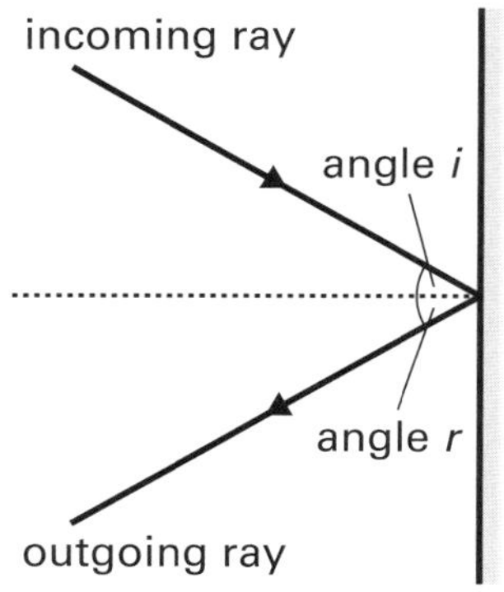

incoming ray
angle *i*
angle *r*
outgoing ray

Angle i is larger than angle r	☐	A mirror image is reversed, left to right	☐
Angle i equals angle r	☐	Light is refracted by a mirror	☐

3. This question is about cells.

3 marks

(a) Complete the sentences below about plant cells by choosing the correct words from the box.

cell wall	chloroplast	cytoplasm	nucleus

The ____________ forms the outer layer of the cell that supports the organism.

The ____________ absorbs light for photosynthesis. The ____________ controls the activities of each cell.

(b) The diagrams below show some different types of cell.

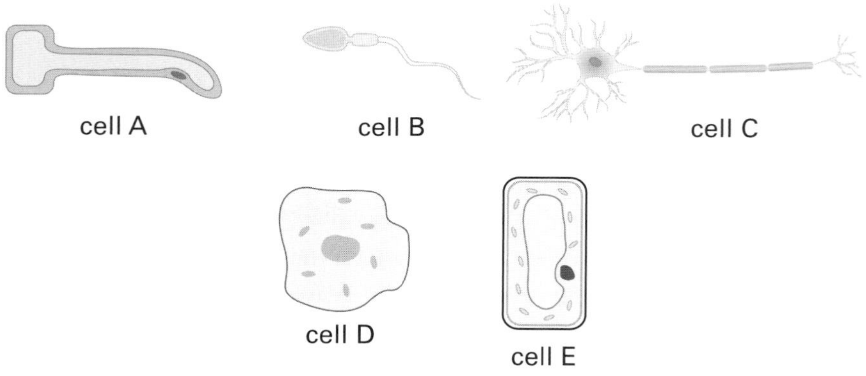

cell A
cell B
cell C
cell D
cell E

1 mark

(i) Give the letters of the two types of plant cell.

____________ and ____________

(ii) Which cell is involved in reproduction?

_____

(iii) Which cell communicates with other parts of the organism?

_____

(iv) Name the structures close to the nucleus in cell D.

_____

(v) What process is involved in the movement of gases in and out of cell E?

_____

GCSE required practical.

4. Lizzie is carrying out an experiment with a spring.

She adds different masses and measures the increase in length of the spring.

(a) Lizzie measures the force produced by the masses in units with the symbol N.

(i) What does this symbol, N, stand for? Tick the correct box.

Neutral ☐   Neutron ☐

Newton ☐   Nitrogen ☐

(ii) What type of force are the masses producing on the spring? Tick the correct box.

Compression ☐ Push ☐

Squash ☐ Stretch ☐

(b) Lizzie's results are shown below.

Force in N	Increase in length of spring in mm
0.0	0
0.5	20
1.0	40
1.5	60
2.0	80
2.5	100

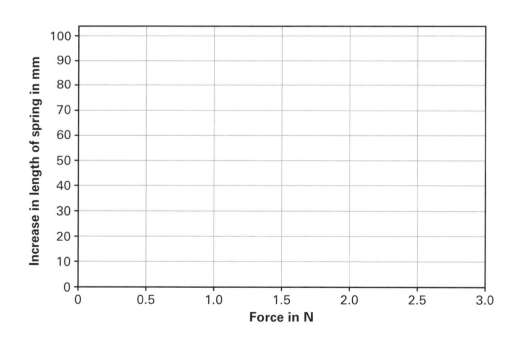

(i) Plot a line graph in the grid above.

(ii) Draw the line of best fit through the points.

(iii) Describe the relationship between the force and increase in length of the spring.

2 marks

_____

_____

_____

5. This diagram shows the structure of the human lungs.

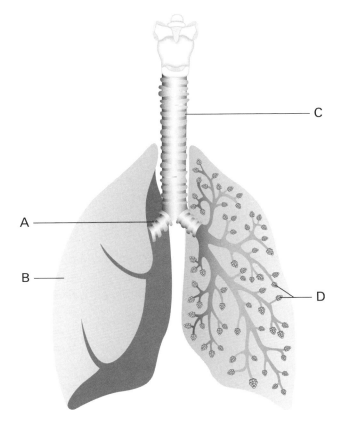

(a) (i) Which letter on the diagram labels the trachea? Tick the correct box.

1 mark

A ☐   B ☐

C ☐   D ☐

(ii) Which letter on the diagram labels the bronchus? Tick the correct box.

1 mark

A ☐   B ☐

C ☐   D ☐

SUBTOTAL

(b) Jodie's teacher sets up a model of the lungs in class.

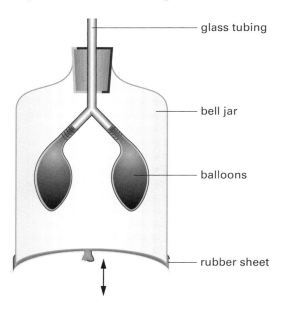

glass tubing

bell jar

balloons

rubber sheet

(i) Which part of the model represents the lungs?

_____

1 mark

(ii) What does the rubber sheet represent?

_____

1 mark

(iii) Explain how changes in the chest result in air being breathed in.

_____

_____

_____

_____

_____

3 marks

6. The diagrams below show the arrangement of particles in a solid, liquid and gas.

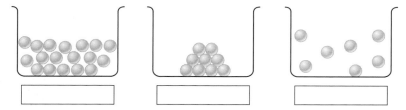

(a) Label the diagrams as solid, liquid or gas.

1 mark

(b) When a liquid is heated, it evaporates. Describe what happens in this process.

_____

_____

_____

_____

2 marks

(c) Explain why it is easy to compress a gas, but very difficult to compress a liquid.

_____

_____

_____

_____

1 mark

7. Larry is a sound engineer in a recording studio.

(a) He uses a digital oscilloscope to look at sound vibrations from his music.

Some of these are shown below.

A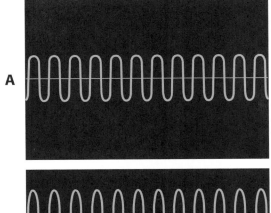

C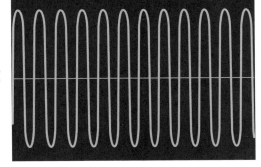

B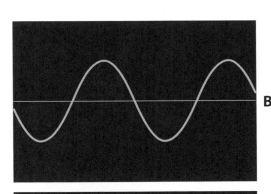

D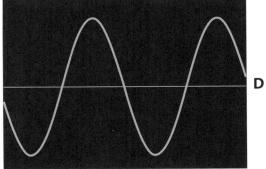

SUBTOTAL

(a) (i) Which sound is quietest?

Tick the correct box.

A ☐ B ☐

C ☐ D ☐

(ii) Which sounds have the lowest frequency?

Tick the **two** correct boxes.

A ☐ B ☐

C ☐ D ☐

(iii) In which unit is frequency measured? Tick the correct box.

Amplitude ☐ Decibels ☐

Hertz ☐ Lux ☐

(b) Larry sets up microphones for a recording session.

What energy transfer takes place in a microphone?

_____

8. Humans have an internal skeleton.

(a) Give **four** functions of the skeleton.

1 _____

2 _____

3 _____

4 _____

(b) Jason is weight training. He wants to measure the force produced by his biceps muscle.

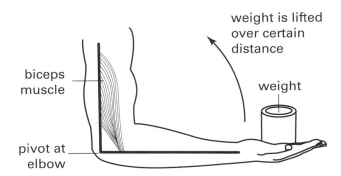

weight is lifted over certain distance

biceps muscle

weight

pivot at elbow

Give three measurements that he needs to make, or values he has to record, to be able to do the calculation.

1 _____

2 _____

3 _____

3 marks

9. The table below gives the names and formulae of some acids.

Name of acid	Carbonic	Ethanoic	Hydrochloric	Hydrocyanic	Nitric	Sulfuric
Chemical formula	H_2CO_3	CH_3COOH	HCl	HCN	HNO_3	H_2SO_4

(a) Which element is found in all of the acids?

_____

1 mark

(b) The chart shows the pH scale and the colours obtained with Universal indicator.

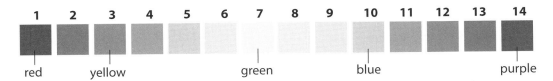

1 2 3 4 5 6 7 8 9 10 11 12 13 14

red   yellow   green   blue   purple

(i) What is the pH range of Universal indicator?

_____

1 mark

(ii) What colour would sulfuric acid give with Universal indicator?

_____

1 mark

(iii) What colour would pure water give with Universal indicator?

_____

1 mark

SUBTOTAL

(c) Owen decides to use a pH meter to find a liquid's pH.

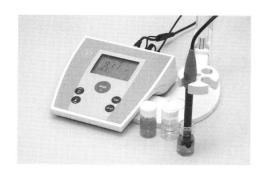

Give one advantage and one disadvantage of using a pH meter to find the pH of a liquid.

Advantage: _____

_____

Disadvantage: _____

_____

10. Jasmine is looking at the energy requirements of different females.

Female	Energy requirement in kJ per day
8 year old, active	8000
15 year old, active	12 000
Woman, office worker	10 000
Woman, breast-feeding	18 000

(a) Label and plot a bar chart of the energy requirements of different females.

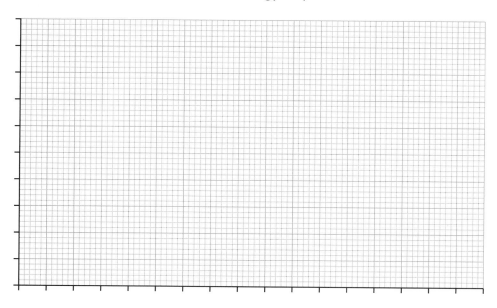

(b) Explain the need for extra energy for the mother who is breast-feeding.

1 mark

_____

(c) Suggest how and why the energy requirements of a 15-year-old male would be different from a 15-year-old female.

2 marks

_____

_____

11. Scientists researching the way our atmosphere has changed have published the following data:

Gas	Today	Number of millions of years ago			
		1000	2000	3000	4000
Carbon dioxide %	0.04	1	3	10	20
Nitrogen %	78	77	72	54	35
Oxygen %	21	10	1	0	0
Other gases %	0.96		24	36	45

(a) Complete the table by calculating the percentage of other gases in the air 1000 million years ago.

1 mark

(b) Draw a pie chart to show the composition of the atmosphere 4000 million years ago.

2 marks

(c) Animals are thought to have appeared on Earth around 750 million years ago. Suggest why they did not appear before then.

1 mark

_____

SUBTOTAL

12. Jenny lives in an old house.
The drawing shows what percentage of heat energy is lost through different parts of it.

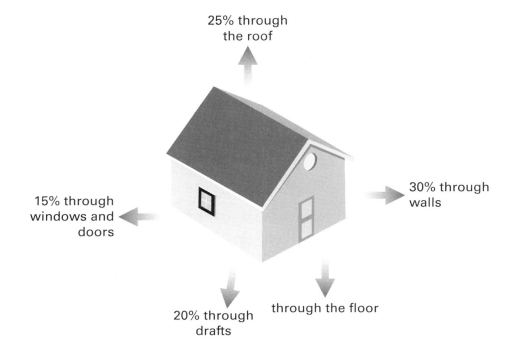

25% through
the roof

30% through
walls

15% through
windows and
doors

20% through
drafts

through the floor

(a) What percentage of heat is lost through the floor? (Assume that heat is lost in no other way except for those shown.)

1 mark

_____

(b) Jenny looks at the cost of some methods to reduce heat loss from her home. These are shown in the table below.

Method of reducing heat loss	Cost in £
Cavity wall insulation	350
Double-glazed windows	1500
Draft excluders around doors and windows	100
Loft insulation – 100mm	300
Loft insulation – 270mm	450

(i) Jenny has a limited budget. Explain why she should not spend her money on double-glazing.

2 marks

_____

_____

(ii) Jenny decides to have her loft insulated.

She is told by her energy company that:

- if she has 100mm-thick insulation, she will save £25 per year on her energy bills
- if she has 270-mm thick insulation, she will save £150 per year.

With savings she would make, calculate how long it will take her to cover her costs if she has:

100mm-thick insulation _____

_____

270mm-thick insulation _____

_____

_____

2 marks

(c) Complete the sentences below by choosing the correct words from the box.

2 marks

conduction	convection	radiation

Heat energy gets transferred through the walls, roof, windows and floor of our homes

by _____

Cold air entering the house as a draft can take heat energy into the loft by

_____

SUBTOTAL

13. The table below shows the feeding relationships of organisms in a UK woodland.

Organism	Feeds on
Robin	Caterpillars
	Earthworms
	Woodlice
Caterpillar	Plants
Earthworm	Plants
Shrew	Caterpillars
	Earthworms
	Woodlice
Hawk	Robins
	Shrews
Woodlouse	Plants

(a) What type of organism is the producer in the food web?

_____

(b) Draw a food web to show the feeding relationships.

Test Paper 2

year 9.

First name _____

Last name _____

Date _____

Instructions:

- The test is **75 minutes** long.

- Find a quiet place where you can sit down and complete the test paper undisturbed.

- You will need a pen, pencil, rubber and ruler. You may find a protractor and a calculator useful.

- The test starts with easier questions.

- Try to answer all of the questions.

- The number of marks available for each question is given in the margin.

- Show any rough working on this paper.

- Check your work carefully.

- Check how you have done using pages 101–112 of the Answers and Mark Scheme.

MAXIMUM MARK	75	ACTUAL MARK	

1. Josh is investigating the electrical resistance of a length of wire.

He sets up the circuit below.

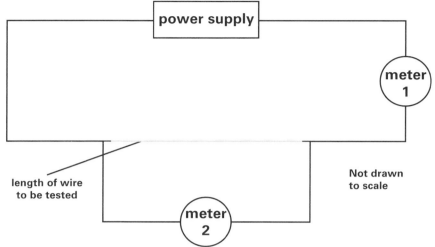

length of wire
to be tested

Not drawn
to scale

(a) He measures potential difference and the current.

Which does he measure on:

Meter 1? _____   Meter 2? _____

(b) He records a potential difference of 1.10V and a current of 0.65A.

Calculate the resistance of the wire using the formula:

Resistance in ohms $= \dfrac{\text{potential difference in volts}}{\text{current in amps}}$

Resistance = _____ ohms

(c) Suggest one way in which Josh could improve his estimation of the resistance of the piece of wire.

_____

_____

(d) The wire that Josh investigated was made from nichrome. Nichrome is a mixture of the elements nickel, iron and chromium.

(i) What is the name of a substance such as nichrome, made from a mixture of metals?

_____

1 mark

1 mark

1 mark

1 mark

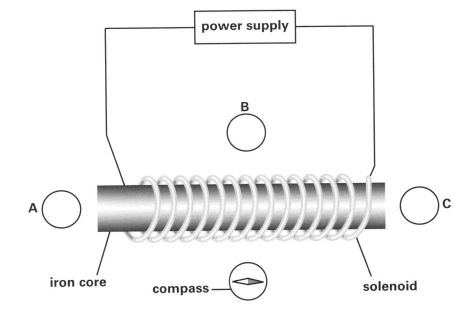

(ii) Josh measures the resistance of other metals.

He obtains the following results:

Metal	Resistance in ohms
Aluminium	0.04
Constantan	0.83
Copper	0.03
Iron	0.16

Which metal would be best to use for wiring? Explain your answer.

_____

_____

_____

(e) Josh replaces a piece of wire with a solenoid with an iron core to make an electromagnet.

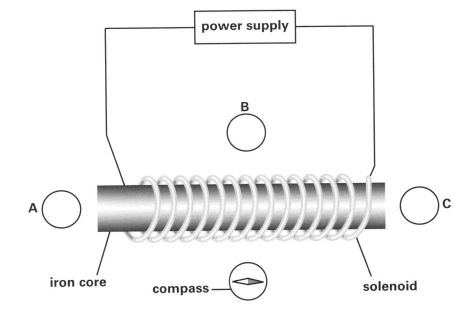

(i) What is a solenoid?

_____

(ii) Josh places a compass next to the solenoid, as shown.

He then moves the compass to positions A, B and C.

On the diagram above, show the direction each compass will point.

2. Three students have been growing some plants in the school greenhouse.

(a) They decide to measure how tall the plants have grown.

The diagram shows the position from which the students make their measurements.

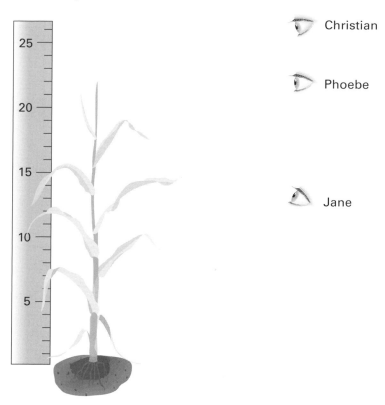

(i) The measurements they make of the plant's height are:

Student	Measurement made of height of plant in cm
Christian	21
Jane	24
Phoebe	22

Which student's measurement is likely to be closest to the true height of the plant? Explain your answer.

_____

_____

_____

_____

(ii) What do we call a measurement that is close, or identical, to its true value?

_____

(iii) The students go on to measure their other plants.

All the measurements made by two of the students have errors.

What is this type of error called?

_____

1 mark

(b) Jane cuts a slice through one of her plant's leaves.

This is what she sees when she examines it with a microscope.

2 marks

Give the name of:

Cell A _____

Structure B _____

(c) What is structure C called, and what is its function?

_____

_____

_____

2 marks

(d) Write down two ways in which the leaf has adapted for photosynthesis.

_____

_____

_____

1 mark

SUBTOTAL

3. Ashraf is reacting some iron filings with dilute sulfuric acid.

(a) What gas is given off when iron and other metals react with an acid?

_____

(b) Ashraf measures the volume of gas produced. He tries out the experiment at different temperatures. He carries out each experiment for the same length of time.

Here are his results:

Temperature in °C	Volume of gas produced in cm³		
	Experiment 1	**Experiment 2**	**Experiment 3**
10	100	105	110
20	218	205	208
30	300	100	310
40	405	400	402
50	505	510	495

(i) Ashraf says that one of his results looks incorrect. Suggest which result this is.

_____

(ii) What do we call a result that is not consistent with the rest?

_____

(iii) At which temperature are the results the most repeatable?

_____

(c) Ashraf calculates the averages from his set of data.

Temperature in °C	Average volume of gas produced in cm³
10	105
20	210
30	305
40	402
50	503

(i) Plot a graph of these average volumes over temperature.

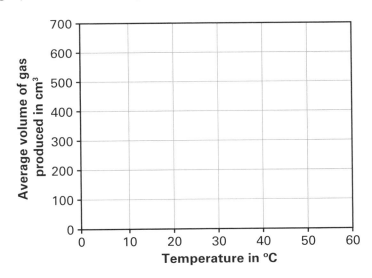

(ii) Draw a line of best fit of the data.

(iii) Describe how temperature affects the volume of gas produced.

_____

_____

_____

_____

(d) The mixture has many unreacted iron filings.

Ashraf would like to produce a pure solution of iron sulfate.

How should he produce this?

_____

_____

4. John is on holiday by the sea. He watches the waves as they move towards the seashore.

He thinks they slow down as they move towards the shore.

John reckons that the depth of water affects the speed of a wave.

(a) What do we call a suggestion or idea based on observations?

_____

(b) When John returns home, he tests this idea. He sets up a tank of water and produces a wave. The tank is 200cm long.

He times how long it takes for the wave to travel up the tank.

He tries the experiment with different depths of water. Here are his results. One has been done for you.

Depth of water in cm	Average time taken in seconds	Average speed in cm per second
1	6.5	
2	4.5	
3	3.8	
4	3.3	
5	3.2	63

Calculate the speed of the wave at the different depths and complete the table above.

(c) To obtain his average results, John did the experiment three times.

Explain why scientists repeat experiments.

_____

(d) What can you say about the results in relation to John's idea?

_____

_____

_____

5. Saima is investigating the solubility of different chemical compounds in water.

She investigates how much of each will dissolve at different temperatures.

(a) What term do we give to a chemical that:

    (i) dissolves in another chemical?

_____

    (ii) dissolves another chemical?

_____

(b) She draws a graph of her results.

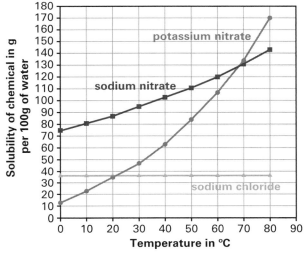

    (i) What is the maximum mass of sodium nitrate that will dissolve in 100g water at 50°C?

_____

    (ii) How does temperature affect the solubility of sodium chloride in water?

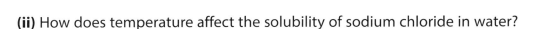
_____

    (iii) At what temperature does the solubility of potassium nitrate match the solubility of sodium chloride?

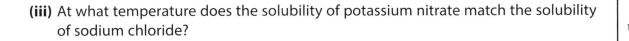
_____

(c) Potassium nitrate and sodium nitrate are both used as plant fertilisers.

In Saima's greenhouse, at 25°C, suggest which fertiliser would be better in terms of its solubility in water.

_____

1 mark

1 mark

1 mark

1 mark

1 mark

1 mark

SUBTOTAL

61

6. Asif is studying a film of a game of cricket.

When a bowler bowls the ball, he times how long the cricket ball takes to travel the length of the wicket.

Bowler	Time to travel length of wicket in seconds	Bowling speed in metres per second
Graeme	0.74	27
Jimmy	0.50	
Mitchell	0.48	
Monty	0.85	
Ryan	0.51	
Stuart	0.49	

(a) A cricket pitch is 20m long. Complete the table above by calculating the bowling speed of each of the bowlers.

3 marks

(b) Asif's own bowling speed is 27 metres per second.

Calculate Asif's bowling speed in kilometres per hour.

2 marks

_____

7. In the science lab, Onnicha is analysing the air she breathes in, and the air she breathes out.

(a) These are her results:

Air	Oxygen concentration in %	Carbon dioxide concentration, in %
Air breathed in	20.90	0.04
Air breathed out	16.00	4.00

(i) Compare the carbon dioxide concentration in the air breathed out with the air breathed in.

By how many times has it increased?

1 mark

_____

(ii) What body process has led to this increase?

_____

(iii) Write a word equation for this process.

$$\underline{\hspace{2cm}} + \underline{\hspace{2cm}} \rightarrow \underline{\hspace{2cm}} + \underline{\hspace{2cm}} \quad (+ \text{ ENERGY})$$

(b) The carbon dioxide concentration in the air 50 years ago was 0.03%.

Explain why it has increased.

_____

_____

_____

8. Steve has looked up car brake systems on the Internet. He finds a webpage that includes a diagram of how car brakes work.

The system shown includes a liquid called brake fluid. There are two pistons at each end. One has a larger area than the other.

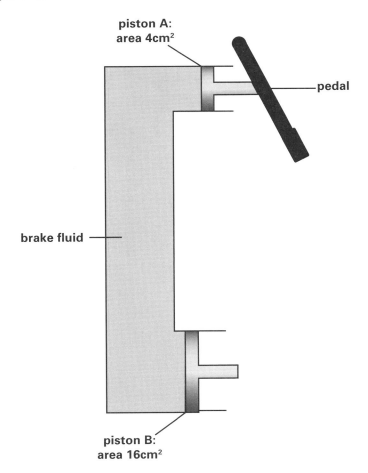

**piston A:
area 4cm²**

pedal

brake fluid

**piston B:
area 16cm²**

1 mark

(a) Give the formula that shows the relationship between pressure, force and area.

____

2 marks

(b) (i) If a person applies a force of 240N on the brake pedal, calculate the pressure of piston A on the brake fluid.

____

____

1 mark

(ii) Assume that all this pressure is applied to piston B.
Calculate the force, in Newtons, on piston B.

____ N

2 marks

(c) Explain why car brakes are filled with liquid and not a gas.

____

____

____

9. The diagram below shows a pregnant woman's abdomen.

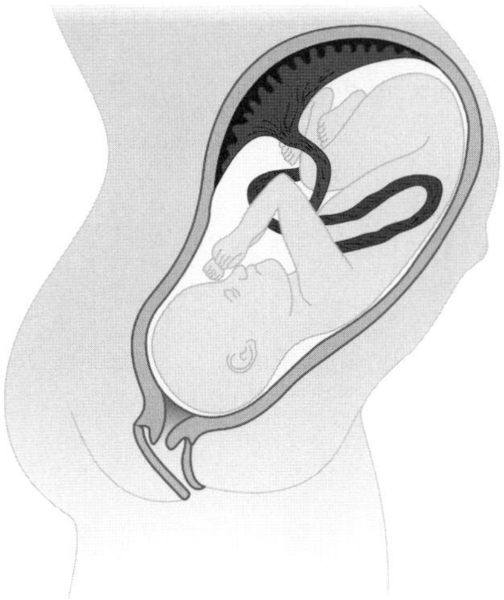

3 marks

(a) On the diagram, label the:

- amniotic fluid
- placenta
- umbilical cord
- uterus.

(b) How does the foetus receive its food and oxygen?

_____

_____

_____

(c) Some pregnant teenage girls are admitted to hospital because of substance abuse.

The data below show percentages of girls admitted to a hospital in the USA in 1992 and 2007.

(i) Describe the changes in percentages of girls admitted for alcohol and cannabis abuse in 1992 and 2007.

_____

_____

_____

_____

_____

(ii) Write down one effect on the foetus of a mother drinking alcohol.

_____

_____

10. In the past few years, scientists have produced certain chemicals as tiny particles called nanoparticles.

Scientists are now putting nanoparticles into sunscreens.

This person is wearing a normal sunscreen and a nanoparticle sunscreen.

before adding sunscreen

nanoparticle sunscreen   normal sunscreen

(a) Give **one** advantage of using nanoparticle sunscreen.

_____

_____

1 mark

(b) Anna is testing how well different types of sunscreen protect against the Sun's rays. She covers pieces of plastic film with each of the sunscreens she is testing.

She places each piece of plastic on a sheet of Sun-sensitive paper.

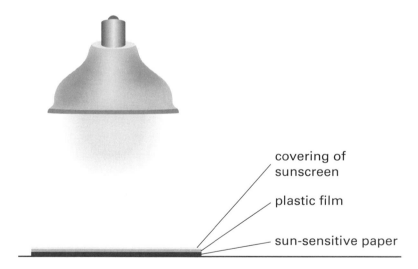

covering of sunscreen

plastic film

sun-sensitive paper

She turns on a sunlamp and records the time taken for the paper to change colour.

(i) Give **two** ways in which Anna can make this a fair test.

_____

_____

_____

2 marks

(ii) How should Anna set up a control for the experiment?

_____

_____

(c) Some nanoparticles are made from zinc oxide.

Give **one** method of producing zinc oxide.

_____

_____

11. Anna, Laura and Mark are practising their archery. They are aiming for the bull's eye. They shoot some arrows into the target.

Anna's arrows   **Laura's arrows**   **Mark's arrows**

(a) Which statement best describes Anna's arrows? Tick the correct box.

Accurate and precise ☐   Precise but not accurate ☐

Accurate but not precise ☐   Neither precise nor accurate ☐

(b) Which statement best describes Laura's arrows? Tick the correct box.

Accurate and precise ☐   Precise but not accurate ☐

Accurate but not precise ☐   Neither precise nor accurate ☐

(c) Write a statement that best describes Mark's arrows.

_____

1 mark

1 mark

1 mark

1 mark

1 mark

SUBTOTAL

Test Paper 1

Science

First name _____

Last name _____

Date _____

Instructions:

- The test is **75 minutes** long.

- Find a quiet place where you can sit down and complete the test paper undisturbed.

- You will need a pen, pencil, rubber and ruler. You may find a protractor and a calculator useful.

- The test starts with easier questions.

- Try to answer all of the questions.

- The number of marks available for each question is given in the margin.

- Show any rough working on this paper.

- Check your work carefully.

- Check how you have done using pages 101–112 of the Answers and Mark Scheme.

Test Paper 1

MAXIMUM MARK	75		ACTUAL MARK	

1. The local reservoir has turned bright green. Adrian, from the water company, is called in to investigate.

Adrian collects a water sample. He then looks at it with a microscope. This is what he sees.

(a) Adrian looks at the structure of the cells in the organism.

(i) Which part of the cell is the cell membrane? Tick the correct box.

A ☐   B ☐

C ☐   D ☐

1 mark

(ii) Which part of the cell is the nucleus? Tick the correct box.

A ☐   B ☐

C ☐   D ☐

1 mark

(b) Suggest **two** reasons why Adrian knows that the organism is a plant.

_____

_____

_____

2 marks

(c) Suggest an explanation for the reservoir having turned bright green.

_____

_____

_____

2 marks

SUBTOTAL

2. This diagram shows white light passing through a prism.

(a) (i) Add labels to the diagram to show the colours missing from the spectrum.

(ii) Which term shows what is happening to the light as it passes through the prism? Tick the correct box.

Absorption ☐   Dispersion ☐

Reflection ☐   Subtraction ☐

(b) In the days before Isaac Newton, people thought the colours came from the prism.

Describe an experiment to show that the colours of the spectrum come from the light, and not the prism.

_____

_____

_____

_____

_____

_____

3. Rio runs his car on liquefied petroleum gas (LPG).

Many other people use LPG for their central heating or for portable appliances such as camping stoves.

LPG is supplied pressurised as a liquid, but burns as a gas.

(a) LPG contains the hydrocarbons propane and butane. What kind of chemical is LPG?

1 mark

Tick the correct box.

Element ☐   Compound ☐

Impure ☐   Mixture ☐

(b) The diagram below shows the properties of propane and butane.

propane   temperature in °C

| 25 | 0 | −25 | −50 | −75 | −100 | −125 | −150 | −175 | −200 |

boiling point (at −50)   freezing point (at −175)

butane

| 25 | 0 | −25 | −50 | −75 | −100 | −125 | −150 | −175 | −200 |

boiling point (at 0)   freezing point (at −125)

(i) At −25°C, in which state are propane and butane?

1 mark

Propane is a _____

Butane is a _____

(ii) At −145°C, in which state are propane and butane?

1 mark

Propane is a _____

Butane is a _____

(c) When propane (and butane) burns, it uses oxygen in the air to produce carbon dioxide and water. Write a word equation for the combustion of propane.

1 mark

_____

_____ + _____ → _____ + _____

SUBTOTAL

2 marks

(d) Some gas suppliers change the proportions of butane and propane in the summer and winter. Suggest **two** reasons why they do this.

____

____

____

4. The diagram below shows the structure of the human digestive system.

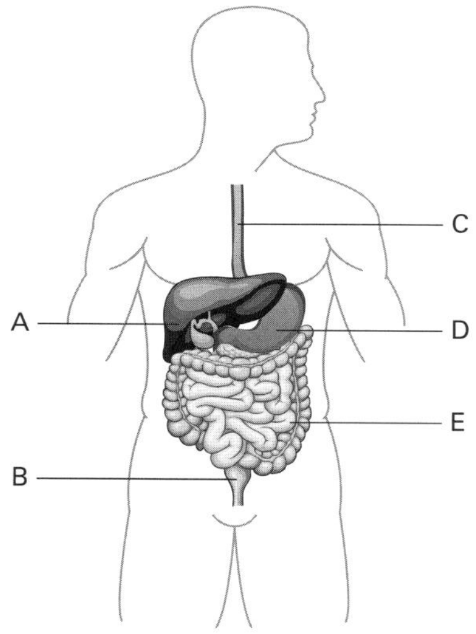

1 mark

(a) (i) Which letter on the diagram labels the oesophagus? Tick the correct box.

A	B	C	D	E
☐	☐	☐	☐	☐

1 mark

(ii) Which letter on the diagram labels the liver? Tick the correct box.

A	B	C	D	E
☐	☐	☐	☐	☐

1 mark

(iii) Which letter on the diagram labels the small intestine? Tick the correct box.

A	B	C	D	E
☐	☐	☐	☐	☐

(b) What is the name of the part of the digestive system:

(i) in which the digestion of protein begins?

_____

(ii) where most of our food is absorbed into the blood?

_____

(c) What **type** of chemical speeds up the digestion of our food? Tick the correct box.

Acid ☐   Enzyme ☐

Saliva ☐   Starch ☐

5.   Jenny is replacing her electric filament light bulbs with energy-saving bulbs.

She reads about the energy efficiency of the bulbs.

$$\text{energy efficiency in per cent} = \frac{\text{useful energy transferred}}{\text{energy supplied}} \times 100$$

(a) A diagram shows her the energy transfer in a filament light bulb.

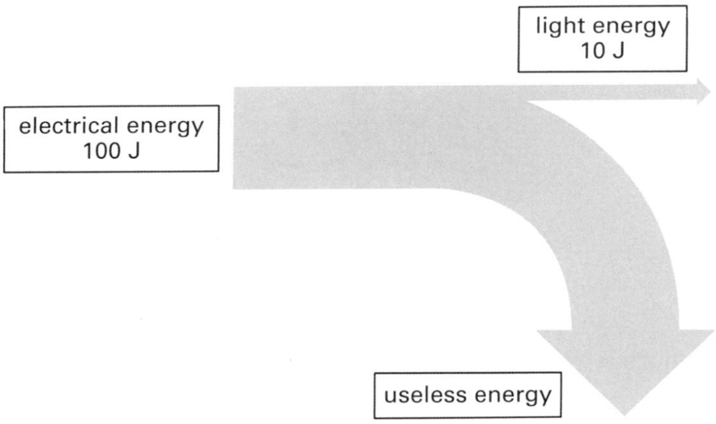

light energy
10 J

electrical energy
100 J

useless energy

(i) How much energy is transferred to useless energy?

_____ J

(ii) In what form, or forms, is this useless energy?

_____

(iii) Calculate the energy efficiency of the light bulb.

_____

(b) An energy-saving bulb is supplied with 1500J of energy in one minute.

600J of energy is transferred to light.

Calculate the energy efficiency of the bulb.

_____

(c) Jenny is looking at the power used by some of her electrical appliances.

Complete the table:

Appliance	Power in W	Power in kW	Time appliance is used for in hours	Units of electricity used in kWh
Hair dryer		2.0	1	
Kettle	3000		2	
Light bulb	100		20	
Toaster		1.3	1	

6. The diagram shows the structure of the human arm.

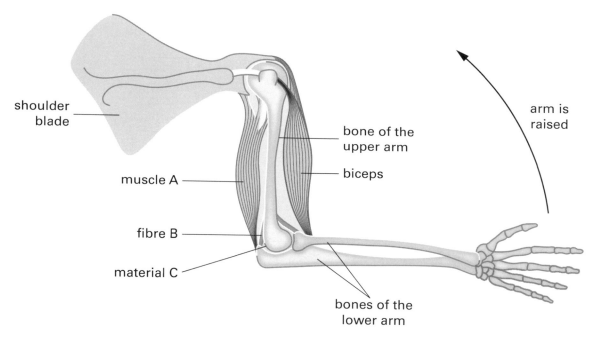

(a) (i) Give the name of muscle A.

_____

(ii) What happens to the biceps when it is used to raise the arm?

_____

(iii) Explain why muscles of the arm work in pairs.

_____

_____

_____

(b) Describe the function of:

Fibre B: _____

Material C: _____

7. Sam is using some nail polish remover. It contains pentyl ethanoate and propanone.

(a) The formula of pentyl ethanoate is:

$$H-\overset{\overset{\displaystyle H}{|}}{\underset{\underset{\displaystyle H}{|}}{C}}-\overset{\overset{\displaystyle O}{||}}{C}-O-\overset{\overset{\displaystyle H}{|}}{\underset{\underset{\displaystyle H}{|}}{C}}-\overset{\overset{\displaystyle H}{|}}{\underset{\underset{\displaystyle H}{|}}{C}}-\overset{\overset{\displaystyle H}{|}}{\underset{\underset{\displaystyle H}{|}}{C}}-\overset{\overset{\displaystyle H}{|}}{\underset{\underset{\displaystyle H}{|}}{C}}-\overset{\overset{\displaystyle H}{|}}{\underset{\underset{\displaystyle H}{|}}{C}}-H$$

(i) Which elements are present in a molecule of pentyl ethanaote?

_____

(ii) How many atoms are present in a molecule of pentyl ethanoate?

_____

(b) Pentyl ethanoate is irritant. Propanone is highly flammable and irritant.

(i) Which symbol, or symbols, would you find on a bottle of pentyl ethanoate?

Tick the correct box(es).

(ii) Which symbol, or symbols, would you find on a bottle of propanone?

Tick the correct box(es).

(iii) Give one safety precaution Sam should use when using her nail polish remover.

_____

_____

_____

8. Zoe is a research scientist in the car industry. She is investigating the motion of a car.

(a) Zoe is test driving the car.

(i) Complete the following sentence.

Force from the car's _____ is causing the forward movement of the car.

(ii) Name **two** forces that are resisting the movement of the car.

_____

_____

(iii) Zoe drives the car at a steady speed around the track.

What can you say about the forces on the car?

_____

_____

(b) Zoe is testing the car on different road surfaces on the track.

She measures the car's fuel use on the different road surfaces.

Type of road surface	Fuel use in cm³ fuel used per km
Tarmac® with small chippings	67
Tarmac® with large chippings	69
Concrete with small chippings	70
Concrete with large chippings	72

Draw a bar chart that shows the car's fuel use on different road surfaces.

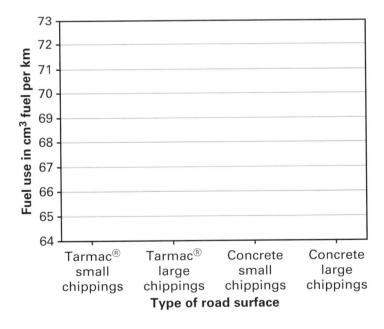

9. The picture below shows Aiysha's kitchen.

(a) Several types of material are shown in the picture.

(i) What type of material are wall tiles made from? Tick the correct box.

Ceramic ☐   Composite ☐

Metal ☐   Polymer ☐

(ii) What type of material is the plastic storage jar made from? Tick the correct box.

Ceramic ☐   Composite ☐

Metal ☐   Polymer ☐

(b) Stainless steel is an alloy. What is meant by an alloy?

_____

_____

(c) Describe how granite is formed.

_____

_____

10. Vicky is investigating electromagnets.

She winds a coil of insulated copper wire around a rod of pure iron. She then connects the wire to the power supply.

She counts how many paperclips the electromagnet will pick up with different numbers of turns in the coil.

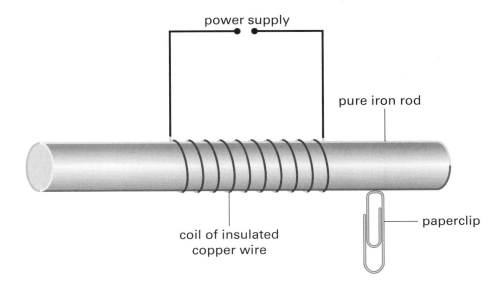

power supply

pure iron rod

coil of insulated copper wire

paperclip

(a) Her results are shown below:

Number of turns in the coil	Number of paperclips picked up
10	1
20	2
30	3
40	4
50	5
60	6

(i) Describe the relationship between the number of turns in the coil and the strength of the electromagnet.

1 mark

_____

_____

_____

(ii) Give one other way in which she could increase the strength of the electromagnet.

1 mark

_____

SUBTOTAL

(b) Vicky turns the power supply off.

(i) What would happen to the paperclip(s)? Explain your answer.

_____

_____

_____

(ii) Vicky repeats this with a steel rod instead of the iron rod. Explain why the paperclips remain attached.

_____

11. When a pollen grain lands on the stigma of a flower, it begins to grow.

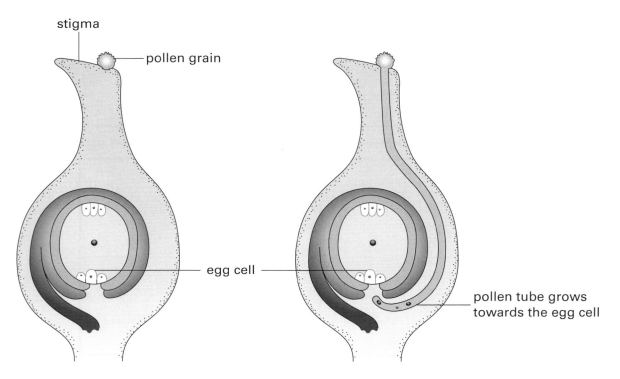

Jodie collects some pollen grains from a spider flower.

She places them in sugar solution on a microscope slide. She watches them as they grow.

She investigates the effects of several different concentrations of sugar solution.

Here are her results:

Concentration of sugar solution in %	Pollen grains that have grown after one hour in %
0	0
5.0	43
7.5	67
10.0	88
12.5	83
15.0	72

(a) Plot a graph of Jodie's results. Draw a line of best fit through the points.

3 marks

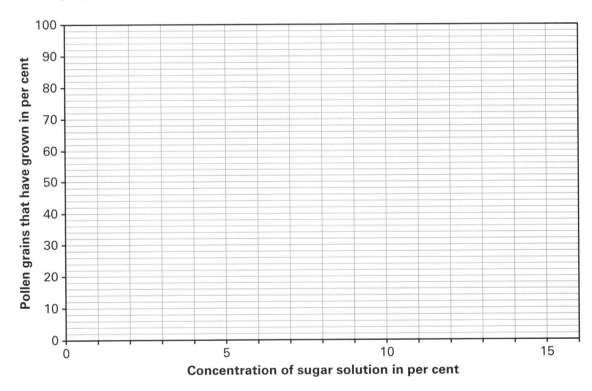

(b) In Jodie's investigation:

(i) Give the dependent variable.

1 mark

_____

(ii) Give one variable that she kept constant.

1 mark

_____

SUBTOTAL

(c) Describe the pattern of her results.

_____

_____

_____

_____

(d) Suggest one reason why the pollen grains needed sugar to grow.

_____

_____

12. Erica is going to recycle her mobile phone.

She looks at some information on the Internet on the metals used in mobile phones.

Element	Total mass in the world's mobile phones in 2010, in tonnes	Concentration in Earth's crust, in part per million (ppm)*
Aluminium	4200	82000
Copper	21000	50
Gold	140	0.0011
Iron	4200	41000
Palladium	30	0.0006
Platinum	1	0.001
Silver	700	0.07
Tantalum	28	2

*Number of parts of the element per million parts of Earth's crust

(a) Which metal is most used in the world's mobile phones?

_____

(b) Using information from the table:

    (i) Which is the **most** abundant element in the Earth's crust? Tick the correct box.

Aluminium	☐	Gold	☐
Iron	☐	Palladium	☐

    (ii) Which is the **least** abundant element in the Earth's crust? Tick the correct box.

Aluminium	☐	Gold	☐
Iron	☐	Palladium	☐

(c) Erica says that it's more important to recycle metals such as gold from mobile phones than it is the aluminium.

    (i) Explain why.

_____

_____

_____

    (ii) Erica reads that to recycle aluminium, the cost is only 5% of that needed to extract it from its ore.

        Give **two** other reasons why it's often better to recycle metals than to mine and extract more.

_____

_____

_____

Test Paper 2

First name   _____

Last name   _____

Date   _____

Instructions:

- The test is **75 minutes** long.

- Find a quiet place where you can sit down and complete the test paper undisturbed.

- You will need a pen, pencil, rubber and ruler. You may find a protractor and a calculator useful.

- The test starts with easier questions.

- Try to answer all of the questions.

- The number of marks available for each question is given in the margin.

- Show any rough working on this paper.

- Check your work carefully.

- Check how you have done using pages 101–112 of the Answers and Mark Scheme.

MAXIMUM MARK	75		ACTUAL MARK	

1. Sarah's teacher sets up a large glass tube.

In one end she puts a piece of cotton wool soaked in ammonia solution.

In the other end, she puts a piece of cotton wool soaked in concentrated hydrochloric acid.

cotton wool soaked in ammonia   cloud of chemical particles   cotton wool soaked in hydrochloric
solution gives off ammonia gas   acid gives off hydrogen chloride gas

(a) The cotton wool soaked in ammonia solution gives off ammonia gas.

The cotton wool soaked in concentrated hydrochloric acid gives off hydrogen chloride gas.

(i) Explain why particles of ammonia gas and hydrogen chloride gas move along the glass tube.

2 marks

_____

_____

_____

(ii) What is this process called?

1 mark

_____

(iii) What are the particles of ammonia and hydrogen chloride called?

1 mark

_____

SUBTOTAL

(b) Within a few seconds of putting the pieces of cotton wool in the glass tube, a white cloud forms part way along the tube.

(i) What has happened to produce the cloud of chemical particles?

_____

_____

1 mark

(ii) Suggest why the cloud forms closer to the hydrogen chloride end of the tube and not in the middle.

_____

_____

1 mark

2.   Tony is laying some slabs in his garden. They are made from limestone.

(a) Each slab is 0.3m × 0.3m and weighs 72N.

Calculate the pressure that would be exerted on the ground by one slab.

_____ N/m^2

2 marks

(b) Limestone is a natural material.

(i) What type of rock is limestone?

1 mark

____

(ii) How is this type of rock formed?

2 marks

____

____

____

____

(c) Marble is a rock that is formed from limestone.

(i) What type of rock is marble?

1 mark

____

(ii) How is marble formed from limestone?

1 mark

____

____

SUBTOTAL

3. Coral reefs are important marine ecosystems.

(a) What is meant by an ecosystem?

_____

_____

(b) Carbon dioxide reacts with water to form carbonic acid.

Write a word equation for this reaction.

_____

_____ + _____ → _____

(c) Emissions of carbon dioxide and other gases are causing the sea to become more acidic.

Acidic seawater destroys coral.

(i) Give **one** source of emissions of carbon dioxide.

_____

(ii) The graph opposite shows how the pH of seawater has changed since the first measurements were made in 1850.

Values of pH shown on the graph have been compared with those of 1850.

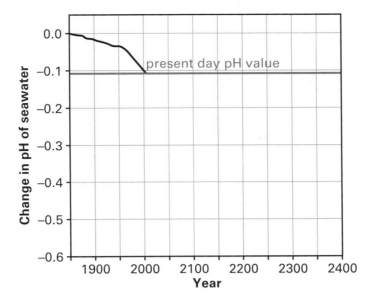

Describe the change in pH from 1850 to the present day.

_____

_____

_____

(iii) What is the overall change in pH during this time?

_____

(iv) Extending the line, use the graph to predict the year when the pH will have decreased by a value of 0.5 since 1850.

_____

(v) What did you assume when you made this prediction?

_____

_____

4. The table below gives the properties of Group 7 elements of the Periodic Table. They are in group order.

Group 7 element	Melting point in °C	Boiling point in °C
Fluorine	−219	−188
Chlorine	−101	−34
Bromine	−7	59
Iodine	114	184
Astatine	302	380

(a) (i) Which elements are solid at room temperature?

_____

1 mark

(ii) Which element is liquid over the greatest temperature range?

_____

1 mark

(b) The properties of elements change as you move down (or up) a group.

(i) Using information from the table, describe how **one** property changes as you move down the Group 7 elements.

_____

_____

_____

_____

1 mark

(ii) Using other information, not in the table, describe how **one** property changes among the Group 7 elements.

_____

_____

_____

_____

1 mark

(c) Here are Ben's results:

Type of fuel	Temperature rise in °C			Average rise in temperature in °C
	Test 1	Test 2	Test 3	
Ethanol	16.5	17.0	16.8	
Propanol	19.0	18.8	19.3	
Butanol	20.5	21.2	21.0	

(i) Calculate the average rise in temperature for each fuel.
Fill in the end column of the table.

1 mark

(ii) Which fuel releases most energy when burned?

1 mark

_____

(d) What is the name given to chemical reactions that give out heat?

1 mark

_____

9. Helena is a marine biologist. She is studying the hearing range of some marine animals.

(a) The graph below shows the hearing range of two animals.

1 mark

It shows the limits of their hearing across a range of frequencies.

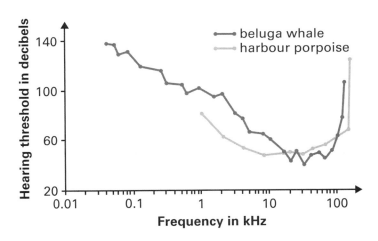

SUBTOTAL

1 mark

(i) What is the quietest sound that can be heard by the beluga whale?

_____

1 mark

(ii) What is the lowest pitch sound that can be heard by the harbour porpoise?

_____

(b) The hearing range of most humans is 20–20 000Hz.

1 mark

(i) Mark this range on the graph on p 95.

3 marks

(ii) Compare the hearing range of humans with that of the beluga whale and harbour porpoise.

_____

_____

_____

_____

_____

_____

_____

10. Sulfuric acid is made on a large scale. It is one of our most important chemicals.

2 marks

(a) The table below shows some products made using sulfuric acid.

Product made	% of sulfuric acid used
Detergent	19
Dyes	7
Fertilisers	4
Fibres	3
Paint	20
Plastics	4

1. (a) (i) A *(1 mark)*

Helpful hint: *Students often confuse the cell membrane and cell wall. The cell membrane is pushed up against the cell wall.*

(ii) B *(1 mark)*

(b) Two answers from:

(Its cells have) cell walls;

chloroplasts;

large vacuoles *(2 marks)*

Helpful hint: *Animal cells often have vacuoles too, but they're never this large. They're also not permanent structures in animal cells, but don't write this, as you can't tell this from the diagram.*

(c) The reservoir contains very large numbers of these green organisms/algae; *(1 mark)*

because of eutrophication/large amounts of fertiliser in the reservoir *(1 mark)*

2. (a) (i) Orange *(1 mark)*

Green *(1 mark)*

Violet *(1 mark)*

Helpful hint: *There are a number of mnemonics for remembering the colours of the spectrum, e.g. **R**ichard **O**f **Y**ork **G**ave **B**attle **I**n **V**ain, or **R**un **O**ff **Y**ou **G**irls – **B**oys **I**n **V**iew. But you can also work them out, as the primary colours – red, green and blue – overlap.*

(ii) Dispersion *(1 mark)*

(b) If another prism is placed after the first (that has produced the spectrum); *(1 mark)*

the colours are recombined *(1 mark)*

or

If light from **one** of the colours of the spectrum from the first prism is passed through another prism; *(1 mark)*

it will not produce a spectrum

(1 mark; maximum 2 marks)

3. (a) Mixture *(1 mark)*

(b) (i) Propane **gas**

Butane **liquid** *(1 mark)*

(ii) Propane **liquid**

Butane **solid** *(1 mark)*

(c) propane + oxygen *(1 mark)*

($\rightarrow$)

carbon dioxide + water *(1 mark)*

(d) Two marks from: Temperatures are colder in the winter/warmer in the summer *(1 mark)*, so (changing proportions) will make mixture more fluid (less viscous)/flow more easily in winter; *(1 mark)*

and change how easily the LPG ignites *(1 mark)*

4. (a) (i) C *(1 mark)*

(ii) A *(1 mark)*

(iii) E *(1 mark)*

(b) (i) Stomach *(1 mark)*

(ii) Small intestine *(1 mark)*

(c) Enzyme *(1 mark)*

5. (a) (i) 90 (J) *(1 mark)*

(ii) Heat *(1 mark)*

(iii) 10% *(1 mark)*

(b) 40% *(1 mark)*

Helpful hint: *The calculation is (600/1500 × 100)%.*

(c) *(1 mark per row)* *(4 marks)*

Appliance	Power in W	Power in kW	Time appliance is used for in hours	Units of electricity used in kWh
Hair dryer	**2000**	2.0	1	**2**
Kettle	3000	**3.0**	2	**6**
Light bulb	100	**0.1**	20	**2**
Toaster	**1300**	1.3	1	**1.3**

Helpful hint: *In questions where you have to fill in tables, you will often get one mark for each correct row.*

6. (a) (i) Triceps *(1 mark)*

(ii) Contracts/shortens *(1 mark)*

(iii) Muscles cannot get longer – they can only contract (or be relaxed); *(1 mark)*

so they have to work in (antagonistic) pairs – when one contracts, the bone is moved one way, when the other contracts, the bone is moved the other way *(1 mark)*

(b) (Fibre B, a ligament) is used to link a bone to another bone *(1 mark)*

(Material C, cartilage) acts as a shock absorber between bones at joints *(1 mark)*

7. (a) (i) Carbon, hydrogen and oxygen *(1 mark)*

Helpful hint: *Note that you need all three elements correct to get the mark. This is often the case in straightforward questions.*

(ii) 23 *(1 mark)*

(b) (i) *(1 mark)*

(ii) *(1 mark)*

Helpful hint: *Do not confuse the oxidising symbol with the flammable symbol.*

(iii) Use in a well-ventilated space/do not breathe the vapour/keep away from flames when using/contact avoid with eyes and (prolonged) contact with skin *(1 mark)*

8. (a) (i) engine *(1 mark)*

(ii) Air resistance/drag
Friction (between tyres and road surface)
(2 marks)

(iii) (Forward and retarding) forces are balanced
(1 mark)

(b)

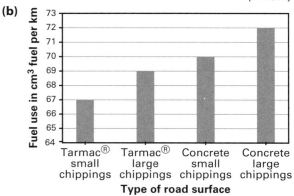

(2 marks for all bars drawn correctly; 1 mark for three or two bars drawn correctly) *(2 marks)*

9. (a) (i) Ceramic *(1 mark)*

(ii) Polymer *(1 mark)*

(b) A mixture; *(1 mark)*
of more than one metal or a metal and other elements *(1 mark)*

(c) From the solidification/slow crystallisation of magma/molten rock *(1 mark)*

10. (a) (i) The greater the number of turns, the stronger the electromagnet *(1 mark)*

(ii) Increase the current *(1 mark)*

(b) (i) The paperclips would fall off; *(1 mark)*
as a magnetic field is only produced when current flowing *(1 mark)*

(ii) Steel forms a permanent magnet/ stays magnetic when current is turned off. *(1 mark)*

Helpful hint: *Remember that electromagnets can be switched on and off by turning the electricity on and off. Permanent magnets are needed in electric motors, generators, microphones and speakers.*

11. (a)

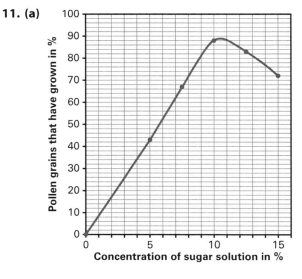

(2 marks for all six points plotted correctly; 1 mark for three, four or five points plotted correctly) *(2 marks)*
Appropriate line of best fit *(1 mark)*

Helpful hint: *Unless you're told to, don't just join the points. Look for a trend in the data and draw a line of best fit. Decide whether the line of best fit should be a straight line or a curve. Draw a line as close to the points as possible. Balance the number of points below and above the line.*

(b) (i) Percentage of pollen grains that have grown (after one hour) *(1 mark)*

Helpful hint: *Many students are confused as to which is the dependent variable. The dependent variable is usually what you measure in the experiment.*

(ii) Type of plant/spider flower or length of time/ one hour or number of pollen grains *(1 mark)*

(c) The percentage germination increases as the sugar concentration increases; *(1 mark)*
and reaches a maximum at around 10/11%; *(1 mark)*
then decreases *(1 mark)*

(d) One answer from: (Raw material for) growth **or** respiration/for energy *(1 mark)*

12. (a) Copper *(1 mark)*

(b) (i) Aluminium *(1 mark)*

(ii) Palladium *(1 mark)*

(c) (i) Gold is a very rare metal while aluminium is in plentiful supply *(1 mark)*

(ii) The world's natural sources of a metal are finite/ would one day be used up (even though they might be in plentiful supply now); *(1 mark)*
it reduces waste (that has to be disposed of somehow); *(1 mark)*
mining (for more metals) destroys the environment/landscape *(2 marks)*

Set C, Test Paper 2

1. (a) (i) (They move) from a high concentration (on the cotton wool); *(1 mark)*
to a low concentration (in the tube) *(1 mark)*
(ii) (They move by) diffusion *(1 mark)*
(iii) Molecules *(1 mark)*
(b) (i) A chemical reaction (between the ammonia and hydrogen chloride) *(1 mark)*
(ii) The ammonia diffuses more quickly/the hydrogen chloride moves more slowly *(1 mark)*
Helpful hint: *This is because ammonia has the lower relative molecular mass (is 'lighter'), but if you give this answer, it doesn't quite answer the question.*

2. (a) Pressure = force/area
The area is $(0.3 \times 0.3)m^2 = 0.09m^2$ *(1 mark)*
∴ Pressure = 72/0.09
= $800N/m^2$ *(1 mark)*
Helpful hint: *Show your working. One mark is awarded for this.*
(b) (i) Sedimentary *(1 mark)*
(ii) Formed when shells, sand and mud/layers/sediments are deposited at the bottom of water; *(1 mark)*
layers are compacted into rock *(1 mark)*
(c) (i) Metamorphic *(1 mark)*
(ii) Formed when limestone is subjected to heat and/or pressure *(1 mark)*

3. (a) The combination of the organisms and their environment that make up a particular habitat *(1 mark)*
Helpful hint: *In your answer, you must make sure that you mention* both *the organisms and the environment.*
(b) carbon dioxide 1 water *(1 mark)*
(→)
carbonic acid *(1 mark)*
Helpful hint: *In a chemical equation, examiners usually award 1 mark for getting the reactants correct, and one mark for the products.*
(c) (i) The burning/combustion of fossil fuels/trees/waste or volcanoes *(1 mark)*
Helpful hint: *Your answer must refer to burning/combustion, unless you have written 'volcanoes'. The respiration of organisms also releases carbon dioxide, but you wouldn't usually refer to this release as an emission. Your answer would be accepted, however.*
(ii) Slow decrease from 1850 to 1950 *(1 mark)*
More rapid decrease from 1950 to the present day *(1 mark)*
(iii) −0.11 *(1 mark)*
(iv) Continuation of line (extrapolation) shown appropriately *(1 mark)*

2250 (or appropriate answer) *(1 mark)*
Helpful hint: *You will be allowed some tolerance with your answer. You may not have found that it was the year 2250. You must draw a line on the test paper from the current gradient of the graph. You must read off where it corresponds with a decrease of 0.5.*

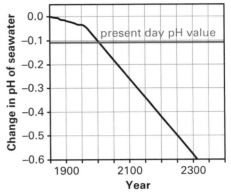

(v) That the decrease in pH will continue at the present rate *(1 mark)*

4. (a) (i) Iodine and astatine *(1 mark)*
(ii) Astatine *(1 mark)*
Helpful hint: *Some of the values are close together, so you need to be careful with your calculations. Jot them down as you do them.*
(b) (i) The melting point increases as you go down the group (from fluorine to astatine) **or**
The boiling point increases as you go down the group (from fluorine to astatine) *(1 mark)*
(ii) The reactivity decreases as you go down the group (from fluorine to astatine) **or**
The reactivity increases as you go up the group (from astatine to fluorine) *(1 mark)*
(iii) Bromine and potassium chloride are produced *(1 mark)*

5. (a) (i) Genetic (variation) *(1 mark)*
(ii) Better camouflaged on the ice/in the snow; *(1 mark)*
so more able to catch prey *(1 mark)*
(b) Pale-coated bears pass on these genes; *(1 mark)*
so over time become paler and paler, and become a new species *(1 mark)*

6. (a) (i) 28 days *(1 mark)*
(ii) By the Earth's gravity *(1 mark)*
Helpful hint: *To get the mark, you need to say it's the Earth's gravity.*
(b) (i) 5 *(1 mark)*
(ii) At phase 1   A *(1 mark)*
At phase 7   G *(1 mark)*

7. (a) The number of bubbles of gas is affected by/depends on the amount of light/brightness of light/light intensity *(1 mark)*

Set C, Test Paper 2 cont.

Helpful hint: A hypothesis is a suggestion a scientist makes to try to explain something they've observed. Scientists then do experiments to test the hypothesis to see if it can be supported by the data they collect.

(b) (i) (The sodium hydrogencarbonate) is a source of carbon dioxide *(1 mark)*

Helpful hint: You may know the answer because you've done this experiment in school. But if you haven't, the clue is also in the chemical formula.

(ii) Photosynthesis *(1 mark)*

(c) (i)
carbon dioxide + water $\xrightarrow{\text{light energy}}$ glucose + oxygen *(2 marks)*

(ii) $6CO_2 + 6H_2O \rightarrow C_6H_{12}O_6 + 6O_2$ *(2 marks)*

8. (a) Two from: Volume of water; volume of fuel; distance between the spirit burner and the boiling tube *(2 marks)*

(b) (i) Flammable: keep away from flames
Toxic: use in a fume cupboard/avoid breathing vapour/use in a well-ventilated area *(1 mark)*

(ii) The hot spirit burner, boiling tube or water/ use of the glassware or thermometer *(1 mark)*

(c) (i) 16.8; 19.0; 20.9 *(1 mark)*

Helpful hint: The results are recorded to one decimal place in each result, so you can't have more in the average. You could lose marks if you write down more.

(ii) Butanol *(1 mark)*

(d) Exothermic *(1 mark)*

9. (a) (i) 40 dB *(1 mark)*

(ii) 1 kHz *(1 mark)*

Helpful hint: Use a ruler to line up the points on the graph with the value on the y-axis, or better still, draw a horizontal line.

(b) (i)

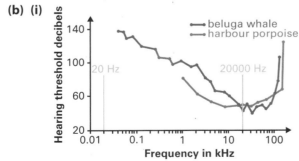

Both lines or points correct *(1 mark)*

Helpful hint: Be careful with units. 1 kHz = 1000 Hz. You need to make the conversion.

(ii) The hearing range shows some overlap with that of the beluga whale and harbour porpoise; *(1 mark)*

but the beluga whale and harbour porpoise can hear sounds of a higher pitch/ frequency; *(1 mark)*
while humans can hear sounds of a lower pitch than the harbour porpoise, and to some extent, the beluga whale *(1 mark)*

Helpful hint: Your answers might not quite correspond with those above. Like all answers in science, it will be judged on quality, and not quantity.

10. (a)

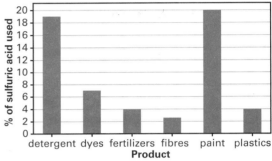

(2 marks for six correct bars; 1 mark for five, four or three) *(2 marks)*

(b) (i) Oxidation *(1 mark)*

(ii) The mass of the product is the same as the mass of the reactants. *(1 mark)*
One molecule of sulfur trioxide is formed from one molecule of sulfur dioxide. *(1 mark)*

(iii) $SO_3 + H_2O$ *(1 mark)*
$(\rightarrow)$
H_2SO_4 *(2 marks)*

11. (a) Two answers from:
Slow overall decrease in smoking from 1948 to 1970;
in two stages/with some small rises around 1956 and 1960;
then steady decrease between 1970 and 2010 *(2 marks)*

(b) (i) There has been a decrease in the rate of smoking and lung cancer *(1 mark)*
The decrease in lung cancer lags behind the fall in smoking *(1 mark)*

(ii) Lung cancer has other causes/not everyone who gets lung cancer smokes *(1 mark)*

12. (a) A substance that dissolves another substance *(1 mark)*

(b) Chromatography *(1 mark)*

(c) So that he could compare the distance travelled between the cocaine and the sample from the crime scene; *(1 mark)*
so as to identify any cocaine (in the sample from the crime scene) *(1 mark)*

(d) Contains cocaine; *(1 mark)*
and two (unknown) substances *(1 mark)*